# Becoming an Anthropologi

## A Memoir and a Guide to Anthropology

By

Gerald Mars

Cambridge
Scholars
Publishing

Becoming an Anthropologist:
A Memoir and a Guide to Anthropology

By Gerald Mars

This book first published 2015

Cambridge Scholars Publishing

Lady Stephenson Library, Newcastle upon Tyne, NE6 2PA, UK

British Library Cataloguing in Publication Data
A catalogue record for this book is available from the British Library

ISBN (10): 1-4438-7692-5
ISBN (13): 978-1-4438-7692-6

# TABLE OF CONTENTS

# ACKNOWLEDGEMENTS

Anthropologists know well that fieldwork is dependent on informants in the different cultures they have researched. In my case I have found that many have been generous and tolerant beyond measure – despite the blundering intrusions that are inevitably part of the job. Some became good friends and others indeed acted as co-researchers. To them all I offer a deeply felt thank you.

In addition, in preparing this book I have been especially fortunate in having contacts, friends and colleagues who have unselfishly offered effort, encouragement and criticism. It has benefitted enormously from their support and inputs, and it is a pleasure therefore to record my grateful thanks to: Alan Bennett, Sandy Bower, Richard and Katherine Bradley, Ruth Cook, Jennifer Iles, Ragnar Johnson, David Nelken, Perri 6, Tom Selwyn, Tony Sharkey, Mike Thompson, David Weir and not least, members of the family: Adrian, Sarah, Len, Mel and Mike Mars.

Those who know me, realise how much I owe my wife Valerie. Her constant monitoring, support and criticism are the mainstay of everything I attempt, not just this book.

# PREFACE – AND A GUIDE TO THE BOOK

This is a book that I hope will appeal to people who want to know about the social bases of behaviour. It has been written so that readers with no knowledge of social anthropology can take it as it is and read it as narrative. But for those who wish to take it further – the extensive footnotes supply elaborations of the text and a guide to further reading. It should also appeal to those interested in applied anthropology as well as to teachers of the subject.

The book demonstrates that how people's lives are organised, determines not only their behaviour but also their perceptions and values. It is an account too of a rather odd profession, of how its members work, how I became a member of it, and of how I came to understand something of the cultures in which I grew up, worked and did research.

It was in my mid-twenties that I began training as an anthropologist. But it was the 'pre-professional' years that provided the bedrock to becoming one. Giving especial attention to these early years, and with the benefits of professional hindsight, I can now put flesh on the cultures in which I grew up, lived and worked. The accounts speak through the stories and the language of those involved.

Part I of the book therefore, explores in some detail the early years of childhood – of life in a close working-class community in wartime Manchester – with its mix of bombing-raids, rationing and the black market, its residents' disdain for education ('it'll snap your brain') and its cynicism of government and officials that ran counter to wartime assertions about 'all pulling together'. Growing up in Manchester sharply contrasted with what followed – adolescence and work in a seaside holiday resort – the ultra-entrepreneurial, competitive, booming and crime-prone Blackpool of the fifties and sixties. Here, the dominant competitive ideology was to 'make it' – and fiddling and 'knockoff' were routinely accepted and often colluded in by bosses. The names of numerous people have necessarily been changed.

Work in over thirty jobs, taught me the extent and practices of workplace fiddles as practised by both bosses and workers – often in collusion. Work on the Golden Mile and the Pleasure Beach revealed the methods of spielers (barkers), the techniques of mock auctioneers and the secrets of clairvoyants. And as a boarding house child I was well set to explore the gentility of landladies. Later, I was to experience what it was to work in a Dickensian factory. By now, an early involvement in several cultures was working, by comparison, to sharpen understanding of them all.

Part II explores a yet different culture, the RAF, with two years National Service in the ranks spent surveying its rituals, participating as a scapegoat, observing hierarchic coercion and being involved in forms of lower level resistance. Here, a complete same-age cohort lived together irrespective of class or education. We could hardly ignore comparisons about ourselves and others. It gave many conscripts, including me, wider visions of a different life on demobilisation. 'If he can go to university then I'm bloody sure I can,' was a not uncommon response.

Part III describes various short-term involvements discussing the functions of interviews, the culture of the police, the nature and effects of official target-setting and the irrationality of organisation in a secret Royal Ordnance Factory.

Part IV discusses Cambridge and how 'learning the ropes' meant learning to navigate in a strange land with different rituals and new behavioural nuances. Here women behaved very differently from their counterparts in the North and the exercise of authority was much subtler than any I'd previously met. Cambridge of course offered training: some understanding of research methods, social science theories and a comparative knowledge of other cultures. I could now look back with sharpened understanding at the communities I had left – and forward to those I would research as a professional.

Part V: Becoming an anthropologist involved practical training. It meant spending two postgraduate years in intensive fieldwork drinking with Canadian longshoremen, analysing their mode of joking and exploring the implications of their conflicts. It explored the built-in antagonisms of fathers and sons that affected all aspects of their lives. Appreciating their sophisticated methods of pilferage - allied to a strong but atypical morality – involved teasing out the sociology of their work gangs and the integral role these played in industrial relations. Finally a more light hearted account of expatriate life in the University community shows that fieldwork wasn't all work.

Part VI: Using Anthropology is a miscellany and discusses different jobs and their anthropological analyses at home and abroad. Work, consultancy and fieldwork over fifty years has involved exposure to a wide array of cultures and organisations. Only a selection is given here but they demonstrate the wide range that applied anthropology can cover. There is a case-study of the place of magic in a multinational company, made explicable by comparison with the magical beliefs of other cultures. A brief spell in Nigeria offers alternative viewpoints about corruption; the imposition of what to us, appear savage punishments, and the means by which nepotism is avoided – or alternatively embraced. What it revealed about the ethnocentricity[1] of expatriates – and of our own 'western' culture was as interesting, and as useful, as much of what I learned about Nigerians and theirs.

Account is given of work in a polytechnic and of the structures that facilitate scapegoat selection. Its student militancy is understood by comparison with union militancy in Newfoundland. A major study set in the Soviet Union researched its black economy – which brought me up against both the CIA and the KGB. Neither is recommended.

Closer to home I examine the culture of the police and of responses to 'control through targeting'. Studying and working in organisations reveals the mechanics of their politicking and of what makes an organisation 'tyrannous' – a condition on the increase but which is under researched and is discussed here with relevance to a university business school. I then describe life in a secret government factory and assess the negative nature of its 'need to know' practices. Chapter 18 discusses a growing social constituency of 'free spirits', whose dominant value and aim is to be autonomous – being free as far as possible of the constraints of social, bureaucratic and financial involvements. These are the 'Autarchs' who are theoretically identified in Chapter 18.

Part VII, Episodes, discusses why we in the West find bereavement more difficult to cope with than do most of the world's peoples – influenced as we are by the dominant role of organisations in our society, a reduction in functions performed by families and their geographical dispersal. Closer to home and somewhat tongue in cheek, I then look at life in bourgeois Hampstead with its incipient hypochondria.

Part VIII gives attention (in Chapter 21) to the theoretical framework that has guided and moulded much of my work. Known as Grid/Group, Cultural Theory or CT, readers are invited to return to the accounts to see its relevance.[2]

---

1  'Ethnocentricity' is the assessing of another culture from the standpoint of one's own (as in: 'they have superstition: we have religion'). It is considered the prime anthropologist's sin.

2  This is the core of Mary Douglas' later work and of her followers who describe four (some say five) archetypal situations found in all cultures and which reveal a clustering of values, attitudes and behaviours appropriate to each. See chs 8 and 21 of this volume for a discussion of the fifth solidarity.

Part IX, The Conclusion, *Becoming an Anthropologist* attempts to pull these strands together and to show how the total experiences of a life have been brought to bear in becoming an anthropologist. It discusses the application of anthropology's principal tenets and shows how they mesh with the complex of experiences before, during and following work with people of different cultures. Hopefully, this account might encourage lay observers to examine and learn more about their cultures and their own activities.

# PART I:

# A SOCIAL HISTORY: TWO CULTURES COMPARED

# INTRODUCTION TO PART I

Part I of this book describes and compares two very different cultures – the first, a close-knit, traditional, working-class community in wartime Manchester, characterised by hierarchic values, conformity, gossip and shame, where the visits of Sid, the black-market egg salesman, were regular and welcome – while the waves of German bombers though unwelcome, seemed, equally regular.

And then, when I was twelve, and in marked contrast, the family moved fifty miles away to Blackpool – an individualist, competitive and boisterously vulgar seaside resort in the north of England where everyone seemed to be 'on the fiddle'.

My mother's aim was to open a boarding house. It didn't work – the interest on mortgage payments, competition of other boarding house keepers, a father in a dying trade, a sick mother and four children, saw to that. But for me the move involved a massive culture-shock.

At twelve, in a town hungry for labour, I could readily get part-time work in the wide range of jobs that cater to tourists. Later I was able to 'go native' in fairgrounds and in numerous cafés, shops and offices. At fifteen I worked full-time in a pretentious gentlemen's outfitters and then in a horrific Dickensian factory. In the ten years between leaving school and university I had worked in over thirty jobs and spent two years in the RAF. Fiddling was endemic in nearly all of them.

The contrast between living in a culture where people accepted their place to one where 'making it' is integral to their way of life emphasised how understanding cultures by living in them benefits from comparison. I was to learn too how understanding workplace fiddling offered similar insights into the varied worlds of work.

CHAPTER ONE

# MANCHESTER BEGINNINGS

## From the Ghetto to 'The Avenues'

Not everyone does badly in a slump. My parents were among the lucky ones. Those in work during the great thirties slump benefitted from deflation – a reduction in the price of most goods that were cheaper than they had been for years. Houses were especially cheap, and new estates sprang up throughout Britain. Hard-pressed builders, desperate to unload speculatively built houses, cut their prices to the bone. They competed not just on price, but on incentives – a coal-shed full of free coal, a fully furnished lounge. For those in a job there was cheap and easy credit. In 1935 a Civil Service Clerical Officer could buy a new four-bedroomed semi in Croydon for £350 – a years' salary. Artisans in work, like my dad, were able to afford a smaller semi on a new estate in Manchester for £250 – a years' wages.

With the growth of new estates, Mam, ambitious and forceful, saw her chance. The daughter of a destitute Jewish dentist from a family of ten, she had married the ghetto-born son of immigrants who had no English (none when they arrived and still none when they died fifty years later). [1] Now with me, her first child, she determined to escape from renting in a dark, poky, Victorian terrace and aspired to owning one of the bright new semis. Though she did not realise it, she was in at the beginning of a new movement: home ownership. Up to then nearly everyone – from the upper middle classes down – still rented their houses.

---

1 One cannot help suspecting that the present clamour over language qualifications for immigrants has more to do with populist anti-immigration rhetoric than the reasons stated. Most of my grandparents' immigrant generation, who never learned English, produced, if not children, then certainly grandchildren who moved smoothly into the professional classes. Many were to make distinguished contributions to society.

We were reasonably well-off. Dad, a clothing factory's top 'sample presser', regularly earned five pounds a week. His skill was to make the samples displayed to the shops look to be of better quality than they were. He earned extra by placing bets for his bosses on dogs and horses. Street bookmaking was then illegal so 'putting a bet on' wasn't easy and only trusted to someone known as honest and reliable. With these extra earnings it wasn't too difficult to pay a mortgage.

In 1935 my parents put a twenty-five pound deposit on 5 Rowood Avenue, one of three new avenues that with Glover and Caradoc were known as 'The Avenues'. It formed a self-conscious enclave of 'owner-occupiers' in an area of rented Victorian terraces.

Set on the lower slopes of a hill, the estate's forty-five identical semis were airy and spacious. Cleverly marketed as 'sunshine-semis', they had a family room the length of the ground floor with large windows at either end. I had my own bedroom. There was even a spare room – and more luxurious still – a garden – all in sharp contrast to the tiny mean terraces that housed the majority of the northern urban working class.

In those days buying a house was a radical move. Both sides of the family thought the venture not just risky but it confirmed Mam as 'stuck-up' and snobbish. Owning one's own house in an 'Avenue' – a word new to most folk – confirmed it.

The most wondrous difference between old and new was that new estates were connected to the electric grid while the Victorian terraces were lit by spluttering gas mantles that gave a poor yellow light. We marvelled at the benefits of clean electricity. As soon as we were settled, Mam went off to buy an iron, a stove, a kettle, a radio and a vacuum-cleaner – all electric, all 'on the HP'.[2] Many terraces had to wait until after the war before they were connected to the grid.

Residentially we were now part of a minority. Coming from a totally Jewish neighbourhood, we found the new avenues nine tenths Christian. For Dad, mild and reticent, the move was difficult. He had been born and spent his whole life in Cheetham Hill, a Yiddish-speaking ghetto where he learned English only when taught it at school, and where life revolved around the bonds of neighbourhood, the synagogue and Jewish festivals. Even the factory had Yiddish as its *lingua franca*. Naturally he was anxious about moving to The Avenues.

I soon became aware – as a Jew living in a non-Jewish area – that I was straddling two cultures. The perpetual observation of their differences

---

2   HP: Hire Purchase, which took off in the thirties as commerce attempted to clear its stocks in a slump. Its post-war mass appeal contributed to an emergent and new capitalist phase – consumerism.

was a source of constant interest. I was unaware then that at a very early age I had stumbled on a central tenet of anthropological method – the importance of comparison.

By spending my childhood in 'The Avenues' I was later to appreciate how a small intimate community was kept together. Here children were early incorporated into adult affairs in a way largely alien to the middle classes. As such we picked up social mores and mechanisms at a comparatively early age. Well before I was twelve I saw how people were ranked and prestige allocated. I not only observed but was of course, party to how children were reared and how gender differences developed and were amplified. I came to appreciate the ingenuity and co-operation involved in the search for food that bypassed stringent wartime rationing. And I could not but grasp the unifying experience of the Blitz with its recurrent possibility of sudden and violent death.

## Respectability and Gossip

The Avenues soon melded into a community where every family's personal details were known to all. It was a community bonded and controlled by gossip, censure, ridicule and ideas of respectability. And the controls worked: people didn't dump rubbish on the street – the street was seen as communal and any dumping would be noted; litter and graffiti were also absent. There was no vandalism. Every adult was expected to check, even to 'clout'[3] any obviously naughty child. When my friend Harold Higginbotham complained to his Mam that he had been 'clouted' by a neighbour – and she found it was for 'being cheeky' – she clouted him again. All adults automatically had authority over all children.

A family's prestige was primarily based on the husband's job. Jobs were carefully rated – except for clerks who were thought of as outsiders and seen as parasitical. Their jobs were 'not real jobs' and somehow not masculine. A clerk's family, the Rimmingtons, lived next door to us at number 7 but they 'kept their distance' – there was no visiting between houses. Mr Rimmington's job, in a reserved occupation, was one considered vital to the war effort and meant he was excused military service. Reserved occupations, of clerks in particular, were much resented.

The most respected jobs were those of skilled tradesmen and those that offered steady employment. At number 3 lived Mam's great friend Mrs Green, a Christian, whose husband was a railway signalman, a skilled job, vital to the war-effort and justifiably rated as a 'reserved occupation'. The

---

3   To 'clout': Northern dialect for 'to hit'

Greens were also respected because railways, like the council, were one of the few employers that gave pensions and paid sick leave.

But besides the husband's job, a family was assessed by whether its members were quietly sober, its children well-behaved and cleanly turned out, its front room curtains kept neat, and whether its windows showed ornaments that faced out. And when it snowed, I was often told to clear snow for sick or aged neighbours – with no question of payment.

It was expected that front steps be 'wetted' every few days, then scrubbed with 'step-stones' given by itinerant 'rag and bone men' in exchange for recyclable waste. Our 'rag and bone man' came every fortnight with a horse and cart and the cry 'Rags Bottles and Bones'. But Mam, ever the individualist, did not use step-stones – she did our step with red Cardinal polish.

There was little conspicuous consumption in The Avenues – not just because war meant there was little to buy but because it went against pressures to conformity. Anyone attempting to 'show off' would attract both gossip[4] and ridicule.

It was not until well after the war that competitive consumerism really came into its own. So although this was a new community, its values re-asserted those of the pre-war, conformist, Northern working class – or rather that section of it concerned to be respectable. Men would stop and raise their hats to a passing hearse and at the end of cinema performances everyone stood for the national anthem: it would have been shameful to be seen not doing so. When a doctor or a priest was due to call, women would slave for hours to clean their houses. This was a culture of deference and conformity – but not deference to all authority: governments weren't much respected – neither were bosses – or teachers.

Living across the road was our self-employed local window cleaner, Mr Hughes. At the lower end of the status ratings, the Hughes's had an impressively large collection of gnomes in their front garden but this only aroused suspicion. Once, while queuing in the corner shop, I heard two neighbours, heads and voices lowered, discussing the collection. 'You know where he gets them from, don't you?' [5]

---

4   See Dennis *et al* (1956), also Hoggart (1957) who well demonstrate how not conforming to common standards is disruptive to communality which is why conspicuous consumption is not a feature of tightly-knit communities such as those of miners but more appropriate to neighbourhoods of competitive individualists. See Tönnies (1887) for the distinction between *Gemeinschaft* and *Gesellschaft* types of social organisation. See footnote 30, page 24.

5   The dialogues reported here are reconstructions that, as I hope and believe, are close to the original.

'No, where?'

'On his rounds. Hides them in his bucket. You know he cements them down don't you? No-one'll get *them* back!'

I never heard any evidence for this – or of anyone 'losing' their gnomes – but the Hughes's were not considered respectable – and so were vulnerable to accusations.

Mothers with children were excused war-work in the factories. They stayed at home and shared cups of weak rationed tea, borrowed half cups of flour or sugar, took care of each other's children – and gossiped. [6]

I well remember how gossip-obsessed were these women. Gossip was exchanged in lowered voices and had frequently to do with health and illness: it interested me intensely.

One afternoon the Avenue's arch gossip Mrs Johnson, a pinched, acetic widow of about sixty called to borrow half a cup of tea from Mam – and then as usual stayed for an extended chat. Mrs Johnson was a specialist at recording and discussing illness – especially women's illnesses. She always looked around her before she spoke then, in a whisper, hunched over her tea and hardly audible, would deliver her latest gems of gossip, innuendo and medical horrors. Why, I wondered, did women always whisper when discussing medical matters? So I quietly rearranged the toy soldiers in my fort and listened hard. Thanks to her, by the time I was nine, I too was something of a specialist, probably the neighbourhood's top child expert, on the female body in all its forms of illness and collapse. But this time, Mrs Johnson's new interest wasn't medical but psychological. You know what's happened to the Reeves' boy, don't you? Their Tom?' 'No. What's happened?' enquired Mam.

The Reeves' lived across the road and I liked Tom, a quiet affable lad of fifteen. Unusually he would talk to us smaller boys and exceptionally was at the Grammar. I listened harder.

Mrs Johnson glanced round, settled herself and lowered her voice still further. 'Ooh! You haven't heard? (A long pause). His brain's snapped! Too much book learning; he always has his head in a book'.

There followed accounts of Tom's increasingly bizarre behaviour culminating in rudery and outrage that had apparently terrified Mrs Rigg, a next-door neighbour. There were 'oos' and 'you'll never believe it...' and

---

6   Concern with gossip was initially fired by Gluckman (1963) who saw it as contributing to community cohesion. Paine (1967) saw it more as enhancing individual motivations and aspirations. A synthesis (via symbolic Interactionism) was offered by Havilland (1977) and Heilman (1978). Merry (1984) updated the discussion.

'I always knew it' but despite straining hard, I missed the more lurid details.

Tom's 'brain-snap' could not have been too serious. He soon returned to school but his case was often quoted as an example of the dangers of education. For most Avenue people, education was seen as a threat to mental stability as well as to working-class culture.

Gossiping, largely a female activity[7] – was never 'idle.' Gossip provided the shared knowledge that reinforced common values and it buttressed the maintenance of communal standards. It was gossip that asserted and confirmed feminine identity, and young girls were incorporated as women by their membership in gossip groupings. Gossip was one of the principal means by which The Avenues melded into a community.

## Failure in the Dreaded Eleven Plus

Teachers often found difficulty in persuading parents to let bright children take up scholarships. Success in the Eleven Plus decided which children would go to grammar schools and eventually to professional jobs; failure destined them to the senior schools and a proletarian life. Many working class people however, were strongly defensive of their way of life – a position that only began to be eroded after the war. They saw grammar schools as representing the middle-class values they despised. Mrs Dempsey – a typically assertive, Northern mother made her position clear. 'I'm not going to lose our Tom. He's going to no grammar. 'And, despite the appeals of his teacher, like many others, nor did he.[8]

Jews and clerks, in contrast, were keen on 'book-learning'. They did not believe in 'brain-snap' and were distraught if their children failed the Eleven Plus. My failure hit Mam like a death. When the hoped-for success-letter failed to arrive, she was not just upset at this slight on her golden boy and her hopes: she was angry. Dad, more sanguine, always the fatalist, tried to persuade her there were some things in life you had to accept. This only annoyed Mam further: she went into battle.

'I'll show 'em,' she asserted: 'I'm going now.' She buttoned on her coat and set off to storm the Education Offices. When she returned she gave us a full account.

---

7    But of course, most of the community's men had been drafted into the armed services.
8    Richard Hoggart (1957) explores how this view reveals the self-confident assertion of working-class culture that has now been absorbed into middle-class aspiration.

'I saw a horrible man. He wouldn't tell me anything – just kept saying, "We can't discuss the examination. That's council policy." I ignored him. Just stood there till he went away. Then a young girl came over, a lovely girl, very helpful. I explained you were near the top of the class and expected to pass. "Wait a minute," she told me, "I'll just have a quick look and see what I can see." When she came back, she said [I] was "close to the top of the failures". She was sure we would hear something very soon.'

The next day the letter came: she had fixed it. I had a place at Chorlton Central School, on the far side of Manchester. Though central schools ranked below grammars they were rated above senior schools. Mam was satisfied.

I have often pondered about that anonymous young woman. From the purest of goodwill she had possibly risked her job to bypass a rigid system.

My time at Chorlton was ghastly. It being wartime, all the staff had been dragooned back from retirement. Mr Moore, the PT master, was the sole male teacher under sixty. And he had only one leg.

At Chorlton I was the school's sole Jew. Most prejudice I faced was relatively mild – jibes and being nobody's friend – but it was constant and depressing. One day however it got out of hand and I was rescued – just in time – from the enthusiastic attention of my classmates. They had put a cord round my neck and were about to hang me from a beam in the school lavatories.

The isolation that comes from prejudice turned me from a social participant to more of a watchful observer. This too was invaluable to an emergent anthropologist. One becomes tuned to notice and be sensitive to nuances in behaviour and speech that might otherwise be missed. Allied to awareness of comparable differences in cultural standpoints, it gives what has been described as 'stereoscopic vision'. This, it has been suggested, is why South African Jewry – who are simultaneously involved with a multiplicity of cultures – different kinds of Black, Brown, Boer, and their own Jewish culture – have contributed a disproportionate number of distinguished anthropologists.[9]

The place at Chorlton meant that later, when we moved to Blackpool, I was able to transfer to a school of equivalent status, still not a grammar school but a 'secondary technical', where I was to benefit from two inspiring teachers.

---

9   For example, Max Gluckman, Adam, Hilda, Leo and Jessica Kuper, Isaac Schapera, Meyer Fortes and Cecil Helman among others. See Kuper (1973).

In The Avenues, surveillance was effective well before CCTV was thought of. With hardly any cars, The Avenues were safe for even small children: we played on the road and were visible from a variety of windows, doors and gardens.[10] We were often chaperoned by officious girls as part of their female apprenticeship. Girls a few years older than us were delegated by our Mam's to shepherd us about. They enjoyed it far too much. Eleven-year-old Betty Higginbotham from Caradoc Avenue, was especially insufferable – she wiped our noses every two minutes, checked our language – and threatened to report us to our Mam's if we weren't obedient to her capricious control.

By the time we reached nine or ten however, boys had joined same-age gangs and were relatively free of controls – though we were vulnerable to other gangs. We roamed nearby bomb-sites and un-built-on parcels of land (called 'crofts') where we played 'capture and pursuit'; cowboys and Indians, Germans and British. We swapped army badges and shell and bomb shrapnel (those with copper from shell bandings being especially valued). We trespassed on the electric railways, put pennies on the rails for trains to squash flat and penetrated 'enemy territories' belonging to other gangs we fervently thought dangerous. We selected suspect 'German spies' and followed these often bemused individuals – sometimes for miles. This often involved travelling long distances on buses – without of course, paying – we went on the upper deck and hid under seats. We were free, fearless and feral – but despite present day fears and paranoia, none of us came to harm – and none of us met a pederast.

When girls reached thirteen or fourteen, after menarche, the gender divide began in earnest. Whenever my Aunty Annie visited with my cousin Vera – eight months older than me – she was increasingly brought into their gossip groups while I, after I reached eleven or so, was excluded and sent out on errands.

The girls gloried in their emerging status; they could not wait to be grown up. On a bus trip with Vera, she insisted on paying the adult fare though she was only thirteen – and it wasn't payable until she was fourteen! What annoyed me was the relish with which she asked the conductor for 'one and a half'.

---

10 Oscar Newman (1972) specifies that crime will reduce if a residential area's physical characteristics permit residents to see what is happening in their adjacent public space. He defines this as their 'defensible space'.

# Anti-Semitism: the Church to the Rescue

Boys were expected to get into minor fights but Jewish boys were prone to be victims rather than antagonists. At eight, I was often persecuted by two bigger lads, the scruffy McGibbon brothers. Well-known as bullies, they were Catholics from Eckford Street who tended to pick on smaller Jewish boys, especially those from The Avenues. One day, returning from the corner shop in Bunyard Street, I was waylaid. Pinning me to a wall and chanting – 'Dirty Jew, dirty Jew,' they punched me and bloodied my nose.

Luckily, it happened that among Mam's closest friends was a respected trio of devout Catholics, the MacNally sisters. Celia and Lucy kept a hairdressing salon on nearby Queen's Road, and Molly, the eldest and most assertive, was a cobbler and – as she proudly asserted – 'the only woman cobbler in all Manchester'. The sisters had high prestige in the Catholic community: not only were they pious but their brother was a priest.

Molly, steeped in literature and knowing much of Dickens' works by heart, was a toughie who would tackle anyone. When she heard about the McGibbon brothers, she readily took charge. 'We'll stop this, you'll see. I'll have a word with Father MacRae (the local priest). He'll settle them – for sure.' He did indeed. The next time we met they looked sullen, but said never a word and crossed the street.

Catholic priests possessed considerable authority over their working-class congregants. Their moral authority was buttressed by their welfare role and the access they had to limited funds to alleviate hardship. They would intervene to gain employment for out-of-work parishioners, organise parish-wide collections in cases of domestic disaster and were valued for arbitrating disputes. They would intercede with local authorities – and occasionally with the police in cases of minor delinquency. Priestly interventions could therefore carry considerable weight. It was understood however, that their enthusiastic support might diminish if a parishioner's family was less than respectably pious. Since families, not individuals, were collectively labelled as respectable or not, the removal of a priest's support from one family member could prove an effective sanction against the whole family. It wasn't surprising then that after Father MacRae's intervention the McGibbons' bullying stopped – and stopped permanently. I was intrigued when later, as an anthropologist in Newfoundland, I found that there both Catholic and Protestant ministers occupied similar roles.

Contrasts in The Avenues between the social distance of Catholics and their priests and the more egalitarian relationship of Jews to their rabbis were marked. Rabbis were certainly respected – but that did not prevent them being argued with.[11]

## The Brutality of Hebrew School (Cheder)

As well as being pressed to be clever and hard-working at school, Jewish boys from age five or six, had to attend Hebrew classes *(cheder)* seven days a week, for two-hours after school and at weekends.

Jewish folklore abounds with tales of sadistic *malamudin*, the teachers of young children. So it was at Rebbe Balkind's *cheder* in Bignor Street. The *Rebbe* was a learned and kindly man but Mr Finsberg, his assistant, was a stereotypical *malamud:* fierce and unyielding, he rarely smiled. To punish us he wielded a leather machine strap, circular in section, and applied with force to our outstretched hands. One day I misbehaved and was given a swipe that raised an angry weal.

When Mam saw it she was appalled. She marched with me as living evidence of outrageous abuse to Rebbe Balkind's house and hammered at his door. The *Rebitzin*, his shy young wife, nervously opened it. Seeing my angry Mam she hesitantly explained: 'Rebbe Balkind can't see anyone today: he's unwell; he's in bed.'

And retreating, she attempted to close the door. 'He'll see me,' said Mam grimly, forcing her way into the hall and dragging me along in the rear. Given a year to live at fourteen, later warned against getting married and then on having children; she had never given way to her own chronic illness[12] and didn't lightly cater to those of others. The *Rebbetzin*, recognising an irresistible force, went to see her husband – then came to usher us upstairs.

Rebbe Balkind, propped on pillows, was every inch the bearded patriarch. He listened gravely as Mam expounded on the outrage done to her first-born. Then, after I had been pushed forward, he examined the damaged hand with its undeniable evidence of outrage. He paused judicially, nodded, appeared to be struggling with a difficult matter of doctrine then slowly pronounced his judgement.

'Mrs Margolis,[13] believe me, if you had thirty children in your class like your Gerald – then you'd hit them. You really would.'

'Oh no I wouldn't,' Mam flashed. 'I certainly wouldn't.'

---

11  Indeed, there is a long tradition of Jews actually arguing with God. My friend David Nelken, a scholar of Jewish history (and other subjects), confirms that God has laughed when admitting that sometimes he loses the arguments.
12  Damaged heart valves from rheumatic fever.
13  See p. 24 for an explanation of when and why the family name was changed.

'Believe me, Mrs Margolis you would. You really would.'
'No! – I wouldn't hit them.'
'You think you wouldn't, Mrs Margolis.'
'You're quite wrong, Rebbe Balkind. I wouldn't hit them. *I'd kill them!*'

She paused – then having the *Rebbe's* full attention, she very quietly delivered her *coup-de-grâce*: 'That's one reason I'm not a teacher.'

The Rebbe Balkind, scholar of the Talmud and master of rabbinic argument had met his match. He had to agree that, 'On this occasion, perhaps a word to Mr Finsberg might be in order; that perhaps, yes, there might indeed have been a punishment here that… maybe had been a little excessive…'

From then on, it was impossible to play one off against the other: Mam and the *Rebbe* were united by mutual respect.

# War

I was six when war started and twelve when we left 'The Avenues.' It was during the war that I learned to listen, an invaluable injunction of Mam's being: 'always keep your ears and eyes open' – valuable advice in wartime when resources were scarce – and priceless as an inbuilt habit for a potential anthropologist.

With war came evacuation. In September 1939, city children became 'evacuees' and were sent to the country to save us from air raids – each with a gas mask and a name label. Children from my school were sent to farms around Belmont – not too far from Manchester. But my evacuation lasted only a week – though it was a wonderful week. I was billeted with my best friend Harold Harris in the charge of an elderly, kind but ineffectual farming couple with no children, Mr and Mrs Pierce.

The Pierces' farm was a boyhood paradise. We were introduced to a whole range of new knowledge and experiences – finding that milk for instance, came from cows. And the Pierces who had never had children of their own, with kindness, and completely out of their depth, fed us every day on hoarded tinned fruit – a rare luxury – and, as an added bonus – did not require us to wash. We mucked out the pigs and were taught how to milk the cows. But then my Auntie Dora, who had somehow wrangled a job with a car and petrol, came to see how I was getting on. She found me covered in pig-shit with Harold alongside trying to milk a cow. She needed only to glance at our filthy clothes and happy unwashed faces to be appalled. She stormed at the Pierces' and I was snatched up and brought home. Then she contacted the Harris's who arranged a similar rescue for

Harold. Mam, who had been doubtful about evacuation from the start, pronounced: 'If we're going to die, then we'll all die together.'

This view took hold in The Avenues despite officialdom's policies, as more evacuated children began to reappear. If any of our houses had been bombed there might have been a change of mind – but government advice was never taken as gospel round our way.

Dad, 'called up' to the army early, had soon been invalided out and went back to his factory – now making uniforms. Those in 'reserved occupations' though excused military service, doubled as auxiliary – part-time – ARP (Air Raid Precautions) wardens or as 'Specials' (Special police constables) with authority to enforce wartime controls. Unsurprisingly, they attracted antagonism.

Mrs Webb, a stout, belligerent woman was antagonistic to anyone who crossed her – but ARP wardens were her pet hate. Much of their time was spent checking unshielded lights in the blackout that just might be visible to enemy aircraft – and Mrs Webb was 'a slack black-outer'.

One morning, seeing Mam returning from the corner shop, she crossed the road and, with waving arms and vivid grimacing, told how the night before; she had 'really wiped the floor with that Robinson.' Mr Robinson, a clerk in a reserved occupation, was an ARP warden. He enjoyed the job enormously, and with his thin body and bony inquisitorial nose would spring into officious action at even a glint of any unauthorised light. But he was no match for Mrs Webb.

> Do you know what he said? He came banging on my bloody door and do you know what he said? He told me to "put that light out!" [the standard air raid warden's cry]. Then he had the cheek to say "Eh Missis, don't you know there's a war on?" [another standard cry]. I gave it to 'im. "Oh yes," I said, "Oh yes – I do know there's a bloody war on. I bloody ought to – my man's in it; not like you! Now bugger off!" And he did!

Mam was full of sympathy and praise: wardens weren't popular. And though she had never had much time for Mr Robinson – she had a lot in common with Mrs Webb. They were both bulky Northern women and in the North especially, the more bulky they were, the more tough, and aggressive they could be. This was particularly evident during the war when women had sole responsibility for the care of their families.

## Public Shaming

Mam was high in the assertion league – particularly if anything appeared to threaten her family's food supply. She demonstrated this when facing Mrs Reid, the stingy proprietor of a grocer's shop at the bottom of Eckford

Street. Avenues women tended to meet there to exchange gossip. It often acted as a crowded social centre – especially since people could not shop around but had to be 'registered' at a specific grocer's.

Ronnie Frankenberg, an anthropologist, when doing fieldwork in a Welsh border village, tells how he was sent by his landlady to buy a loaf of bread. When he returned she noted how quick he had been. 'But it's only two minutes' walk away,' he answered. 'Huh,' he was told, 'it takes me an hour to buy a loaf of bread'.[14] So it was at Reid's corner shop.

One day, after collecting our rations, Mam found one of our weekly ration of eggs was broken – a big loss as rationing limited us each to one egg a week. Mam went to the shop for a replacement but Mrs Reid wouldn't deliver. Mam insisted. Not realising her vulnerability, Mrs Reid still foolishly refused. Mam told her that she expected grocers would receive an allowance to cover breakages and she believed Mrs Reid was keeping these back for her own family. Mrs Reid denied this. Apparent deadlock. But every local area had a Food Office – an outpost of the Ministry of Food. Mam immediately went there, put her case, found her hunch was correct and obtained details of the permitting regulation.

Armed with this she waited until the week's busiest time. When the shop was full she elbowed her way to the front and, confronting Mrs Reid, recounted the deception, quoted the appropriate regulation and publicly demanded recompense. A humiliated Mrs Reid was forced to pass over a replacement egg and, having suitably shamed her before a shop full of customers, Mam then announced she would be changing our registration to Cooper's,[15] the rival grocers at the corner of Bunyard Street. A number of others, also with accumulated grievances, did so too – even though this meant paying off their ongoing debts that were then a standard feature of the grocer/client relationship among the working class.[16]

Mam's hunch – that there was likely to be an allowance to cover broken eggs – offered a lesson I later applied when studying workplace fiddles: that once you have a key to a person's motives and a structure that can satisfy them, then you have a key to their likely, albeit hidden,

---

14  Frankenberg (1990)
15  Wartime rationing required people being registered to deal at a specific shop.
16  Ongoing debt relationships give credit to families needing regular provisions but whose incomes are erratic (Melville, 1973). Later I found similar arrangements were offered by grocers in Newfoundland to the families of casually-employed longshoremen. (p. 159). They are common too in India and around the Mediterranean. This early introduction to both public shaming and to debt relationships offered valuable insights when I later researched the tight-knit community of Newfoundland's longshoremen.

behaviours. This approach involves not accepting roles as they appear or are presented. I learned to look for people's hidden agendas, to deduce what was in their interests and to uncover how these interests could be accommodated.

Public shaming – common in many parts of the world[17] – and enhanced as it is by gossip[18] – is found in tight communities wherever social relationships are visible and intimate. Shaming, like gossip, affirms shared moral standards and reflects not only on the individual but on their family. Its effects are more powerful and direct than gossip. This is why there are so often sanctions *within* the family when one of their members breaks a communal norm. The intervention of the priest with the two McGibbon brothers, described earlier, worked because it involved the reputation of the whole family.

## The Black Market: 'Keeping Your Ears and Eyes Open'

Car use was strictly controlled and petrol tightly rationed. Dr McBride, our GP, had a car to visit patients on his rounds, and Sid Williams, our neighbourhood black marketer, had another to service his round – supplying black-market eggs to eager customers – at eight shillings a dozen.[19]

Everyone was always pleased to see Sid, who sported the thin moustache and drape suit of the stereotypical wartime 'spiv'. Dapper, always smiling, Sid was a great flirt and always popular with the women – not surprising given the shortage of men. But his visits were erratic. He would frequently disappear – when the Military Police caught him – and then, failing to keep him, would return a month or two later, smiling as ever. I later realised how Sid must have been part of an organised and extensive black economy circuit, a system oiled by bribery and covering production from the farms, with him doing the distribution via his illegal car that ran on illicit petrol. Of course, the whole circuit had to be based on a willing, participative clientele, one rather different from the government's 'all pulling together, Britain can take it' propaganda line. [20]

Buying food on the black market raised no concerns in The Avenues. 'Mad' Frankie Fraser, one of the notorious Kray gang in London's East End, explained how he had begun his apprenticeship as a wartime

---

17  For example, see Campbell (1964, pp. 310-320).
18  Gluckman (1963)
19  Then costing about four hours' work at average prevailing wage rates.
20  Smith (1996)

gangster, with black market crime. He reported that for many like him, the war offered wonderful opportunities and was supported by a necessary groundswell of popular collusive support.[21] 'We never had problems getting hold of 'duff stuff' or getting rid of it. Difficulties were smoothed away – there were always people keen to have their palms greased.'[22]

So it was in The Avenues. Everyone kept an eye (and an ear) open for 'duff stuff' – especially food, without worrying too much about where it came from: foot-high bags of broken biscuits would occasionally appear – brought round by Lily, a friend of Mam's, who worked in the nearby biscuit factory. A large amount of their produce it seemed, when broken, was taken by staff as a perk. We always passed some to Lucy and Celia, Mam's hairdressing friends. They in turn tipped us off when their neighbour, the local greengrocer, had a rare delivery of oranges. These were available only on children's green ration books and only then to those who were quick to claim them. In this way, by reciprocity.[23] people carefully nurtured their networks.

Information spreads fast in a tightly-knit community. One day after school, at my friend Michael Olsberg's house, the two of us were engrossed in playing with his Meccano when his *bobba* (grandmother) came rushing in, breathless, to see Michael's Mam and announce: 'They've got [cooking] oil at Johnson's'[24] (their corner shop).

His Mam immediately set off. I said *'I've got to go,'* and rushed home to tell my Mam. She didn't wait, buttoned on her coat and stopping only to pass the news to a friend, dashed to join what she found was a huge queue.

---

21  *Bad Boys of the Blitz* (2005). The wartime government was keen to project the image of a nation, all unitedly pulling together and to deny any disturbing publicity about deviants or gross profiteering. To this end Herbert Morrison, the Home Secretary, on 5 March 1942, threatened to ban the *Daily Mirror* after it published a cartoon by Philip Zec that criticised and therefore acknowledged war profiteering. My experience was that residents of The Avenues were not fooled. See Smith (1996).

22  'Mad' Frankie explained that looting was common during air raids and that his fellow gang members would readily don ARP (Air Raid Precautions) and firemen's uniforms to give them authority. They had no difficulty getting hold of uniforms.

23  Reciprocity – the exchange of gifts, services (and, as here, information) – was first discussed by Mauss (1954) and later shown to be a fundamental and universal feature of social process. Mair 1992, 2nd Ed. ch. 11, considerably extends the discussion.

24  Highly prized among Jews for cooking, though largely unknown then to non-Jews

She returned an hour later, triumphantly clutching her bottle. There was glowing praise for me for 'having kept my ears open'.

People were ingenious and often unscrupulous in getting extra. My Auntie Dora, an actress manqué, went to the local Food Office and 'speaking cockney', claimed to have been 'bombed out' in London with the loss of all her belongings including her precious ration book and identity card. When she returned she re-enacted, in dramatic detail a stunning tale of tragedy, pathos and death. 'Everything gone – the whole house – all the furniture – just matchsticks and rubble – all gone – even... (here she broke into sobs) even... Jessie, the dog.'

They gave her an emergency ration card for two weeks. We laughed and gloried at her triumph. So did our neighbours who heard the story. Again it indicated how few in The Avenues were taken in by the 'one nation' propaganda.

At eleven when I moved to Chorlton Central School in the suburbs. I found a richness of horse chestnut trees – a rarity in urban Cheetham. Now I too could join the 'enterprise economy'. I collected large conkers in the lunch hour to sell at Hebrew school to a ready market at a penny each. Then my glamorous grown-up cousin Evelyn – who had a reputation as 'fast' because she went out with US officers – had them collect the comic sections of American papers for me. These too were readily saleable at a double page for a penny. What did not sell at Hebrew school, I brought back and sold in The Avenues. Though there was a shortage of comics during the war and a block on the manufacture of toys, there was no shortage of money. Indeed the main feature of the wartime economy was never shortage of money but a shortage of goods.

## The Blitz

Though our parents' lives were dislocated by war, we children were freer of anxieties: to us war offered immense adventures – despite Manchester, with its heavy munitions factories, being a prime target for German bombers. Throughout 1944 the Blitz was intensive. During night-long air raids lasting up to ten or more hours, we took cover in our Anderson family shelter – a cleverly designed, corrugated zinc construction, half buried in the garden but invariably waterlogged and, when we were lucky to get them, lit by candles. I was always far too excited to sleep, even if it had been possible against the drone of aero engines, the whistles and explosions of bombs and the periodic dull 'whump' from nearby anti-aircraft batteries.

Dad told how he had seen Zeppelins in World War I as they bombed Manchester. Now he found the air raids as thrilling as I did. During raids we both crowded to the shelter's entrance, gazing up at the night sky to follow the battle as it raged above. It was spectacular – lines of luminous tracer bullets criss-crossed the skies, and waving searchlight beams tried to randomly highlight bombers and fix them for the ack-ack guns. [25] Often they lit up inflated barrage balloons tethered to cables and designed to prevent the bombers flying low, while flares periodically flashed and lit up wide expanses of sky. And over all was the roar and rumble of high-explosive bombs and the pulsating drum of aero engines.

Mam would get angry at both of us as she tried to keep us from the entrance – falling shrapnel was a real fear. But she had little effect. We craned to watch the drama, tried to fix the direction of a bomb's mounting whistle as it hurtled to earth, attempted to sense its final landing place and guess at whether an engine's drone belonged to 'one of ours' or was 'one of theirs'. These games never palled.

One night, at the height of the Blitz, we were both crowding the entrance, when a piercing whistle mounting to a shriek was followed by the loudest of ear-splitting explosions. The ground quaked as if a giant thunderclap had directly struck. Dad said only, 'That was close.' And then went quiet. When, later we saw an orange glow in the nearby sky, heard the crackling of fire and smelled pungent, acrid smoke, Dad said: 'Seems like Blacks has got it.' Blacks, a big nearby factory, produced packaging, and Dad was right. Blacks that night *had* got it – with considerable loss of life.

After a month or more of consecutive ten-hour air raids, Mam had had enough. Fed up with our cold, wet Anderson, she devised a shelter in our lounge by turning our heavy three piece suite on its sides and creating a space into which we could lie in comfort. Shortly after her brainwave, we had a visit from her favourite brother, a hero of mine, Uncle Lionel who, though in the RAF, always seemed able to fiddle the odd day off. He was staying the night when once more, the sirens went. As Mam started to prepare our internal shelter, Uncle Lionel rocked with laughter. A jovial soul who, as a youngster before the war, had been a feckless ne'er-do-well until forced into the Services by a not-uncommon police ultimatum of the time: 'Sign on – or we'll throw the book at you.' The Air Force channelled his love of risk-taking by having him jump out of planes to test the design of parachutes. He knew about bombs and explosives too. 'What' he asked,

---

25  Ack-ack guns: anti-aircraft guns

'will you do if there's a fire?' Within seconds we were back in the Anderson.

The Avenues were fortunate. We were some distance from the main targets, the munitions and the Ford vehicle factories at Old Trafford (where Auntie Dora worked for a spell) and well away from the city centre's railway terminals. None of The Avenue's houses was hit – though a couple of small incendiary bombs fell impotently on our garden.

## VE Day and the Street-Party

What united Avenue people against 'the outside' was not just the war, but that we lived in 'modern' houses and were owner-occupiers (despite the mortgages), unlike the denizens of Bunyard and Eckford streets at the bottom of the hill who rented their Victorian 'back-to-backs'. There was no visiting their houses. Their children did not play with us in our 'Avenues' nor we with them in their 'Streets'.

I was eleven when VE Day (to celebrate Victory in Europe) was announced. A group of fifteen or so women from The Avenues then met in the road to arrange a children's celebratory street party. I went out to listen. Our next-door neighbour Mr Rimmington, clerk in a reserved occupation, happened to be passing. Foolishly he joined in. Worse, he suggested extending the party to the children of Bunyard and Eckford streets. 'Wouldn't it be best,' he asked mildly, 'to have one big party?'

This brought a barrage of abuse:

'Who do you think you are?'

'This is for women. You've no place here.'

When he persisted the abuse turned vicious.

'You – you're not a proper man – you're a clerk – in a reserved bloody[26] occupation, aren't you.'

The cry was taken up.

'Bloody coward – excused army service, isn't he?'

'You've been having a 'cushy' time at home while our men are away fighting, haven't you?'

Vainly he attempted to talk of unity but was shouted down by this instantly mobilised feminine front. Again he half-heartedly tried to put his view but quickly gave up, and disheartened, slunk away. The Eckford and Bunyard Street mothers – not being 'people like us' – were left to arrange their own street party.

---

26 'Bloody' was by far the most common expletive in use by both sexes at this time. Fuckin' was largely restricted to men and only used in male company.

# The Move to Blackpool – and the End of Childhood

By war's end three brothers had arrived: Len, Mel and Mike, and with post-war development came economic boom. Mam became restless. She was worried about opportunities for her children in Manchester and had heard that schools were much better in Blackpool, a seaside resort fifty miles away. Dad however, preferred to stay within the cocoon of his Yiddish-speaking Manchester workshop. But Mam had a sister and a brother in Blackpool – both assertive entrepreneurs – one with a boarding house, the other, a hotel. They were doing well and were persuasive. 'Come to Blackpool,' Auntie Kath assured Mam, 'and open a boarding house. There's good money to be made.'

Big earnings could indeed be made. Holiday-makers clamoured to spend their demob gratuities (a money grant given to servicemen on discharge) together with Post War 'Credits' (a refund of excess tax paid during the war by civilian workers). It was all part of a wash of money successfully designed to kick-start a post-war Keynesian boom. This too, was the beginning of 'holidays with pay,' an early introduction by the newly-elected Labour government. It was a time of optimism and change.

'Accommodation in Blackpool is scarce,' insisted my Uncle Wilf. 'Why – they'll even pay to sleep in the bath.' And he apparently knew what he was talking about. After all, he owned the Collingwood Hotel on the Promenade.

So Mam determined to move to Blackpool and open a boarding house. Getting a mortgage would present no problem – credit was readily available, and selling the sunshine-semi would raise enough for a deposit. Dad, never one to move unless he was pushed, had therefore to be pushed. One day Mam took a day excursion train to Blackpool leaving the family in charge of Auntie Dora who was staying with us on one of her periodic extended stays. Mam returned late that same evening to announce she had bought a four-bedroomed Victorian terraced house – ideal as a boarding house if we all squeezed in together. Dad had no choice.

With Mam firmly in charge, we moved to 16 Devonshire Road, Blackpool and prepared to make our fortune – with Auntie Dora as main help and with four children – me, the eldest at twelve, and Michael the youngest at three months.

Dad was to keep his job, and this meant travelling each day to his workshop in Manchester. It was a move that would shift him firmly into the background – a common role for the husbands of landladies.[27] But our

---

27  Walton (1978, ch. 4)

move to Blackpool was to reveal an aspect of his character that startled me then and has intrigued me since.

Dad was normally awkward and self-effacing even at family gatherings. He would stand lost on the edge of a group, taking little part in the swirls of conversation surrounding him: it seemed as if he had little to say. It was a characteristic that annoyed Mam who, vociferous and outgoing, could not understand his long silences and lack of sociability. But there was more to him than he revealed.

Once a year when Manchester closed for 'wakes weeks' (the annual holidays when all work in a Northern town ceased), its workers would swarm into Blackpool. And those who were Jewish gathered on the North Pier – to meet those they normally met during the rest of the year. North Pier was known with good reason as 'Jews' Pier'.

One year I went with Dad to meet his co-workers. There I saw a man transformed. He was speaking Yiddish. He even had a different name – they referred to him not as 'Ellis' but as 'Elkie', and he was animated. He waved his arms, joked, responded and laughed. Here he interacted as I had never known him do before. My taciturn, silent father was now vibrant, eloquent, amusing. I could not understand a word these gesticulating, jolly men were saying, and felt isolated but I was pushed forward to be proudly introduced – and then Dad went on to gabble again in this strange tongue from his past that I could not decipher.

This transformation lasted only while we were on the pier. Dad never stopped being an urban 'ghetto Jew'. Years later when visiting my brother Mel's house at Bala in North Wales – an area of great natural beauty and designated a National Park – he was massively unimpressed. 'Call this a park? Where are the bandstands? Where are the bowling greens? And the tennis courts? It's just grass and water.'

As soon as the last of his secularly educated sons had left the family home Dad, then a widower, was quick to pave over the front garden. By means of red and grey paving stones arranged in a chess-board pattern he proudly displayed his urbanite distaste for nature. The same approach is evident in all London's Jewish quarters. In Golders Green and Stamford Hill, for example, nearly all the gardens are paved over. In the perpetual battle between nature and nurture, Jewish urban culture usually wins.

Mam was enthused by the move to Blackpool. She decided no-one would stay at a boarding house with a proprietor called 'Margolis'. 'They think they'll get greasy foreign food.' Our family name therefore, had to be changed. Dad was not consulted about this loss of his name. So we dropped 'Margolis', became 'Mars'[28] and advertised in the *Manchester Evening News*:

Mrs Mars' boarding house
Blackpool's North Shore
Full Board 12/6d a day

And we waited – hopefully – for guests who would, if necessary, sleep in the bath. We did not make our fortune – mortgage repayments,[29] illness and four growing children saw to that – though the schools *were* better.

Blackpool was very different from The Avenues – and contrasts sharpened the comparison. Here, neighbours appeared not to know each other. There were few of the social controls that made The Avenues such a tight community[30]: no public shamings, no debt relationships. Gossip had little place – people took only minimal interest in their neighbours – or much cared what they thought.

---

28  Years later 'the Brothers' got together and agreed to change our names back to Margolis. But it would, we found, have raised big problems since by then professional qualifications were involved. And as we wished to retain the same name for all of us, the idea was, reluctantly, dropped.

29  At that time the valuation of houses suitable as boarding houses was at a premium of roughly £1,000 a bedroom.

30  Tönnies (1887) had early noted a duality between the characteristics of small face-to-face communities such as The Avenues, that he termed *Gemeinschaft* – based on feelings of togetherness and mutual bonds, and *Gesellschaft* – groupings more typical of urban settings such as Blackpool, where people are more individualist, competitive, relate on less dimensions, and are maintained by serving their members' individual aims and goals.

CHAPTER TWO

# BLACKPOOL

## Blackpool's Vulgar Aesthetic

To its millions of working-class visitors, Blackpool presented a new and exotic world, one in marked contrast to the drab conformity of their industrial towns. As soon as they emerged from their trains and charabancs they were engulfed in a maelstrom of exuberant, brightly-painted stalls, primary-coloured posters and cafés with twenty-foot high menus – all with their staffs beseeching custom: salesmen bellowing at them to buy TV sets at five pounds; fountain pens – 'as good as a Parker 51' – were pressed upon them for less than the price of a portion of fish and chips. They were implored to see 'the dreadful effects of mutilating drug addiction', to gape at a genuine mermaid, a two-headed giant, the biggest rat in the world. And not least, to gaze at the nude, albeit stationary beauties at *Le Palais d'Etranges Demoiselles.*[1]

Blackpool portrayed a world as different from their day-to-day experience as it was possible to get. In this it was far more successful than its nearest rivals – Morecambe and Southport.

From the first, I was captivated by Blackpool's excess, its surfeit of colour and energy, its essential 'otherness', so unlike the dour industrial Manchester where I grew up. Here for a brief period every summer, holiday-makers enjoyed carnival time – when they could carry to extremes behaviours that were normally constrained.[2] So they drank to excess, sang on the streets in raucous groups, and spent their saved –up money without restraint. Here their low industrial status was reversed. They were courted, deferred to, called 'Sir' or 'Madam.

Exaggeration, fantasy and vulgarity became the norm. A famous advertisement in 1887 invited visitors to: 'Come to the Winter Gardens for

---

1 Stage nudes were only allowed to move after 1967 when the Lord Chamberlain's powers of stage censorship were removed.
2 Victor Turner (1967) used the phrase 'time out of time' to describe 'situations where usual social rules and roles are disbanded'.

sixpence and spit on Bill Holland's 100 guinea carpet.' This 'vulgar' constituency represented the aesthetic – if not of all holiday-makers, then certainly of a defining core.

To be sure, a minority asserted a different identity. Repelled by what Blackpool offered they holidayed at places like St Annes further down the coast where they could demonstrate moderation, restraint, a preference for muted colours, temperate behaviour and more restrained interaction. A Blackpool joke went that in St Annes, 'Sex is what the coal comes in.' Whether for or against, both used taste to confirm their identities, to mark out not just who they were but most importantly, who they were not. And in their choices they both condemned what each despised in the other. It has been well observed that: 'Tastes are perhaps first and foremost, distastes.'[3]

Blackpool then, allowed working-class holiday-makers to assert their identity in opposition to the genteel and the aspirant. It relished its vulgarity and took every opportunity to assert it. The *Daily Express* once sent a young reporter to do a feature on the town. Naïvely seeking to get a cheap rise, he interviewed the chief librarian, F.E. Cronshaw, who was also curator of the town's art gallery. 'Mr Cronshaw,' he was asked, 'wouldn't you agree, there isn't much culture in Blackpool?' Cronshaw, no effete artistic administrator but a bluff, no-nonsense, Northerner, firmly asserted the town's perspective on culture – and on intrusive Southerners: 'Culture? Why, Lad, Blackpool stinks of culture.'

The town savoured this story. Those with a sense of history recalled William Holland's famous carpet.

## The Road to Rapid Growth

In 1840 Blackpool had been a genteel middle-class watering place with a population of two thousand. When the railway from the hinterland to the coast was laid in 1846, cheap day trips followed and the town's growth became exponential. And at its forefront marched an army of entrepreneurs.

By 1905 Blackpool had travelled far from the genteel. By then, a raucous 'fun factory', its resident population had reached 50,000; the Tower, the Pleasure Beach and three piers had been built, the shoreline straightened, and seven miles of Promenade created – with hotels and boarding houses lining its length. In the centre of town, as the vaunted 'silent trams' roared and rattled their way along the new promenade, the

---

3   Bordieu (1984)

'Golden Mile' emerged. And along the North Shore, concrete cliffs were built to supplement the natural sort that were deemed inadequate: Blackpool had eradicated nature.

With the thirties slump the town had a relatively quiet time but after World War II, suppressed demand and growing prosperity together fuelled an insatiable demand for holidays. All Lancashire's resorts boomed – but Blackpool boomed fastest. From 1946, workers and their families flocked to the town – and the ambitious, the energetic and the greedy swarmed after them. Blackpool became a gold-rush frontier town and the new boom lifted it to new excesses. It offered a roller-coaster of bent rules, officials' corruption and rampant short-termist exploitation. This account of Blackpool is essentially as it was from the end of World War II to the middle of the 1960s, the period I know best.

## Making It the Blackpool Way

During its post-war heyday, most Blackpool folk shared a simple aim: to make their fortunes as fast as they could. To do so they competed to get money off their seven million visitors,[4] most of whom regularly returned every year. Not all by any means were rampant entrepreneurs but there were enough to create an overall climate – a cultural bias[5] – of vigorous enterprise that set the tone for the town as a whole.

While the boom lasted, the town throbbed with energetic enterprise and its corollary – exploitation, both of visitors and employees. Even as schoolchildren we saw ourselves as cunning predators, with the visitors as hunted innocents. We were buoyed by the town's confidently asserted mantra, heard whenever there were protests at sharp practice or outrageous prices: 'We've got to live in the winter.'

I only heard this disputed once – when an angry Scotsman objected to the local practice of imposing a sixpenny discount on Scottish one pound banknotes: 'Live in the winter? Aye – but not in the bloody Bahamas!'

By the time we left school at fifteen many of my classmates already had several years' work experience. Since there was big money to be made, laws controlling labour, including child labour, were bypassed and planning regulations and hygiene rules routinely overlooked. Corruption was rife in the Town Hall and the police. The Town Clerk, faced with

---

4  These were predominantly staying visitors. By the year 2000 the number had increased to 20 million but these were mostly day-trippers travelling by car who spent relatively little money in the town. (Blackpool residents have always called its holiday-makers 'visitors'.)

5  Douglas (1982a, ch. 9)

undeniable evidence of his department's systemic corruption, committed suicide. Earlier the Home Office had forced Lancashire's Chief Constable from office (he had recently been Blackpool's Chief Constable prior to his promotion).[6] This boisterous exuberance, reminiscent more of the Wild West than life in an English seaside resort, well reflected the mood and tenor of the town.

I and my brothers all had part-time jobs well before we left school. Throughout the holiday season, at weekends and school holidays, a juvenile labour force worked before school and after, in cafés, hotels and shops. Saturday mornings saw crowds of us jostling at the town's main railway stations to meet the incoming excursion trains with our home-made wheeled trolleys ('gyders'). We competed to take people's luggage to their boarding houses since the working class used taxis only in grave emergencies or for rites of passage.

Others of us would nobble holiday-makers as they queued for accommodation lists at the council's Information Bureau. Since a high proportion never booked their accommodation ahead and came 'on spec', residents would attempt to siphon them to their own family's boarding houses. It was a contest to get to visitors before the Bureau's clerks who, with their official lists, offered their own suggestions. We all knew they were paid off by the hotels and the bigger boarding houses.

The clerks, realising they were being bypassed, moved to stop touts from grazing off the queues. But survival means adaption. Two highly adaptive touts were my brothers Mike and Mel. From the age of eight they would queue *with* the visitors, until they got to the counter, then shout: 'We've got rooms. Why haven't you sent anyone to my Mam at 14 Banbury Avenue?' Those visitors sweating at the back of the line would hear them, queue-jump to the front, and clamour: 'We'll come to your place, lad, just take us to it.'

My brothers' next hurdle was to get them to the bus station and keep them talking as the bus went further and further inland and farther and farther from the sea. By the end of the journey, burdened with luggage and children, and cheerfully welcomed with tea and biscuits, they were usually resigned to accepting what they'd got.

Blackpool folk fostered ingenious ways to exploit their visitors – and each other. One of my classmates, Aubrey Firewater, scraped the cash to buy a cheap Kodak camera and had cards printed showing he was a photographer who specialised in every branch of photography that could

---

6  The *Glasgow Herald* of 11 May 2011 reported the Town Clerk's suicide on 20 Dec. 1955, and recalled the Chief Constable's dismissal in 1977.

ever have existed. He spent his every spare minute after school and at weekends on the sands handing out his cards to visitors as he pretended to take their snaps. Only when they showed interest, would Aubrey use film.

As an alleged specialist photographer of portraits, factory sites, animal studies and groups, Aubrey's enterprise sadly counted for little with the local magistrates who were keen for the town to get a share of his profits. He paid over 140 fines in three years for unlicensed selling – a typical score for that occupation – and a bearable overhead but calculatedly not enough to deter him. Aubrey and his fellow photographers shared a rich market; it was not until the sixties that cheap cameras and working-class affluence brought widespread camera ownership.

I never kept up with Aubrey after he entered full-time work. But at a seminar of scholars in the behavioural sciences, I sat next to Harold, another old Blackpool confederate. An ex-grammar school lad, he had been one of the Mile's most accomplished spielers – a skill he too had polished whilst still at school. His father, a market trader, had gone to the same Hebrew school (*cheder*) as my father. Later Harold morphed into a suave and distinguished Oxford professor and college fellow. We swapped notes about our subsequent jobs, the work we were doing, the politics of academe, and our shared grumbles about university administrators.

'But do you know, Harold,' I said, 'of all the things you've done, there's one I especially admire, quite apart from your academic work.'

'No,' he said, 'What's that?'

'Remember that time you were spieling[7] on the [Golden] Mile? You were so good your pitch stretched right across the promenade? You blocked the traffic, and got fined for obstruction? That was terrific! Remember it?'

He did not.

One can understand how Aubrey and Harold became so adept at developing their exploitative skills. With few bonds of community and no place for childhood, the role of the town's schools was central. Palatine Secondary Technical School was superb in fostering this aspect of our individualist education: the school playground was a thriving marketplace.

---

7   From 'spiel, a persuasive patter; one who delivers such patter especially of a salesman or market stall holder' – hence spieler – one who spiels (*Cassell's Dictionary of Slang*).

# A School for Dealing

Moving from Manchester to this maelstrom was a revelation but it was the change of schools that startled me most. I was twelve and from a Manchester school where boys chased each other around the playground or fought. But during breaks and at lunch-times, the playground at Palatine was largely deserted. Few played tag and few were chased. Instead most pupils gathered in small inward facing groups and kept close to the walls. They were playing brag or pontoon, and not for matches: as 'a school' Palatine was distinctive.

In post-war Britain, luxuries were as scarce as they had been in the war. A government slogan of the time insisted we had to 'Export or Die', and the home market was kept deprived. But luxuries, as in the war, were available – at a price. During breaks, two or three older boys could be seen moving from group to group with attaché cases. These they opened to offer scarce exotics such as nylon stockings and artificial silk ties: our playground simulated a trainee wholesale market.

Like all good schools, Palatine prepared us to make the best of what was on offer. I was not surprised to learn later that one of my old classmates had pioneered a new kind of direct selling. During his National Service he had distributed navy tobacco and blankets – to the North Koreans. Other schoolmates became accomplished and highly paid spielers on the Golden Mile or the Pleasure Beach or dealers in anything from property to plastics. Palatine was surely one of Britain's first business schools. Here personal development focused on 'making it'.

The chairman of our school governors, Councillor Charles Higginson, was a kindly, well-intentioned local butcher. A tubby, fresh-faced, smiley man, he often gave sixpences to Palatine pupils he met in town. The Councillor had done well and in middle age looked exactly what he was – a comfortable, benign, satisfied, and slightly flash tradesman with a small chain of shops. As an archetypal small-town Conservative, Councillor Higginson was the ideal choice as our chairman of governors – his approach to education so perfectly represented the town's robust entrepreneurialism.

Known affectionately as 'Ch-Ch-Ch-Charlie' because of a stammer, his annual speech introducing the guests on Prize Giving Day was the delight of the school year and was eagerly and cruelly awaited. But, despite his delivery problems, Charlie always persevered.

One speech day, after painfully manoeuvring his way through, 'Honoured guests, Mr Headmaster, teachers, parents, boys and girls,' he announced that, before introducing the main guest, he would like to pass on some good advice he had had from his mother. It was then he began to unravel. 'A l-l-long time ago,' he began, 'm-m-m-my m-mother said to me,' a long pause, then it came: 'Ch-Ch-Ch-Charlie...'

It was too much: the school, pupils and teachers alike, rocked – totally out of control. Charlie though, persisted and tried again – and again – until finally he did succeed in putting over his message. 'M-m-my mother always s-s- said "Education is wonderful." It's a m-m-marvellous thing to have – so get out there and see you g-g-grab as much of it as you c-c-can.' His idea of education as commodity predated Thatcher by forty years...

Not that Palatine School ignored educational tradition. Speech days always ended with a full-throated rendition of the school hymn, *Non Nobis Domine*, sung entirely in Latin. This represented a recurrent triumph for Miss Thompson, our music teacher, since Latin had never been taught at Palatine – despite the school having a Latin motto: *Per Ardua Ad Alta*.[8]

Palatine, as a secondary technical school, was unhappily intermediate between the grammar schools that did have Latin and the secondary moderns that had very little of anything. The political theorists had planned that one would produce professionals via higher education whilst the other was for the seventy percent of Eleven Plus 'failures'. We, the middle ten percent in our 'sec-techs' (and central schools), would either sink to the level of the sec-mods; rise through technical apprenticeships (there were none in Blackpool), or become clerks. But to make it as a clerk or a library assistant in Blackpool's local government – where real careers were thought possible – you needed the bent ear of a bent councillor. Very few of us had this benefit, while hardly anyone went on to higher education. Luckily for us, Blackpool offered the sort of alternative career aspirations that theorists could never have planned.

---

8   'By hard work to the top'

CHAPTER THREE

# THE GOLDEN MILE

## Spielers, Gees and Illusions

Nowhere was enterprise more rampant than at the town's two great hubs
of exploitation – the Golden Mile and the Pleasure Beach. They were well
placed; the Mile straddling the Central Promenade, opposite the last
section of sand to be covered by the tide; the Pleasure Beach at the
Promenade's southern edge – where there is nowhere else to go. Many of
Palatine Sec-Tech's pupils graduated to one or the other after leaving
school.

The Mile, like much of Blackpool, is an overstatement. Occupying a
quarter mile stretch of Promenade between the North and Central piers, the
Mile gradually grew as entrepreneurs took over what had been the gardens
of promenade boarding houses, called forecourts. In the sixties
competition for space was high and every forecourt was occupied.[1]

Here, holiday-makers massed to spend their savings at the amusement
arcades, shooting galleries, 'mock auctions', pubs and cafés. They were
harangued by spielers to patronise bagatelle stalls with games offering
prizes or stalls selling rock. They queued to gape at clever optical
illusions: 'Cleo – the Mermaid in the Goldfish Bowl' whose image was
four inches long but who waved and smiled. And they stood astonished at
'The Most Gruesome Sight You've Ever Seen – The Headless Lady'.
Women queued at the tents of its two fortune-tellers, and crowds thronged
the forecourts of the live shows. The bizarre has always had a place on the
Mile. A still famous exhibit in the thirties had been the unfrocked and
scandalous Rector of Stiffkey, exhibited for no good reason in a barrel,
who was eventually killed by a circus lion.

---

1   The Mile's valuation assessment (gross value) was £55,000 in 1958
    representing 'reasonable' average rents with the tenant paying rates but not
    maintenance. Its rateable value was £33,000 at the then poundage of 13
    shillings and 9 pence (68.79p).

There were usually at least two shows exhibiting curiosities.[2] In my time there was a dwarf couple in a miniature house and 'The Largest Rat in the World' – with an outsize sign asserting it had been 'captured on a Liverpool bomb site.' I gazed through its bars at this two foot or so of smelly rodent with its long yellow fangs. But it had its day when it escaped, causing panic as it ran south along the Promenade. The crowds parted like the Red Sea, with waves of shrieking women and girls running to escape this relatively harmless monster that wasn't a rat, just some sort of Asian raccoon. It was never seen again.

As a schoolboy I was fascinated by the Mile and spent every spare day and most weekends, when I wasn't working, moving in and out of the arcades, attempting to cheat the slot machines, smuggling myself into the shows and working as an unpaid gee. Gees[3] pretend to be members of the public and in listening to the spielers, aim to draw a crowd behind them. They are vital since punters will never patronise an empty forecourt or be the first to join a bagatelle game. An adolescent who proved useful as an unpaid gee and wasn't too small, might be paid something and as a junior insider, be served in the cafés at insider rates. But the real benefit of geeing, at least to me, was in learning how to spiel – and you learned this best by listening to the live shows spielers.

Many spielers start as gees. The live shows each employed three or more gees who spread across the forecourts listening to the spiels. When enough of a 'pitch' has gathered behind them, the gees shuffle slowly forward, hopefully bringing the pitch with them. When the spieler climaxes his spiel and announces the price, the gees briskly lead the way to the pay-desk then melt back into the crowd, to reassemble for the next spiel.

## The Exhibition of the Liverpool Museum of Anatomy

One of the Mile's shows had an immense fascination for adolescent boys. This was 'The Exhibition of the Liverpool Museum of Anatomy'. The 'Museum' comprised Victorian wax models of parts of male and female

---

2   Older workers on the Mile insisted that pre-war, the Mile had emphasised exhibits of freaks but that the post-war development of television made the bizarre no longer strange.

3   Workers on the Mile assumed that 'gee' derives from work with horses, since their job is to 'gee up' likely customers. *Cassell's Dictionary of Slang* gives the derivation as '19th century + Australian from *Gee* as one who *gees up* potential customers into a sideshow etc. hence *Geeman*' (a term not used in Blackpool).

bodies set out in glass cases with a hell-fire script dating from about the 1880s. The Museum employed no spielers since it claimed the dignity of an educational institution and was instead staffed by two middle-aged, motherly women kitted out in nurses' uniforms. Customers were firmly segregated, men and women occupying alternate fifteen-minute sessions – a clever device that increased sexual frisson, and ensured a fast through-put.

I recall fifteen different wax impressions of the female breast at different stages of pregnancy and lactation, together with a catalogue of homilies about health, morality and the pure life.[4] One exhibit however, haunts me still. It showed a woefully withered penis and the notation: 'This exhibit shows the dreadful effects of onanism. This subject rapidly sank into second childhood. Oh what a terrible account of himself he will have to give on Judgment Day!'

I was stopped at my fourth entry by one of the 'nurses,' who firmly and correctly observed: 'I think you've had quite enough for one day, sonny.' They don't make adolescence like that, nowadays.

The top spielers at the live shows were at the peak of the Mile's prestige pyramid. Live show spielers (who were never women) earned more than other Mile workers simply because the prosperity of whole undertakings depended on them. But there are spielers and spiels. Even the lesser league stalls and bagatelle games needed spielers to entice and cajole – but their spiels were formulaic and uninspired compared to those of the live show spielers. The top spielers were charismatic; they exuded confidence and spoke with authority. Their first task was to excite interest by referring to the unexpected, the exotic and the bizarre.

In my time, in the fifties and early sixties, there were three live shows: *Le Palais d'Etranges Demoiselles* with its gaudy placards and nude poses, the *Theatre Montmartre* with can-can girls, and the third, *Samson – the Strongest Man on Earth with the Beautiful Delilah*, a harridan who posed blindfold holding a sword and who we gathered, periodically beat Samson up after work.

Each live show had seventy or so seats set in a miniature theatre. Performances lasted around fifteen minutes and spiels carefully reflected differential targeting. Every spieler introduced his own variations. The best, carefully honed, delivered with verve and gravitas, were discussed, assessed and rated by the Mile's staff. Among the finest was Harry at *Le Palais*.

---

4    A couple of years ago I noticed the Liverpool Museum still in place on the Golden Mile – but it was now a bland, modernised affair, very different from its grim Victorian predecessor. And it had dropped its moralising.

# Le Palais d'Etranges Demoiselles

*Le Palais* was noted for the quality of its spielers, their *double entendres* and scarlet placards with lettering two feet high.

PRIOR TO WORLD TOUR
SEE THE TERRIBLE EFFECTS OF DRUG ADDICTION
HERE IS THE LEADING CONTENDER FOR THE TITLE
OF 'MISS EUROPE' IN 1956
IT WAS HER FATHER'S FAULT
NO PHOTOGRAPHS BY ORDER

Harry, a slight man in his early thirties was the *Palais'* principal spieler. He was sallow, skinny and unimpressive – until he began. But as his pitch grew, punters, gees and visitors alike were enthralled.

Harry always began by pointing to the notices and then would elaborate on each. What audiences would see was available only for a limited period. Soon the show was to begin its world tour – it was booked to visit twenty capitals of the world in twenty months. After sternly warning that no photographs were allowed, Harry would then launch into his spiel with a heady mix of the sexily exotic, the weird and the shockingly repulsive.

'Inside the portals of this air-cooled and air conditioned theatre ('Huh!' a rival spieler would mutter, 'only when the doors are open!'), you will see the leading contender for the title of Miss Europe in 1956… ('1926 more like!') You will have a rare chance to feast your eyes on the exotic and ravishing Mademoiselle Fifi – here fully revealed – fully revealed – prior to her completely booked world tour.'

And then in an uplifting move to the moral: 'Come inside and learn a dreadful lesson. Here you will see for yourself the exposed and horrible effects of mutilating drug addiction.' ('Pox, if you ask me,' the rival would mutter).

Titillating descriptions of 'Russian Henry' were heavily laced with *double entendres* neatly applied to exploit the ambiguities of a hermaphrodite. 'Come inside and see Russian Henry. See why it was her father's fault. First he stands on one leg. Then he stands on the other leg. And between the two, she earns his living'.

Harry's spiels always ended with a flourish – and a leer. 'If you want your entertainment… *in a continental way* [a pause as he scanned the pitch and leered], then this is your show.' He would announce the price, the gees led the rush, and Harry would take a break and a smoke before his next spiel.

Spielers had to be careful of their timing. Harry was precise; every performance took exactly twelve minutes – a skill I never quite mastered. In the late fifties, largely due to Harry, *Le Palais* was able to double its entry charge, to two shillings,[5] without noticeably reducing the number of punters.

But some spielers were quite unaffected by standards or competition. These were the 'inside spielers', those who worked inside the theatres and announced the show's sequences to audiences already 'captive' because they had already paid for their entrance.

When I spieled at *Le Palais d'Etranges Demoiselles,* the inside spieler was Edgar, a weary, wizened old man of about seventy who arrived wheezing each morning with a large green box of 100 Woodbines. Standing at the side of the stage, fag in place, in a bored, gravelly monotone, he would uninspiredly announce each act. 'Now we have Mademoiselle Fifi – as Botticelli's nymph.' On the word 'nymph,' he sagged against a rope, the curtains opened and Mademoiselle Fifi stood revealed – a tall, well-built woman, standing in front of a large gold picture frame her arms outstretched, stiff, stationary – and far removed from any of Botticelli's nymphs. She was in her late thirties, but in very good shape, black haired – and in another sequence – 'The Leading Contender for the Title of Miss Europe in 1956.'

Mademoiselle Fifi held her nude poses for about thirty seconds. The only parts of her that moved were her glittering black eyes as they raked her audience of mostly over-expectant male adolescents. At the slightest murmur from any of them, those eyes would swivel and – like Medusa's – turn them instantly to stone. As with her audiences, I too was intimidated by Mademoiselle Fifi. Offstage, she tended to be distant, austere – and certainly not readily given to chat. But then, I too was just another over expectant, over-heated adolescent.

But in a class of their own as providers of entertainment and ingenious exploiters of the gullible, were the Mock Auctioneers.

## Mock Auctions[6]

Ladies, you should know that Jayne Mansfield [a noted Hollywood 'sweater girl' of the fifties who opened Blackpool's illuminations in 1959] called in here yesterday afternoon. Yes – she did Ladies. She did. She bought two of these lovely cushions. [Throws two cushions in the air

---

5   10p in decimalised money
6   For an unappreciative sociological view of mock auctions, see Clark & Pinch (1992).

and catches them like a juggler]. You buy 'em Lady and you'll have a
pair – just as good as what Jayne Mansfield's got.

Alongside its bustling live shows, busy cafés and the raucous cries of its
spielers, the Mile usually contained one mock auction. These mainly sold
allegedly discounted, reject-quality domestic goods, at very high prices,
mostly to housewives. The auctioneers did this by inciting a hysterical
frenzy among their customers and maintaining this for as long as they
could. But to maintain hysteria needs a crowd, and mock auctioneers
therefore ensured their pitches never fell below a critical size – usually
about fifty or sixty.

The mock auctioneer's problem is that auctions are expensive to run –
a large pitch needs a large forecourt that could otherwise house four or
more lucrative stalls. They also need large staffs – up to half a dozen gees.
To sustain all this needs a high turnover.

The spiels of mock auctioneers varied from day to day since they
rarely sold the same goods for two days running. Spielers on the live
shows, in contrast, were selling a constant product, and could stick to the
same spiel for a whole season. As a result, mock auctioneers were the
most versatile, up-to-date and inventive of all the Mile's spielers – the
contemporary reference to Jayne Mansfield being only one example.

Auctioneers first attract but then have to keep their pitches interested.
They do this in part by offering entertainment. They project an imaginative
'stand–up' mixture of hype, flattery, and sexually suggestive *double
entendres*.[7] And they make it difficult for punters to leave a pitch once
they've joined.

Auctioneers perform on a raised stage, their voices massively
amplified as they jump about, throw sales goods in the air and offer
bargains that are too good to be true – all at a pace that allows punters no
time for reflection. Nor any chance to examine the goods.

Their spiels followed a regular sequence based around that staple
market-stall gambit, 'the collapsing price'.

> Not twenty pounds, fifteen or even ten; not eight, seven or even six. Here
> you are, a very special offer. For today and today only, they've all got to
> be cleared: two for five quid – TWO FOR FIVE QUID – **TWO FOR
> FIVE QUID!**

---

7   Their spiels owed much to the *risqué* stand-up Northern comics of the time
    such as Frank Randle and George Formby, both Blackpool-based who
    depended heavily on *double entendres*.

After exciting potential customers on price, the mock auctioneer then creates scarcity by emphasising a limited supply. An assistant brings the spieler a box. He opens it with a flourish and with an assistant's help, holds up its contents.

> See this fine Murphy TV set? I've only got five of these [a voice of veracity from the back storage area: 'No – there's another one here – you've got six'.] All right [with seeming exasperation] – six. But they've all got to go today. Who'll give me fifteen pounds? Thirteen? Twelve then? All right! They've all got to be cleared. I'll let these go to the first lucky six of you – [a pregnant pause] – for five quid each! **FIVE QUID!** No wonder they call me 'Mad 'Arry'. Who wants a top-name TV set – **FOR ONLY FIVE QUID?**

Up, up would shoot a forest of hands. But these bargain 'sales' were all spurious, the 'lucky six' [it is always six] are always the house gees. 'Unlucky', unsuccessful punters then have to be patient and wait – further boosting the size of the pitch. After several similar offers of 'bargains', none of which result in real sales, the punters carefully cultivated frustration mounts.

The spieler will then apply himself to real sales – and all in large quantities at premium prices, rapidly offered and rapidly disposed of – usually in sets: canteens of cutlery, complete dinner services, nests of saucepans, matching sheets and pillowcases.

> What's next? Oh yes – these lovely sets of pure linen table-ware. Only some of you are going to be lucky today. And for the first lucky six I'll throw in this chef's pair of top quality Sheffield stainless steel saucepans. And I'm not asking forty pounds or even twenty five...

The linen is then unveiled, the saucepans held up and clashed against each other as the spiel intensifies – 'listen to that sound – just listen – purest stainless, finest quality, Sheffield steel. And I'm giving 'em away.'

Once more, up would go the hands. Once punters are identified, the gees – then transformed into assistants – quickly take their money. And having paid their money they are now captive – goods can't be collected until the session's end. And as soon as the sales of one item are complete, the spieler moves quickly to the next.

> What do we have here? Oh yes – I've got something very, very special for you today. Look at these high-quality, guaranteed Swiss-made, fully-jewelled, lever-movement watches. [He lifts a handful high in the air.] Not only do these all have guaranteed fully-jewelled lever movements, they're each shock-proof, dust-proof and fully waterproof. You can visit

the Titanic with one of these watches, Sir. I guarantee they're waterproof
to six hundred fathoms deep. You'll crack before they will, Sir.

Mock auctioneers, with good humour, false-deference, imaginative
ribaldry, and a tightly-packed pitch, not only make punters want to stay
but make it physically difficult for them to leave as they continuously
crammed ever more passers-by into their pitch.

Move just a bit more forward please – a little bit more forward – let those
at the back get a look-in. Squeeze in tight. Ooh! you know that's how you
like it. That's right, Love. Let the dog see the rabbit.

With platoons of gees, their astute manipulation of crowds, their fast, witty
and clever patter, the mock auctions were highly profitable. So successful
were they that in the early sixties the authorities made them illegal.[8] I was
sad to see them go.

Sometimes a lesser level spieler – on a stall or selling a product at an
allegedly ludicrous price – would deliver such an original or amusing spiel
that exceptionally he attracted a larger audience than might normally be
merited. Such a one was the 'Executive' Pen Salesman.

## The 'Executive' Pen Salesman

My director said, 'Sammeh, nevah you mind about this cancelled order to
the United States of America. You go to Blackpool. Go to Blackpool,
Sammeh, and give these pens away. Give them away as an advertising
gesture.'

We boys learned spieling by comparing spiels. It did not matter that our
squeaky adolescent voices precluded us from spieling – we were looking
to the future. So we listened and learned. One spieler, 'Sammeh', a short
tubby man, florid, in his fifties, was new to the Mile. He was selling pens
but was different from other spielers in his adoption of the role of a
company executive – complete with condescending delivery, a smart suit
and tie and what might, just possibly, pass as an upper-class or at least a
'managerial' accent.

It was warm that particular day with an absence of the sea breezes for
which Blackpool is famous. The pen-man, hot and sweating, positioned
himself on the far edge of the Mile – as if to stand apart from its vulgarity.

---

8    The Mock Auctions Act 1961 has succeeded in moving them from Blackpool
     and reduced but never fully eradicated their presence elsewhere, though now
     they make only occasional appearances – for a day or an afternoon – and then
     move on, before proceedings can be taken.

Mounting a small box he opened a smart leather suitcase and began his spiel. He presented himself as the epitome of what his customers might expect of a boss – though he acted more posh than any they had probably met. It was soon obvious he had an aversion to small boys. He perhaps thought they detracted from his carefully constructed dignity.

It wasn't just his appearance and adopted *persona* that fascinated me as the singular nature of his spiel. Together with a friend we edged forward.

'Ladies and Gentlemen', he began [a phrase he was often to repeat]. 'Ladies and Gentlemen, I represent a company that manufactures high quality personal pens.' He broke off to mutter at us, 'Now move away sonny, move away.' [Then back to the pitch.] 'My company, Ladies and Gentlemen, had an export order to the United States of America. We heard only last week that this order had been cancelled. Ladies and Gentlemen, my managing director called me in to his office and he said to me, "Sammeh, nevah you mind about that cancelled export order to the United States."[9] Now move away boys, move away... "Sammeh, nevah you mind about that cancelled order. You go to Blackpool. Go to Blackpool, Sammeh, and give these pens away. Give them away as an advertising gesture." So here I am, Ladies and Gentlemen. I've travelled here today to offer you the benefit of our company's very generous advertising program. I'm not selling you these pens. No Ladies and Gentlemen, Oh No! – I'm not selling you these pens – at these prices. I'M GIVING THEM AWAY. Now move away, boys. WILL YOU PLEASE MOVE AWAY. NOW!'

We moved. But he was too different from other spielers, and it was too unusual a spiel to miss. We edged back.

'Now, Ladies and Gentlemen,' he continued, 'how many of you have heard of a Parker 51? How many...?' (He looked over his growing pitch and noted the one or two who nodded. Nodders are the likeliest customers and are given the closest attention.) 'Well, Ladies and Gentlemen, I know I can speak without fear of contradiction when I tell you that the Parker 51 is the finest pen in the world.' (Here he made eye contact and nodded to the nodders, forcing them to nod again.) 'Now, If I was to tell you that this pen...' (and here he lovingly selected one, and holding it up, slowly took off its cap to let its nib glint in the sun.) 'If I was to tell you that this pen was **BETTER** than a Parker 51, then quite frankly, Ladies and Gentlemen, I'd be lying. NO, Ladies and Gentlemen, No. This pen of ours...' (Another pause as his eyes scoured the

---

9   Consumer goods of all kinds were in short supply in the post-war period – certainly up to the mid-fifties – and it was common knowledge that export orders had priority over home sales.

audience). 'No… this pen of ours is **NOT** better than a Parker 51…'
(Longer pause) '…BUT I'LL TELL YOU THIS' (An even longer pause)
'IT'S AS GOOD! – **IT'S AS GOOD!!**'

Then, just before collapsing his price: 'Not a pound, not fifteen shillings,
not twelve, ten or even eight. Here you are – two for…' At this, the high
point of his spiel, he saw we had again wormed our way to the front. It
was then he snapped. Turning brick red and hurling away his posh accent,
he abandoned all claims to gentility. In the broadest of Lancashire accents
he yelled:

'IF YOU TWO DON'T BUGGER OFF – I'LL CLOUT YOU ROUND
YOUR BLOODY GOBS – **NOW** – **FUCK OFF!**'

Then realising he had completely blown it, he abandoned his spiel and his
pitch, slammed his suitcase shut, picked up his box and stalked off.

By the mid-sixties, some live shows were replacing their spielers with
recorded spiels relayed over sound systems. They were cheaper to
produce, shorter than live spiels, were louder and could be repeated more
often. Their quality was often very good but one spiel in particular was
exceptional. This proclaimed the newly arrived 'Paraguayan Two-Headed
Giant'.

## The Paraguayan Two-headed Giant

This spiel blasted over the Promenade every few minutes. My brother
Mike, who was hiring out deckchairs on the sands opposite the show, was
exposed to it for twelve hours a day. Unsurprisingly, he remembers it well:

Here you will see the Paraguayan two-headed giant – eleven feet ten and
a half inches high – weighing over a quarter of a ton – this terrifying
spectacle, the Paraguayan two-headed giant with two complete real heads
– was brought to this country with immense difficulty by two eminent
anthropologists from the depths of the Paraguayan Amazon. We offer
you a thousand pounds if you can produce its equal – alive, real and
genuine – step inside now.

The spiels of course, fooled very few. Mike told how Cyril, the old
Blackpool hand in charge of the stack, was one day chatting with an
elderly woman holiday-maker as the Paraguayan spiel blasted forth.

'Ooh!' She shivered, 'I wouldn't like to wake up in the morning and
find 'im on me pillow.' Cyril's reply was quick and classic: 'Don't you
worry, Love. It's only two 'eads what 'e's got.'

A particularly naïve geography undergraduate was also working on a
deckchair stack. He felt it might be appreciated if he pointed out to the

stall-holder that the Amazon did not in fact flow through Paraguay. At a loss for words, the unappreciative stallholder just shook his head at this enormous culture-gap – and tiredly shrugging his shoulders, muttered: 'Just piss off!'

## Stalls, Games and Cafés

Whereas live show spielers delivered their spiels to an audience, those in the lesser league – on the stalls and bagatelle games – engaged with passing couples and small groups. They tended to the personal, trading mostly in *double entendres*, especially when addressing two or more girls or couples.

For much of one summer I spieled on a 'can-can' stall, set on the forecourt of one of the Mile's cafés, appealing to punters to 'knock the cans off the shelf to win'. To do this they needed to throw lightweight woollen balls at cans piled in a pyramid and to clear them off the shelf.

'Come on girls. Knock the cans off the shelf and win a prize. Play with my lovely woolly balls.' Or, when accosting a couple, 'Go on Miss, let him have a go. You know he's good at it.' The girls would collapse in giggles at this badinage.

The trick was to demonstrate by example that the pyramid of cans could easily be dislodged if placed on the shelf's back edge. But it was almost impossible to dislodge them all – let alone to leave none on the shelf – if they were placed at the front – as they were for punters.

The longer people worked in Blackpool's service jobs, the more many contemptuously came to regard holiday-makers as just a source of earnings. A few stall-holders who worked their winters on the markets, peppered their spiels with abusive Yiddish slang they had picked up from Jewish market traders: 'Come on, you *meshugganers* (madmen), come and try your luck. Hey you, the *shmuck* (prick). Yes, you the *shlemeil* (idiot), you in the hat. Come on, give it a try.'

Considerable ingenuity was evident in separating punters from their money. One day a painter passed my stall carrying a tall ladder, a small pot of paint and a tiny writing brush. I watched as he placed his ladder against a café's twenty-five foot high advertising menu. Painted in scarlet capital letters over two feet high it offered:

EGG AND CHIPS
FISH AND CHIPS
EGG, BACON AND CHIPS
CHICKEN AND CHIPS
SAUSAGE AND CHIPS

CHIPS
TEA, BREAD AND BUTTER[10]

He seemed to be adding something in tiny, illegible lettering to the bottom of the menu. When he came down I asked what he'd been doing. 'Oh,' he said, taking a piece of paper out of his pocket and squinting at it, 'the Council are acting a bit tough [about untruthful advertisements]. So I had to paint on: "or butter substitute".'

I noted when later I worked in these cafés, to find how common it was for families to use food in discriminating against women and children. It was usual to receive an order such as: 'Fish and chips for me; the wife'll have egg and chips – and it'll be chips for the lad.'

This was justified because men were seen as breadwinners on whose well-being their whole family depended. It was in sharp contrast to how Jews order their family meals – where children are indulged as 'princes' and 'princesses' with the best food always going to them, and the parents, if necessary, going without.

# Fortune-Telling and Clairvoyance

One 'penny in the slot' machine told fortunes. It was astutely directed at young girls who invariably wanted to know their prospects of romance, travel and a glamorous future. They would gather in groups of four or five, giggling as they dared each other to go first. There was a telephone type dial at the machine's front and they would dial their birthdays and gender to be connected to the appropriate gramophone disk. Readings were slow, scratchy and solemn and, to further exploit the exotic, a sign advised they were offered by 'A Master of Arts of the University of Cambridge'. The recordist sounded Anglo-Indian.

Each fortune followed a similar formula with variations of detail. All hinted at romantic alliances – always with a stranger: 'You will fall in love and marry a tall dark man from afar.' Each raised the likelihood of travel to exotic places: 'You will travel across seas and over distant deserts.' At the end of every message was the shrewd phrase: 'And I have some particularly interesting information for the person standing at your side.'

---

10  This was before The Trades Description Act of 1968 which codified previous attempts at enforcing sales descriptions. It replaced and expanded the old Merchandise Marks laws dealing with mis-descriptions of goods which were locally operative at this time but only spasmodically policed by local municipalities.

Young girls were always astonished that a mere machine should know about 'the person at their side'. They would eagerly take turns to have their fortunes read, unlike the more considered choices of older women who sought individual readings from gypsies in their private, more expensive tents.

## Gypsy Fortune-tellers

Few women worked on the Mile or the beach and there were no women spielers. Spieling is an active outdoor job and traditional gender divisions precluded them on both counts. The few who did work on the Mile mostly worked in passive roles indoors – in nude shows, as Delilah to an apparently dominant Samson, or as 'nurses' at the Liverpool Museum of Anatomy. The very few who ran their own enterprises – Dorothea, who guessed people's ages, and the Mile's two fortune-tellers, Gypsies Petulengro and Rose-Lee, worked from tents.

Their tents were enclosed and, having no interface to the outside, maintained the divide that precluded women from spieling. Instead their external walls were hung with framed letters from the secretaries to various royal persons. They attracted custom by suggesting an intimacy with the mighty since they typically bore the appropriate royal coat of arms and thanked the stall-holder by name in response to enquiries offered about the royal person's health: 'Dear Gypsy Rose-Lee, I am directed by Her Majesty to thank you for your kind expressions of concern…'

One day, curious about what went on in these tents I positioned myself at the back of Gypsy Rose-Lee's tent, close to a gap between two canvas panels, and waited. Gypsy Rose-Lee was about forty. She looked authentically gypsy-ish, was swarthy of skin and wore droopy gold earrings. She well knew her customers and what they wanted to hear. She announced the rates for reading one or both hands and the crystal. Her charges ranged from 2/6d (12p in decimalised money) to 3/6d.

A large Northern woman, straight out of a McGill postcard entered, plonked herself on the tiny seat before the cerise covered table and asked for a reading. She was typical of the gypsy's clientele: working-class, middle-aged, married, a little more affluent than the young girls who paid only a penny for their slot machine fortunes, and more serious about the nature of clairvoyance and what it could tell her. This client chose the expensive crystal reading at 3/6d for the crystal.

Gazing into her crystal ball, Gypsy Rose-Lee was silent. Then after a full minute, she quietly and carefully, murmured: 'I see, Missus, that your husband is a weak man. A very weak man?' She had scored in one. Her client banged her fist so hard, the frail table shook, the crystal rocked. 'You're right,' she shouted. You're so right. He is. **HE IS!**'

## How It's Done

Like all experienced clairvoyants, Gypsy Rose-Lee was as successful as she was observant. It takes less than half a minute for an experienced clairvoyant to deduce a large amount of useful information about a client. Their age, social and educational level, their affluence and marital-state are mostly apparent at a glance whilst many personality traits and physical conditions are evident almost as soon as a client enters the tent. It is possible to quickly deduce, for instance, if a client is timorous or assertive, in good health or not, married or single, agitated or calm. And it is not difficult to assume they are worried – the clairvoyant being well aware that her services wouldn't usually be required if a client did not have something worrying them. Blackpool's clairvoyants have a further asset: they live outside their clients' own community and therefore, are well placed to receive confidences that would be unlikely to 'leak'.

But a clairvoyant's strength in making her deductions is also based on a keen appreciation of statistical incidence. Most middle-aged women, the majority of a gypsy's clients, have husbands and probably children and these are liable to present characteristically similar problems.

Armed with this background knowledge, the clairvoyant will first establish confidence by suggesting awareness of something in the client's life, the likelihood of which she will have already deduced – say, a weak husband or a troublesome child. This initial foray is not offered too assertively but if confirmed makes plain sailing for the rest of the consultation. With confidence established, the client is then likely to supply further information. If confidence is not initially confirmed the clairvoyant will make a second or a third foray. Once armed with some idea of her client's concerns and with the benefit of her observations she is then in position to offer apparently personalised understanding, advice and reassurance taken from her more standardised packages of the same.

So valued are clairvoyants' services that many clients return to update their readings year after year.

Blackpool fortune-tellers share this awareness of statistical incidence with magicians and shamans throughout the world. I recall the account of an African magician conducting an open-air ritual who, when he failed to demonstrate his powers, was able to quickly restore his reputation. 'It's clear to me,' he told the assembled crowd, 'that my magic cannot work today because there must be a menstruating woman in this audience.' His powers were reaffirmed when four of the assembled women shamefacedly removed themselves.[11]

Years later I visited a celebrated Central European medium in Tel Aviv, strongly recommended to me as 'a powerful witch'. After asking only a few apparently disconnected questions, she made what appeared to be some startlingly accurate personal observations:

> 'I see you don't like dealing with details, do you? You tend to see the wood but not the trees? This causes you problems – doesn't it?' 'Your life tends to revolve around projects doesn't it? I see that you hate routine? You have a tendency to take on more projects than you can finish, don't you?'[12]

Only later when I came across the work of the psychologist Myers-Briggs[13] did I understand her method. Her apparently disconnected questions and insightful deductions were based on her clever use of an attenuated version of Carl Jung's sixteen personality types. Once she was able to allocate a client to an appropriate type she was then able to 'read off' the personality characteristics and the problems appropriate to them. Gypsy Rose-Lee used a less sophisticated procedure but in essence it was the same – except that she was less dependent on her client's psychological make-up and more on their more common social characteristics.

I later used an expanded version of the same procedure – and even some of the same questions – when, as 'a magician', I was one of a team of behavioural consultants who sat on selection boards to recruit fast-track executives for a multinational company (see Chapter 16).

## The Golden Mile: Make-Believe and Collusive Deception

The Golden Mile was a microcosm of Blackpool. And just as the Mile was only a quarter of a mile long, so exaggeration was part of the wider web of deception in which the town's holiday-makers were keen to collude. For them, their holiday offered not just 'time out of time' but 'place out of place'. For one or two weeks they suspended reality and accepted that the town really did deliver magic: that quarts *could* go into pint pots; pigs

---

11  This is an example of the 'bypass loop' by which magic survives because it allows for the negation of unwelcome evidence. See Evans-Pritchard quoted in Gluckman (1955, p. 215). An example of its application to magical beliefs in a contemporary multinational company is given in ch. 16.

12  This analysis was appropriate to a Jungian extravert/intuitive personality.

13  Myers-Briggs (1980)

*were* to be found in pokes; that TVs could be bought for five pounds and that raccoons were really rats. Here, skilfully targeted by accomplished craftsmen and with money to spend, deferred to and treated with unaccustomed respect, their week or two in Blackpool was memorably different from anything the other fifty weeks could offer.

CHAPTER FOUR

# THE PLEASURE BEACH

## Weight Guessing and 'the Weed'

The Pleasure Beach, more an amusement park than a fairground was and still is Blackpool's most effective crowd-puller.[1]

On both the Mile and the Beach, the fiddle is called 'the weed', 'the practice of pocketing a certain amount of cash from the employer's till.'[2] Workers tried incessantly to increase it, and bosses to limit it, while both accepted that the weed could never be eliminated. It was too necessary an incentive and it offered workers a vital *raison d'être*.

In my day the weed' was more important on the Pleasure Beach than the Mile. On the Mile, stalls and shows were mostly singly owned and often run by families who worked on the spot, making it harder for an employee to fiddle. It was easier to fiddle on the Beach since the majority of stalls and games were leased, usually in groups, to single operators and management was therefore relatively distant.

When I was guessing weight on the Beach I was paid half the basic daily rate I had been paid as a tram conductor, and the hours were longer. Work started at ten in the morning, often finishing near midnight. It could mean hard, continuous graft for fourteen hours. Nobody but a simpleton or a naïve works such long hours, seven days a week for so little when there are jobs that pay more for much less effort. Of course, the reward lies not in the wage but in 'the weed'. As I later found, to fiddle as a conductor on the trams was risky, and in any case it took too many transactions at a penny or so a time to make a sizeable 'take': to exploit 'the weed' on the Pleasure Beach was much simpler and far more profitable.

Most of my previous experience of fairground work had been on the Mile and surprisingly, there was little contact between their workers and those on the Beach. When first I tried to work the Beach I knew no-one. If

---

1   The Pleasure Beach is allegedly the most visited amusement park in the United Kingdom, and one of the top twenty most-visited amusement parks in the world (5.5 million visitors in 2007, source: Wikipedia).

2   *Cassell's Dictionary of Slang* (2000)

I had simply gone there and asked for work, I would have been waved away: 'No, everything's full,' they would have said. They didn't know me so why trust me? The way in was to wait for a slack time then chat to one or two of a stall's workers, first making sure they weren't stall owners. I ambled up to a stall called the Kentucky Derby – names derived from the United States were increasingly common in the fifties – and homed in on an affable-looking fellow my own age. Off-handedly I discussed how busy they were. Then, after mentioning my experience on the Mile I casually asked: 'What's the weed then? Any good?'

By then he knew I was 'safe', and might possibly help. It worked. 'Jimmy Crooke probably wants someone,' I was told. 'He's got a few stalls. Been on the Beach for years. He's a sly bastard, mind.'

So I went to search out Jimmy Crooke. I found Crooke spieling on a bagatelle stall. He was a small man, about fifty and burned a dark brown, with grey, tightly waved, greasy hair. I hung around waiting for the game to finish and the pitch to go. 'Are you Mr Crooke?'

He looked me over with a shifty sideways glance. He epitomised what Northerners call 'crafty.' Then, cautiously he answered, 'Aye?'

'I wonder if you've any work going?'

'Um. Any experience in this line?'

'No,' I lied, 'but I'm always willing to learn.'

He liked that: inexperience meant having no expectation of the weed. 'Well then,' he said carefully, 'I think perhaps I can use you – but I can't pay more than...' – and he offered me the Beach's lowest rate. 'Right,' I said.

He paused again, perhaps surprised at my ready acceptance of such a low rate, and then slowly, as if weighing up the offering in his gift. 'Well then. You go up that path there...' and he pointed, '...up that path you'll see a weigher. It's got a string at the side. Your job is to pull that string every time anyone stands on that weigher. Right?'

It was obvious the string worked a recording device that told Crooke the size of the takings. 'Right, Mr Crooke.' I made to set off. He called me back. 'Listen,' he said, 'the bloke on that weigher is called Mel. He'll tell you not to pull the string. You take no notice of him – I'm paying you, and that's what you're paid for. Every time anyone stands on that weigher – you pull that string. Got it?'

'Yes, Mr Crooke.' I went off to see Mel.

The weigher, a Big Red Berkel machine, had a huge circular dial and in front of it stood Mel. He was slightly built, about thirty, a hang-dog with a droopy, ginger moustache. He was in mid-spiel, and had a reasonable pitch of about twenty. But it was a busy time – he was doing at most, only modest trade – and pulling the string, I saw, about one time in four. Mel looked harassed and unenthusiastic. He obviously did not enjoy spieling.

Guessing weight isn't difficult. Most people can quickly learn to guess weight within a pound or two. You get an image of standard people in your mind and rate these against your own height and weight. And weight-guessers in any case, guess within seven pounds. This means seven pounds on either side of the actual weight – giving leeway to guess within a stone.

But even if a weight guesser wrongly guessed a punter's weight, and she won a prize, it was only a derisory couple of Player's Weights, the cheapest cigarettes on the market, costing only half the sixpenny charge.

I waited until Mel's pitch dispersed. 'Are you Mel? Mr Crooke sent me. I've come to pull the string.' Though Crooke may have been taken in by my apparent naïveté, Mel certainly wasn't. He looked even more morose. 'Christ,' he said, 'Now I suppose I'll have to split the fuckin' weed two fuckin' ways.'

It was quickly obvious that Mel, though a very good weight guesser, was a poor spieler. He was too depressive. Within a day or two, I found myself doing all the spieling with Mel doing all the weight guessing. We were a good team, got on well together, ran big pitches, and took in about two or three times the amount I estimated Don had been taking by himself. And of course the more we took in, the greater 'the weed'.

The first step to being a good spieler is obviously to have a spiel that grabs passers-by, that makes them stop and feel involved. The aim then is to sustain the pitch. This takes time and skill but do it well and takings can become continuous for long periods. Then all one needs to do, is cry: 'Who's the next then, who's the next?' Get it right, and as Mel put it: 'Christ – they're hopping on and off [the weigher] like fuckin' rabbits'.

One method of developing a good pitch was to attract a core group – ideally five or six lads who tend to egg each other on. 'Come on, lads, prove me wrong. Prove I can't guess your weight. Beat the guesser – and win a prize'. The lure of competition, of beating the guesser and being the centre of attention often encouraged the entire group to try their luck. To a running commentary, I would walk appraisingly around each in turn. 'How much does this fine figure of a man weigh?' Then I would feel and comment on his muscles. 'Uh huh!' Then, with a flourish: '8 stone 6 pounds!' I was lucky not to be thumped.

Young women were always 'lovely ladies'. There would be a complimentary public discussion of their figures with a cheeky pinch, poke and prod all delivered to a background of giggles. Guessing weight in this way would be unimaginable today.

Mel had recently done a stretch in Strangeways, a prison in Manchester. A lot of workers on the Beach, as Mel confirmed, had records. Fairgrounds, at that time, did not bother with cards, stamps or income tax, and it suited people who liked to take on a job and pack it in quickly without notice – the Beach was a useful refuge.

Mr Crooke quickly came to realise I wasn't as inexperienced as I had suggested: 'he'd been had.' He could tell from the spiel that I had at least *some* experience. But he could judge from our pitches we were doing well, that it was a good combination he had on the weigher. And he could calculate from the proportionate number of Players Weights we gave out as prizes how many sixpences we might be taking in. To counter these calculations I brought in our own supply of Weights. (I glimpsed him once, watching us from the back of our pitch. And his brother-in-law Charlie, who worked a fruit stall opposite, kept 'scanning' our way, sizing up our pitches and obviously passing this back to Crooke.)

Crooke's dilemma was how to keep a bigger share of the increased takings without losing the staff who were taking it. I estimated that before I arrived Mel alone must have been taking in much less than a half of what we were now taking together and that he had been taking out about a half of this each day as his weed. Mel's suggestion that we 'split the weed equally two ways' wasn't kept: he was cheating me by taking out more than we had agreed. My response was to take out a sum equal to that which I reckoned he was taking, while suggesting I was only taking what we had agreed. Both of us knew we were lying.[3]

After I had been on the weigher a week, a new arrival appeared: Jack, a slightly plump twenty-five year old. Spotty and slow, he announced: 'Mr Crooke sent me. I'm here to pull the string.' 'Christ Almighty,' said Mel to me later. 'Now we'll have to split the fuckin' weed three fuckin' ways!'

But I was unwilling to split the weed further, at least as long as I thought we didn't need to. So I said to Mel, 'Look, I don't trust this one. We don't know him, we know nothing about him. If he's happy to work for the basic why shouldn't he?' Mel accepted this logic. So we kept Jack in the cold for three days, with Mel doing the weight guessing, me the spieling, Jack the checking, and Mel and me splitting the weed. We quickly persuaded Jack not to pull the string, but that involved his overt collusion and meant he too would probably soon have to be paid something, if not a full share of the full weed.

---

3    Cheating on one's confederates (a practice well known in Blackpool) and known elsewhere as 'weeding the swag', *A Dictionary of the Underworld. 1950.* See also footnote 8, p. 64.

After three days Mel came back from a dinner break with Jack and, while Jack was away, said, 'Look, I've been talking to him. He's been in Durham [Prison], he's been on the coal fiddle and he's fiddled on the milk.[4] And I just heard him say he'd smash Charlie's face in if he caught him scanning [observing] over here again. He's a real good lad!' So because Jack was such 'a real good lad', he was finally brought into the weed with us. Now, with four parties, including Crooke involved, and with all of us fiddling each other, we had produced what might be called 'a fiddlers quartet'.

This obviously could not go on. Jimmy Crooke wasn't going to pay out for three of us and get minimal checking. When he realised what was happening, he sacked Mel. I was left as spieler *and* guesser, with Jack to do the checking. A day or so later, Jack too left but of his own accord, as Mel had suggested he might. It seemed the police were after him. Before I arrived, Mel had been leaving about a half the takings for Crooke. When I was on the stall alone I was happy to take out only a quarter as my weed. Crooke too was happy.

The weed then, is a form of colluded-in commission. But – and this is its lure – it's the way a worker *pays himself* a commission. The boss, in trying to keep the weed as low as he can, knows if he presses too hard, that he'll not get a good spieler or he'll get someone who is lazy, and his takings will suffer. The worker knows that if he takes out too much he risks being replaced. For him, 'what he takes out is based on what he takes in'. Somewhere in the middle there is an agreed meeting point.

This 'payment system', for that is what it is, did not operate throughout the Beach. There was no colluded-in weed for those who worked on rides operated directly by the Pleasure Beach Company and for which no especial skills or effort were needed – such as the big dipper or the bumper cars where the only task was to take cash and where allocated tickets removed ambiguity. As a result, if the company caught anyone taking even a small amount of cash, they were subject to prosecution. Morality and prosecution depended purely on their setting, with whether a record of

---

4   The 'coal fiddle' was the classic domestic fiddle of 'dropping short.' Once sacks of coal have been emptied it is difficult to assess if the resultant pile of coal represents the number of sacks charged for. The 'milk fiddle', still extant, is again a classic domestic fiddle applied against housewives who have irregular deliveries, keep no systematic record and make irregular payments. Such housewives invariably leave assessments of their bills to the milkman and – as invariably – are likely to be fiddled. For details of the wider generality of occupational crimes, see Mars (1982, ch. 3).

cash receipts could operate, as with the issuance of numbered tickets, and whether or not the employer needed to pay an incentive.

CHAPTER FIVE

# THREE FIDDLERS' ACCOUNTS

## Working on the Trams: the Theft of Time

My first day as a conductor on Blackpool's trams offered a sharp baptism. Allocated to a double-decker, my co-conductor was Lil, a petite, pretty, quick-witted woman of about forty. Her mission was to make me appreciate the realities of the job, which she did early on. She had worked the trams for twenty years and her advice was direct: 'You have to deal with a lot of funny buggers.'

I asked what I should look out for. She wasn't hesitant. 'Watch out for the dirty buggers. They're the worst. Only last Monday I had a couple mucking about on the seat at the back. "You can pack that in," I told them. "I'm not having that sort of thing on my tram." Do you know what?'

'No, what?'

'They'd only left a johnny[1] on the seat – there it still was – steaming hot! The dirty buggers!'

The most important thing she taught me was about breaks. Breaks weren't scheduled – so you had to make them. To do that she explained, you needed to fiddle time by getting the tram to the end of the route earlier than scheduled. She spelled out how. If I linked to a regular driver, I could then move to a regular schedule – instead of, as a casual, getting all the non-preferred routes. But to switch I would have to prove to a regular driver that I could fiddle time. To do it meant picking up fewer passengers.

My chance came when I was put with Ted, fortyish, gloomy and without the mate he had worked with for five years. I knew the job had been getting to Ted when holiday-makers wandered across the track, as they did all the time. Other drivers drove at them with the hooter blaring. Ted, I noticed, would just mutter wearily, 'They think they're on their bloody holidays!'

During an unofficial break towards the end of our first hectic shift, Ted said: 'Y' know, Gerry, I've never known anyone pick up so few'

---

1   'Johnny': a condom

[passengers]. He actually smiled. 'Do you want a regular mate?' This was a compliment indeed.

It was because the timetable precluded breaks that getting them became such an obsession and made a hard job bearable – and even fun. An effective crew will practise and develop all kinds of tricks to exclude passengers. They all depend on the conductor working closely with the driver to beat the timetable: Ted and I were a dream team.

If a conductor is slow at giving his driver the starting bells, or a driver is slow in leaving the stops, then this alone can stop them getting breaks. But apart from being quick on the bells, the best way to fiddle time is not to pick up passengers at all. If you pick them up you have to collect their fares. Then they'll eventually want to get off, which means delay while you stop the tram. When they get off, other passengers will want to get on and in their turn have their fares collected – and they too will want to get off. You become mired in a descending spiral of delay and effort. Picking up few in the first place avoids a load of trouble.

But a tram cannot simply sail through a stop and leave people on the pavement. There are strict rules specifying when a tram must stop. And inspectors check and can sack staff for non-observance. To beat the timetable *and* bypass the inspectors, Ted did exactly the opposite of what passengers expected. At a request stop they would stick out their hands and expect the tram to slow down, then stop. What they *don't* expect is for the tram to speed up! As soon as Ted saw a queue with its hands out he would speed up and roar past. But because we *had* to stop, we would come to a skidding halt – *past* the queue. Nobody then could say we hadn't stopped, that we did not obey the rules.

When Ted did this the queues were at first baffled – then they would run, panting, to the tram. I would open the door – just enough to put my head out – and rapidly give a list of places we were *not* going to. I would say: 'This tram goes to A, B, C, and D' (places at the end of the line that nobody is normally interested in) 'but it doesn't go to E, F, G, and H' (and I would list other places off the route).

That way, instead of saying where we *did* go, the destinations they actually wanted, they would be so doubtful about where the tram was going that they didn't know whether to board us or not. With the door hardly open, I would quickly say: 'OK?' – Ring the bell – and we would be off. But – we had stopped.

Another trick was to practise the opposite: not to take *nobody* on board – but to play being 'God's gift to passengers' – and take *everyone* on board. Many people wanted to go from the same part of town to the same destinations. There were invariably big queues at Cleveleys, the start of the route on Blackpool's northern boundary, most wanting to go to the Central Promenade in the middle of town. If you filled all the seats and had five standing passengers – as you should – then you would find two alighting here and one there with new arrivals able to assert their right to board because you would be carrying less than the legal maximum. But I would stack them in at Cleveleys and play 'God's gift'. Come on now, I'm sure we can get a few more in at the back. Can you squeeze up a bit, Love? There's still room for a few more back there.'

This way I could get, not five, but up to twenty standing passengers and everyone would squeeze up and be good-natured about the crush. Then I would give Ted three bells – which meant 'no stopping to pick-up' and we would sail past the gesturing queues with impunity. If you had to stop to let someone off, at least you never had to pick anyone up. You could always say: 'Look, I'm absolutely crammed – I'm only allowed five standing and see, I've already got about twenty.'

This trick had another advantage – a conductor can fiddle money when the tram is packed since a lot of people get off at the same stop. They can't easily collect all their fares so passengers are likely to shove money at him as they get off – without waiting for tickets. Some conductors made two or three times the daily rate. I never did fiddle on the trams because the number of transactions at a penny or so a time involved just too much risk and anxiety; the inspectors were vigilant and there were no tolerated levels, as with 'the weed'.

But there was a managerially-inspired encouragement to fiddle cash. If you were found to be 'down' when 'paying in' at the end of the day, the amount you were short would be deducted from your pay – whereas if you were 'up' the surplus was always taken by the corporation. There was no balancing up – no weighing of surpluses against losses over a period. Naturally we conductors ensured we were never 'up'. Even without conscious fiddling it was usual to find you had a surplus at paying in time. Unconsciously one is more likely to give short change over the course of a day than to give out a surplus. So you always took out an amount to cover any shortfall when paying in. Nobody 'teaches' these 'wrinkles' – they are learned through hard experience.

A more blatant fiddle that still wakens a chord when I travel on buses is to appreciate their apparent erraticism. Occasionally some buses travel so slowly it would almost be quicker to walk. At other times their crews appear hell-bent on breaking speed records. If the explanation hasn't to do with tea breaks or a concern to keep strictly to the timetable, then it is likely to be in the way overtime is calculated. If a crew are likely to finish their shift eight minutes over schedule they are likely to be paid to the next quarter of an hour – so they slow down to 'earn' their eight minutes. Up to seven minutes over schedule however is not paid for – so they speed up.

## Contempt for the Public: Revenge and Sabotage

Of course, over-filling the cabin can prove dangerous, and conductors' strategies were morally appalling – but so were the job's pressures. Easing them allowed a reduction in pressure though they certainly reduced service. They also led to an unpleasant disdain for passengers. When crews met, much of the talk was about scoring off passengers, especially the more irritating ones. Some stories entered staff folklore. One bright conductor recounted a bizarre encounter.

He had been travelling down the Central Promenade, on the busiest part of the route, at the busiest time of day when a Yorkshireman, with his wife, asked for 'two fares to the Tower' and, without apology, proffered a pound note. Being given a note is harassing at the best of times because it takes time to give change. The conductor then pointed out that the tram was in fact already at the Tower. He indicated its soaring 519 foot height directly outside the window.

'No Lad,' the Yorkshireman insisted, 'no it can't be.'

'Why can't it be?' he was asked.

'Because the Tower's farther down the Prom, of course.'

'Were you here last year?' he was asked.

'Aye.'

'Well that was last year's position. Don't you know they move it every year? Next year it's going further up north. It's what keeps Blackpool from getting boring.'

'By God, I never knew that,' came the startled response. ''Ear that, Mother? They shift it every year!'

Alienative responses were also directed at the administration. One conductor, leaving the job in mid-season on a busy Saturday, spent the whole of his last day singing out: 'Watch out for a ticket with the lucky blue stripe. If you get a ticket with a lucky blue stripe, you'll win a prize.' A blue stripe is printed at the end of each ticket roll to warn the conductor to replace it. And all day long from 7:00 in the morning until 8:00 at night he sang the same mantra. When passengers excitedly offered him their blue striped tickets he told them they had to be presented to the Transport Manager, Mr Blundell, at his office the following Monday morning. The issue must have been discussed in boarding houses all over the weekend for on Monday morning a massive, expectant, and progressively hostile crowd besieged Mr Blundell's office.

There is a postscript. Some years later I wrote a brief version detailing ways of fiddling time in a book that discussed fiddles at work,[2] and mentioned Blackpool's trams. It was noticed by the Blackpool Gazette who asked the Director of Transport for his comments. 'I don't know who this man Gerry is,' he said, 'but he was obviously being taken for a ride by our drivers.' He did not discuss the need to introduce breaks... nor make the connection between their absence and the level of service.

Many service jobs offer disgruntled employees the chance to sabotage their dealings with customers. I recall one disillusioned waitress who when asked to recommend something from the menu would answer: 'I can't recommend anything. The kitchen's short-staffed, cook's off ill. And honestly, the cooking's really dreadful.' Sometimes, if feeling really vindictive, she would recommend a rival café.

There is a celebrated account of a disillusioned rock roller that records: 'They had to throw away half a mile of Blackpool rock[3] last year, for, instead of the customary motif running through its length it carried the terse injunction, 'Fuck off'.[4] This worker, dismissed by a sweet factory had effectively demonstrated his annoyance.

These examples of sabotage[5] point to a dimension of industrial relations often missed – that sabotage is a frequent, if latent sanction – but one not often recognised in service occupations because it is difficult to locate.

# A Bar-worker's Fiddles: 'Chasing the Dropsy'[6]

'As far as I can see the whole business is crooked.'

If the Mile and the Pleasure Beach were supremely designed to extract holiday-makers' cash, then they were almost matched by some Blackpool pubs. These were not your standard small-scale, local pubs. They were larger, more akin to drinking caverns, and serviced by waiters schooled in the arts of siphoning extra earnings. It was to be another forty years before this size of pub came to dominate other city centres. Blackpool had several

---

2  Mars (1982) pp. 50-53.
3  Blackpool Rock: a stick of sugar candy with 'Blackpool' written throughout its length
4  Taylor & Walton (1971, p. 219)
5  See Mars (2001).
6  Dropsy – money, especially accruing as a tip or bribe (*Oxford Dictionary of Modern Slang*). A word 'used by the underworld for any illegal or improper payment' (*Dictionary of the Underworld*, 1989).

of these 'mega-pubs'. All were close to the Promenade strip where the greatest density of holiday-makers congregated.

Alan Snell, had long experience in these pubs. At this time we both worked by day on the same government site in St Annes as clerks and union branch activists – but in different buildings – unimaginatively named Blocks A to F.

With his alert smile and perky moustache Alan looked more like a top hotel waiter than a junior civil servant. Having five children, he was invariably hard up and accordingly hyper alert about the hidden economy. I recall him chortling over a trip he'd made to the butchers.

'I was buying meat in Talbot Road on Saturday. When I got to the front, I thought, I recognise that old feller behind the counter – he looked like a bloke who had worked in the block next to mine. "Weren't you in Block B?" I asked him.'

'He winced', said Alan, 'then glanced round to make sure nobody had heard, and quickly asked "What would you like, Sir." Too late I realised he was thinking of prison blocks!'

'I'll have a couple of pounds of sausages and one and a half of mince, please. "Right, Sir," he said, all efficient. He went to one side, returned with a huge parcel – and winked. I took it home. There were about four pounds of sirloin and what must have been three pounds of liver – as well as the sausages and mince. For the next fortnight we lived like kings!'

Over a period I learned a good deal about Alan's life as a pub waiter.

'I've worked in most of the big pubs in this town. It's the big pubs that employ waiters – not the small cosy locals where drinks are bought from the bar.

Big pubs are mostly the same – the work and the waiters are the same and so are the fiddles. You find two classes of people who work in these pubs: the waiters 'on the floor' and bar-staff who work behind the bar. They're different breeds: bar-staff are conservative – they've got a snobbish pride – like secretaries – they've mostly been working for the same boss for years, so they're more trusted than waiters and to mark it they get a small pay difference.

'Waiters are a mixed lot. You've got a small professional waiting class, the regulars. They have the best stations and the landlord's ear – and then there's a bigger lot, the dishonest extras, part-timers who are more typical. Anyone who's short of a pound can get a job as a part-time waiter. Most are either 'duckers' or 'gentlemen'.

Duckers?

'Because they're always 'short arsing' – they 'short arse' from place to place. Duckers are the lowest of the short arses.[7] They're employed for special jobs and tend to be itinerant.'

'There's often jealousy between regulars and part-timers. Regulars think part-timers avoid a lot of the jobs they have to do – and they let you know it. 'I'm not here just for the fuckin' tips – I'm here at 8 o'clock sweeping out the fuckin' bogs.'

## And gentlemen?

'Gentlemen' are part-timers with a regular job 'on the outside'. You need a mixture of the two to run a place properly. Being a gent, I found managers extremely tolerant of my early ignorance. They reckon gents are less likely to steal or insult the customers or get blind drunk. They're mostly right of course.

'Bar staff and waiters both fiddle – and for both it's the customers they take. Really, there are only two fiddles: serving cheap drinks instead of dear – and short changing. As the night goes on punters get sloshed and can't recognise slight differences in taste. So in serving cheap drinks for instance, you'll put 50% soda water in a John Collins which is more than it should be. And in shandies, where you should put in a Double Diamond you'll use Pale Ale instead. And at Christmas especially, you'll give Tarragona instead of port.

'Short changing is even simpler: when you reckon up an order, you add on – we call it 'putting on the tray'. Usually we 'put on' about ten percent. These fiddles are done by waiters and bar staff alike. Bar staff say the waiter has a better time of it but the waiter says he doesn't get to the till! The difference is that before the evening starts the bar staff will already have taken their lot out of the float and they work to make it up during the night; the waiter has to build up his fiddles as the night goes on.

## How much can you make?

'Well you wouldn't do it for less than the wage – not bloody worth it for less – and you'll get more than that again in tips, so the actual total's about three times the wage. It's a decent amount – nothing extortionate. It varies on the night of the week and the place and how busy things are. But you can usually fix an expectation – what you expect to get – then

---

7   Short-arse: a 'stumpy short person' in 18th-century standard English usage meaning, 'an insignificant person', (or as here, one low in the pecking order), *Cassell's Dictionary of Slang*.

you work towards that. It's called 'the dropsy'. Mind you I know three
people who've never fiddled a penny?

## Why?

'Why? – because they're bloody fools – that's why! But there are limits.
You don't fiddle good tippers for instance. Or regulars. The problem with
visitors is you often don't know what they'll do [in the way of giving a
tip] so you have to put something 'on the tray' just in case. I've known
waiters go back when they've been well tipped and say, 'Sorry, I over-
charged you' – though you get sharks and thieves in all jobs. But
customers who don't tip just ask to be fiddled – or 'thrown a deaf ear'
[ignored when they ask for drinks].

'To a waiter, the most important person is his head waiter. He hires and
fires and he defends you against the licensee. He gives you your station.
He'll settle disputes [with other waiters] and cover for a waiter who is
drunk. But he's particularly useful, if you're new, in advising about the
regulars who're not to be fiddled.

'The equivalent for bar staff is the licensee. He's very concerned to have
honest bar staff – or at least as honest as he can get them. He's less
concerned about honesty among waiters, and in any case there's not
much chance of getting honest waiters. As long as they seem to behave,
he's happy. What he hates most though is collusion between his barmen
and the waiters – that way he can lose a packet. Otherwise it's only the
customers who lose and he doesn't much bother about that. He's not
much bothered about ability either.

'Though there is not usually collusion between barmen and waiters, there
are alliances. Waiters for instance, aren't expected to 'knock the till' – to
argue that they've given the barman a tenner when they've given him a
fiver for instance. It's funny – it's a peculiar kind of honesty you
wouldn't expect.

'There are always alliances between waiters – it's a brotherhood – I've
never seen waiters fight each other. Of course you're drinking together all
night long and you're always passing tips to each other about jobs going
in other pubs. But the main thing that binds you is self-defence. If a fight
breaks out you're all in it together. You've got to be prepared to
converge. I always used to converge with a broom. I've seen waiters go
home together in groups for fear of what's waiting for them.

'At the end of the night there's 'pollying-up'[8] – the collection that's taken among waiters to be given to the one barman who's picked out to serve them – which means he can't fiddle the till as much as the others – so he has to be compensated. It's a token – it's really 'agreed-to blackmail', supposed to be a payment for service – it emphasises the bar-staff's superiority.

'Pollying–up is usually organised by the head waiter. He'll go round collecting. Amounts vary: on a bad night it's less, on a good night it's more. He'll go around the waiters and say: 'What have you done then?' 'Six quid.' 'Fuck off.' 'Ten quid then.' 'OK – that's more like it.' 'Two quid to polly–up.' Or he might just say: 'Pollying-up's two quid.'

'At the end of the night there's always a booze-up when the shutters are up and the bar-staff and waiters all drink together. There's no name, it's just a booze-up when the battle's finished. It's all friendly then – since the customer's the take for both lots and the guards are down. Mind you, only a mug would talk about tips. But there's always banter – usually with the waiters accused of making more. I remember the advice of an old ex-publican who had been a barman for years: 'Only believe a half of what you see – and nothing of what you hear.'

'The booze-up always starts off with the manager – without exception – he gets in the first round. Always. There's an allowance for staff drinks given by the brewery – a pint each. After that drinks are always paid for by the waiting staff in order of seniority, though bar-staff can and do occasionally slide along odd drinks at the end of the session – without paying for it. But here's a funny thing: bar-staff generally don't buy drinks.

'There's a big pretence: everyone suggests they're in it for the drink – not the money. There was a teetotal waiter in one pub I worked in – he would put money up for his round – but he wasn't liked. Some miserable buggers have the staff drink and then go. They're not much thought of either. But I've stayed – sometimes till five in the morning. The manager doesn't join you. He's upstairs counting the cash. There's several thousand quid or more. That's why the brewery gives out staff drinks – it

---

8   Pollying-up. *Dictionary of the Underworld* (1989) states that in the 15th-17th centuries 'to poll' was standard English usage meaning 'to plunder, to fleece'. By 1839 Brandon recorded that it was in criminal use to refer to 'knavish receivers' who would cheat the thief of his share or payment'. However, Hotten (1887) regards poll or polling as 'of ancient usage' and certainly in use as long ago as 1548 to refer to 'one thief robbing another of part of the booty'. In the exchange recorded above it was implicit that attempts would be made to cheat on the share of payment due to the barman and that 'pollying-up' was a way of ensuring more of the share due to him.

keeps eight or ten people on the premises while the manager checks his
cash and puts it in the safe. He's pleased to see the police then – they
usually call in for a quick one after hours.

'As far as I can see the whole business is crooked. After a while when
you've been working in bars, you begin to get a low view of human
nature. Customers are called 'punters' or 'mugs'. It rubs off on you.'

Not long after this account the Civil Service promoted Alan to Executive
Officer and his head of unit, an expatriate Londoner new to the town,
suggested that working in bars was 'inappropriate' to his new grade.
Reluctantly Alan had to give it up. He said he missed the job and its
companionship more than the money.

## The Waitress's Tale:
## 'The more I dug down – the more I dug up'

Away from the Mile and the Beach, Blackpool's women were well
represented in cafés, boarding houses and particularly in hotels – again, all
essentially indoor jobs.

Labour costs make up a large element of a hotel's total costs. And
since, in Blackpool, competition was marked,[9] managements responded by
tightening working conditions. They limited breaks, imposed 'split shifts',
tried to get more time for the same money, haggled over pay levels, and
arbitrarily sacked and re-employed staff. Staff of both sexes naturally
aimed to rebalance this 'benefits balance'. In Blackpool, they did it, as was
shown, not through unionisation, but by fiddling.[10] In most of the town's
hotels, there was constant conflict over fiddling. Managements standardly
attempted to limit fiddles – and there were more or less agreed limits. All
this was expected and understood with – at least for most of the time –
some degree of tolerance.

But employment conditions and levels of competition varied over time,
and agreed limits to pilferage were liable to be arbitrarily amended –
sometimes by managements, sometimes by staff. Kitty, the mother of a
school-friend, a long experienced waitress at a top hotel, told me how
someone had greatly exceeded the tolerated limit: a whole side of a
smoked salmon – to be served at that day's dinner – had 'walked'. (It had
been strapped to a waiter's leg inside his trousers.) Her manager exploded

---

9   See Mars & Nicod (1984).
10  An Individualist rather than a Group response and one particularly appropriate
    to Blackpool where the entrepreneurial climate was strong. See Chapter 21 for
    an elaboration of this distinction.

– not in outrage at the fiddle – but at its scale: 'I know you fiddle. You know I know – but for Christ's sake – LEAVE ME A BIT!'

The threat of purges was a serial experience. After each threat, fiddle levels would again creep back until a new purge was thought necessary. Kitty told me about a purge based on rumour that was part of such a cycle.

> I was at the Embassy then and it used to be very busy. Everyone was fiddling like mad when we got a leak through from the office: they were sending private detectives round the houses. Well, a friend of mine, Molly, told me this was going to happen. She didn't tell everyone – just me and two other girls. I was petrified because all my sheets and tablecloths and all my cutlery and silver were all stamped with the Embassy crest. Well, I didn't know what to do. As I say, I was petrified! So I made an excuse, said I was ill and rushed off home.
>
> I piled everything I could onto a sheet in the middle of the floor and tied up the corners. I dashed into the garden – out there – and started digging a bloody great hole. Laugh – the neighbours must have thought I was bloody crazy! I wasn't laughing at the time though, I can tell you, because the more I was digging down, the more I was digging up! There was a pile of coffee pots, cutlery and rotted linen already in the garden that had been buried there by the waiter who had had the house before me! He must have done exactly the same as I did when the panic hit him. The only difference was that these all had the crest of the Splendide on them.

Rumours of a purge nearly always proved false, and detectives, as far as I knew, were never employed – but the effects were the same – fiddles were kept down. For a time. This rumour was part of a cycle of control, activated when collusive and tolerated fiddles exceeded mutually accepted levels. I have found similar examples in other organisations.

## An Overview of Fiddling

These accounts show that fiddling involves far more than just the gaining of extra pay: it frequently offers companionship in a shared undertaking. And besides helping tip the balance of employer power it often overcomes boredom and grants at least some degree of autonomy to job-holders when a job might otherwise be unbearably tedious. In short fiddling, besides its obvious benefits, can often turn a tedious job into more of a fun job.

As employers frequently recognise, tolerated fiddling can offer an incentive to harder work – a way of offering rewards by which both sides benefit. It is in the personal service occupations where passing trade dominates, where two sides to a transaction typically meet only once,[11] where there is no continuity to their relationships and no possible build-up of goodwill, that fiddling dominates. Seven million visitors a year amount to a lot of passing trade.

In addition, personal services involve what I have called 'triadic occupations'[12] where transactions involve three parties – an employer an employee and a customer, so that fiddles can readily be effected by any two combining against the third. In these situations fiddling may well subsidise an employer's wages bill at the expense of customers. For these reasons then, collusion between management and labour is common, though rarely expressed, especially in service trades.

A common view of fiddling is that it is anarchic, rule-less and if not checked will lead to massive excesses. But this is rarely so; it is more common to find that limits are built in, so that controls on quantities taken are kept within accepted and understood bounds – either set from above or determined by a group where they are likely to be subject to group surveillance and control – as is well demonstrated in the account of dock-work pilferage in Newfoundland (ch. 11). In Kitty the waitress's account, there was an absence of effective groups, and therefore of group controls, that tend to limit fiddles to tolerated levels. Limits were therefore usually less effectively maintained by the threat of periodic purges.

Fiddling at work has a long history[13] but despite this is too often dismissed as aberrant – as the isolated actions of odd deviants – of 'the odd rotten apple in the barrel'. Understanding workplace deviance would better be understood by examining the barrel – or indeed the whole orchard –that is by concentrating instead on the way work is structured. To do this it is necessary to understand the workers' view of their work – without necessarily condoning it.

## Postscript: Why are Seaside Resorts Prone to Occupational Crime?

Much of this account of life in Blackpool has focused on its extreme enterprise, ambition and dynamism. In doing so it has featured its

---

11  Mars (1982, p. 138) N.B. The influence of passing trade is likely to increase with the growth of service trades and 'hypermobility' – the propensity of people to travel more. See Adams (2000).

12  Mars (1982) ch. 6: Fiddle proneness

13  Recorded examples go back at least to the time of the Pharaohs. For an early account of Ancient Egyptian warehouse theft, see Peet (1924). This was identical in its structure to my experience of theft from RAF stores.

proneness to crime – its *criminogenesis*. That the town *was* prone to crime is beyond argument. It ranged from the high incidence of institutionalised bribery and corruption at the top – from the town's chief executive the town clerk, councillors, and the chief of police, down to everyday occupational fiddling at the bottom of the 'food chain'.But it also extended to the widespread ignoring of laws governing both child and adult labour, hygiene regulations and the deferred considerations of planning permissions for seasonal holiday structures which were typically not assessed until *after* the end of each summer season.[14]

The propensity to crime in its various shadings should not surprise. First there was a pent-up demand for holidays post World War II, and Blackpool controlled and excelled in providing a large proportion of the holiday provision wanted by its public – and did it better than its rivals. The second is that the post-war boom attracted risk-taking entrepreneurs from throughout the North of England and beyond, and alongside them came others who had participated in the wartime black economy: now displaced, they sought new opportunities.

Two further reasons for the resort's liability to criminogenesis is that in a tourist centre the vast majority of transactions involve both passing trade and triadic occupations which are dominant features of personal service occupations (as discussed on page 63). At the risk of repetition, passing trade transactions usually occur once only and involve no build-up of goodwill. Holiday-makers are continually 'passing through'. When found alongside triadic relationships they form a powerful alliance.

Triadic relationships involve three parties – employer, employee and customer, so that fiddles can be effected by any two combining against the third. In these situations fiddling may well subsidise an employer's wages bill at the expense of customers. This is a further reason why collusion between management and labour is common – though rarely expressed. It is the prevalence of these two conditions where personal services dominate that permits us to extend its relevance beyond the specific example of Blackpool to include other seaside resorts and pilgrimage sites.

---

14  Walton (1978)

# CHAPTER SIX

# VARIED EMPLOYMENTS

## Landladies: Competition and Gentility[1]

Despite their absence from outdoor involvements, Northern women were (and still are) certainly not passive: Blackpool's women came into their own as landladies.

We had three landladies in our family: Mam and my two aunties, Kath and Rachel. All large women, they were busy, busty and bustling. In dealings with visitors they gave good and cheerful service – but when opposed could be formidable. Auntie Kath, the Irish wife of Mam's elder brother, was the most experienced – and potentially the most vicious. I have seen her switch from motherly matron to formidable battle-axe in an instant. And it was she who advised the other two about dealings with difficult visitors. But because she gave her visitors more food and better service than they expected she normally had few difficulties. One of her much appreciated extras was to take them a pot of morning tea in bed. Since her hotel had six floors and no lift this was a very special service.

Auntie Kath normally ran her hotel with tolerant resignation. One hot summer afternoon, I was at her front door as a family of six returned from the beach. She watched the children as they climbed the stairs, hot, tired and tearful from too much sun and leaving, as they went, a trail of sand and toffee wrappers. Clearing them up, quite unperturbed, she summarised the human condition as it applied to landladies: 'It's all hell's bells – buckets and spades – and scriking[2] kids.'

One afternoon however, when she came to see Mam, she was far from resigned or tolerant: she was furious. 'Those buggers! You won't believe it – *I* don't believe it.' Mam was concerned. 'What's to do?' 'What's to do? They complained the bloody tea was cold! That's what's to bloody do! Cold ? Well it could well be bloody cold couldn't it? You'd hardly expect

---

1   For a social history of the Blackpool landlady see Walton (1978).
2   North of England dialect to describe 'whining, crying children'

it to be boiling bloody hot by the time it got to the top bloody floor, would you?'

Mam nodded sympathetically. She knew Kath's kitchen was in the basement – and that she was then without staff. 'But I taught them,' Kath flashed. 'I got up at five this morning – I don't normally get up till six, but I got up at five. I put the pans on the stove and I boiled that bloody teapot, that milk jug, the bloody sugar bowl, the cups and the saucers – and the spoons – I boiled the whole bloody lot for two solid hours. I had to take them out of the pan with tongs! They glowed! Then I rushed up with 'em to the top floor. That taught 'em. They'll never complain again EVER!'

My Auntie Rachel, Mam's elder sister, was the hardest of the three. She kept a five-bedroomed boarding house in Ashburton Road, close to the town's centre. Built like a cube with tightly waved grey hair, she could readily have doubled as an Ena Sharples look-alike.[3] One winter's day I was at home after school when Auntie Rachel came round to see Mam who saw she was subdued, even perhaps depressed. Mam sat her down and poured her a cup of tea. 'Are you all right Rachel?'

Auntie Rachel sniffed; Mam was moved; this was unlike her elder sister. Auntie Rachel did not usually show emotions other than anger and scorn. She sniffed again – and then out it came. 'My lodger's dead!'

We knew she had a lodger, a 'regular' who stayed with her throughout the winter. Lodgers were highly valued. They helped meet costs through the slackest time of the year. But Mam was surprised at this unusual show of feeling. Was there perhaps more to the relationship than that? 'Oh dear! I am sorry. I didn't know you were so fond of him. Was it sudden?'

But sentiment had little place with Auntie Rachel. 'Fond of him? Don't be bloody daft! He paid monthly and he died last Friday – the day before his rent was due.' Another sniff. 'Mind you,' she paused, 'there was a pile of [returnable] bottles under his bed. So I took them back. It all helps.'

Undoubtedly, part of the mythology of meanness surrounding the Blackpool landlady – and it wasn't all mythology – was due to strong competition in the town. Thus when Auntie Rachel served beans on toast, she spread margarine only around the toast's edges She also salvaged tomato skins from her own family's meals to put in the cheap, tinned, tomato soup she served to visitors. 'It makes 'em think it's home-made from fresh tomatoes. Silly buggers!'

And it was she who was inspired to put a lock on the bathroom door so she could charge a shilling a bath. 'If they're posh enough to want a bath, they're posh enough to pay a bob.'

---

3   A character in an early ITV television programme, *Coronation Street*

Petty meanness was evident in most of the town's enterprises since margins were generally tight, competition keen, small savings important, and in the early fifties there was still food rationing. But there was more to it than just these obvious causes: there was exuberance and a shared ideology that made a big thing out of small illicit benefits. In Singer's, one of the town's main grocery stores, the owner instructed his staff how to get 60 lbs of butter out of every 56 lb barrel– by using heavy paper and the dexterous pressure of one finger on the scales. On Saturdays my brother Len worked in a café spreading margarine on sliced bread. He received high praise from his boss. 'Len, you're a wonder. You must be the best spreader in Blackpool – no-one can make a packet go farther than you.'

It is not surprising that with intense competition, managerial fiddling should be honed to a high level. But is it any wonder that in this climate many Blackpool workers should have equated fiddling for their bosses with fiddling for themselves?

Though Blackpool folk were ambitious and competitive, this was played out very differently between the genders. Men strived for prestige and money and so did women, but women craved gentility even more. It was most evident in their concern with accent. 'To speak proper' was an obsession for swathes of Blackpool women,[4] one that seemed to bypass men completely.

Again, my own extended family provides a classic example. One of Auntie Rachel's problems was a severe pretension to gentility. Another was that she could never sustain it. This made for difficulties with her accent – it was liable to veer in the same sentence from broad Lancashire to 'ultra refeened'. Answering the phone always caused her problems: how to judge the right response without knowing who it was at the other end? Her approach was to answer all calls with a strangled: 'Toew, toew, sax, foive, win,' – then wait. If her efforts were wasted she would revert to her 'rude normal': 'Oh – it's you is it?'

Rivalry between Mam and Auntie Rachel went back decades. Their mother had died when Mam was nine and Auntie Rachel, by then grown up and married, had apparently ignored her motherless younger sister – a neglect Mam never forgot. Mam insisted their rivalry arose from Rachel's jealousy of their father's favouritism. Once, she told me, he had bought Mam a watch that Rachel, in a rage, had stamped on and ground underfoot. They still had regular spats that followed a routine, with Auntie Rachel boasting of her social contacts and Mam squashing her with wit and her association with superior education: three of Mam's four sons

---

4    And not just in Blackpool. It seems to pervade much of the North of England.

were attending grammar schools; Auntie Rachel's only son had failed the Eleven Plus!

One day Auntie Rachel, the devotee of Received Pronunciation, was lauding the daughter of a friend of hers. 'She's very well educated you know – she talks beautiful. She's had elocution lessons.'

She had stepped straight into Mam's territory - education – and Mam also knew the family. 'Her? Talk beautiful ? You can teach a parrot to talk beautiful. That's not education. It doesn't mean she can talk sense.'

'Oh yes!' responded Auntie Rachel. 'But she speaks three languages.'

'Yes, I know her,' replied Mam, 'And I know this – she can't talk sense in any of 'em.'

## A Canine View of Gentility

After two years we moved to a slightly larger boarding house in Cheltenham Road, North Shore, one of a terrace of identical Victorian houses, each presided over by its landlady. Every landlady accommodated the same class of visitor, and in 1948 they all charged the same rate – 12/6d a day for full board. Yet despite their similarities Cheltenham Road seethed with competition. It was based on gentility, and its pace was set by the women. Men were shadows with little economic place except as subordinates to their landlady wives.

Our next-door neighbour, Mrs Keen, claimed ultra-gentility – and had the height, bulk and presence to almost carry it off. Tall, rigidly corseted, her dyed blonde hair was stiffly coiffed. To buy a loaf was for Mrs Keen a full dress occasion involving her prized fur coat, hat, gloves, and matching handbag. So dressed, she regally sailed the 300 yards to the corner Co-op – and then the 300 yards back. Poor Mr Keen was rarely visible. A modest, cowed soul, he was compelled to take off his outdoor shoes before entering the house. There were no little Keens.

At fourteen I was in no position to know Mrs Keen's views on sexuality. But looking back I would guess she was probably 'agin it': it certainly influenced her attitude to dogs. In a rare, 'woman-to-woman' exchange, she had explained to Mam that 'Lady' (her darling pedigree poodle) was never allowed off a lead and had to be kept chained in a kennel in the back yard during 'her season'. She shuddered delicately as she explained that the thought of Lady having puppies was 'too awful' to contemplate. To be fair, puppies arriving in the summer might perhaps be a nuisance to a busy landlady. Though why she had never had Lady spayed, I have no idea. Poor Lady was in fact kept deprived all the year round. Or almost.

My dog Peter, a spaniel/retriever, had seen service as a mascot in the RAF. When his squadron was disbanded and Peter needed a home he was rescued via a contact of my Auntie Kath's. She thought I needed a dog and explained to Mam that Peter was 'fully domesticated' having been 'put through his paces' by the squadron's dog handler. We would, she thought, be very lucky to have him. Mam, unconvinced, agreed grudgingly despite her qualms, to allow Peter house-room.

Peter was a boy's perfect companion. At a signal he would point heavenwards and bay like a wolf – which always discomfited the Salvation Army brass band as it played to capture souls on the Promenade. He would retrieve sticks and balls from gardens that were too dangerous for a boy to traverse. He earned me money by recovering children's beach balls that had bounced over the sea wall during high tide. He could play dead and then, at a signal, leap up snarling viciously to order. And as part of his RAF skills he could scale high walls – the kind of walls that separated our property from Mrs Keen's.

I knew something was wrong when I heard a whimpering from the yard. On going out I saw Peter was hurt. He was whining and limping about the yard though he did not seem to be injured. I stroked him and took him into the house. Then I heard Mrs Keen shouting from her yard. I went out, stood on a box and looked over the wall. An extremely angry, most unrefined Mrs Keen waved a broom at me. 'If that dog comes into my yard again I won't just hit it – I'll kill it! Yes – kill it!'

It seemed Peter had scaled the dividing wall, been caught by Mrs Keen *in flagrante delicto,* was chased out of her yard and while straddling the wall to make his escape, she had banged a broom down on his arched back. Mrs Keen immediately tackled Mam. She was almost incoherent. 'Mrs Mars – your Peter has seduced my Lady.' Further, if Lady became pregnant, she would certainly sue for damages. Mam, for once at a loss for words, could only reply, 'Ooh – the dirty dog!'

If Peter had subscribed to proverbs he would have appreciated that 'revenge is a dish best served cold.' The next day Peter disappeared. Normally he would joyously appear whenever I whistled. This time, despite my whistling, there was no Peter. I found him lying patiently on the pavement outside Mrs Keen's front gate. He wouldn't follow me, and for the first time when I tried to pull at his collar he growled. So I left him waiting for whatever he was waiting for.

A couple of hours later I heard barking on the street. It sounded like Peter but this was not the exuberant barking of Peter expressing himself. This was a measured, regularly spaced, single bark – a 'WOOF' followed by a pause, then another 'WOOF' – with the sequence repeated. I went outside.

Mrs Keen, as dignified as ever, was bedecked for shopping in her full fur ensemble. Peter was following four or five feet behind – and he was barking out his revenge. I followed them both, as Mrs Keen tried her hopeless best to maintain a detached, aloof deportment and pretend this dog at her heels was nothing to do with her. She couldn't sustain it. Half-way to the Co-op she abandoned all attempts at decorum and, impotently waving her basket, started swearing and making wild runs at Peter. Peter, though, was far too agile to be caught again. He skipped away from each foray. Aware she was becoming the subject of a mounting farce, Mrs Keen then attempted to resume her dignified progress and at last reached the sanctuary of the Co-op. Peter though was not finished. Again he lay quietly on the pavement. When she reappeared he repeated the sequence – back to her front gate. Peter kept up his torment for a fortnight.

There are postscripts to this account. As amused neighbours heard the story they came out to watch the fun. We heard that Mrs Keen had tried to get the Co-op to deliver. They said, they couldn't spare the staff. And then we received the anonymous letter. In thick black ink and neat block capitals, full of disconnected abuse it ended: 'This was a respectable neighbourhood until you, your family – and your dog – came to live here.'

Blackpool with its drive to 'making it' and its female-driven aspirations to gentility – especially when demonstrated through a 'superior' accent – would have had no place in The Avenues. There conformity ruled – and everyone knew enough about their neighbours to make such pretensions ludicrous.

## The Man Who Loved Hats

Not all Blackpool's workers were employed in the holiday trades: Blackpool was also a retail centre. So after leaving school in July 1949 I applied for an 'all-the-year-round job' and was taken on, at just over two pounds a week, by H. Hunters and Sons, a very old, extremely respectable, 'gentlemen's outfitters' on Abingdon Street in the town centre.

Working at Hunters was like being a servant in a large Victorian house. The shop was heavy with mahogany and pervaded by rank. It had hardly changed since the nineteenth century, and still had a system of overhead cash containers that winged and swung their way on wires from the counters to a central cash-desk. A core of long-serving, faithful employees staffed its main departments – each in charge of a member of the Hunter family. These were always respectfully addressed, and discussed, by their

first names – but with the appellation 'Mr'. So we had 'Mr Thomas' –
head of shirts, ties and woollens, 'Mr Edgar' – head of suits, and 'Mr
John' who was head of coats and scarves. I however was put into Hats, a
minor department with only one other employee, Mr Fernlea. He
explained on my first morning, that he was 'Head of Hats.'

A grey, arid man of about fifty, Mr Fernlea told me he was responsible
for my training in the technicalities of hat care and maintenance. He would
also teach me how to serve customers. He called this 'being respectful of
the clients'. Since our customers were essentially middle-class they were
therefore *de facto* 'clients' to be respected rather than customers to be
served. According to Mr Fernlea, to show respect involved leaning slightly
forward from the waist, one's head inclined and the adoption of an
obsequious snivel tone.

Hunters' hat department stocked mainly trilbies, and a few Hombergs
but no caps – caps being a symbol of the urban working class. Mr Fernlea
loved hats (and, I assumed, hated caps). He knew everything about them –
their manufacture, history and especially their care. Otherwise as
communicative as a clam, he nonetheless relished the opportunity to pass
on to me his life's knowledge about his specialism – the storing and daily
brushing of trilbies which varied according to their pile. This fell to me
and was apparently essential to my training. When I queried why I needed
to brush each hat every day, since they were sealed behind glass in
cabinets, Mr Fernlea looked thoughtful – and then quietly asked. 'Do you
want your cards?' [5]

This was a warning: asking such questions involved the risk of being
fired. Yet despite my questioning and being bored nearly to death I was
obviously proving at least adequate as a trainee. At the end of our first
month together Mr Fernlea pronounced: 'If you keep your nose clean
Mars, you could well be Head of Hats when I retire.'

Mr Fernlea was not due to retire for fifteen years. This prospect was so
appalling that it triggered an early escape. I gave in my notice and moved
swiftly across the road to Greenwoods (H&O) Ltd, (the initials standing
for 'Hosiers and Outfitters').

---

5   To 'give a worker his (insurance) cards' was an accepted form of dismissal. In
    the historic past it seems there were two cards – hence the common plural.

# The Man Who Loved Ha'pennies

Greenwoods men's outfitters was a family-owned chain of 120 shops, based in Bradford.[6] Its clientele was predominantly working-class so of course it sold caps rather than trilbies or Homburgs. Greenwoods flourishes still, though Hunters long ago sold out to Austin Reed, after a century of non-adaption.

This branch of Greenwoods had a relaxed and friendly manager, Roland Hemingway, a portly, genial man who had flown Lancasters in the war and been a prisoner in Stalag Luft III, the famous 'wooden horse' camp for officers. Its only other assistant, Mrs Mason, was in her thirties, very experienced and smart. What made her day was when customers mistook her for 'Mrs Greenwood'.

Well before I was sixteen I had found that most if not quite all Blackpool employers were exploitative. By then I had worked in a wide variety of part-time and short-term jobs. But for greed, Greenwoods was well in front. I had been there three weeks at the minimum statutory weekly wage, when a note arrived for Mr Hemingway from head office. He passed it silently to me:

> We note you have been paying your new employee, Mr Mars, two pounds two shillings and three pence. We are aware that this extra payment of a halfpenny each week above his entitlement, allows you to operate your books to the nearest penny. In future we suggest you effect this by paying him two pounds two shillings and two pence from next week and two pounds two shillings and three pence on alternating weeks.

Mr Hemingway smiled then spelled out how Greenwoods managed its staff. He explained what was common gossip in the firm: that every ha'penny saved allowed the (absentee) owner, Old Man Greenwood, to spend most of his time in the Mediterranean, on his yacht with his 'fancy woman'. Then I found out about the firm's system of accounting. Each branch had an annual stocktaking. Any shortfall in the balance of 'stock held' against 'stock sold' was deducted from the manager's salary. The reverse however, did not apply: all surpluses were credited to the firm. Nor was credit from any one year written off against losses in subsequent years. This mode of accounting meant of course that fiddling was built-in since managers had to overcharge customers when they could, to ensure they were covered against any shortfall at stocktaking time. This style of

---

6  Now known as Greenwoods (Outfitters) Ltd, it has ninety shops and, I gather, a more modern approach to its staff. I recently chatted to staff at a couple of branches and they were high in their praise of its contemporary management.

accounting was similar to that operating on Blackpool trams (page 53). Is it any wonder that a common expression in the town had it: 'Once you start fiddling for them, you might as well fiddle for yourself'?

Serving at Greenwoods was much more interesting than serving the more socially distant clientele at Hunters. Not only was my boss more amenable but one diversion was to watch the North of England's working-class sex-war being daily enacted in the shop. In some skirmishes, supremacy went to women, in others to men. One day an elderly couple entered the shop, and there was no doubt how the battle was going. He had a large moustache and a big physique: she was small and slight. 'I want a jacket,' he barked, 'like the green one in the window.'

He then wanted to see more jackets so I brought him a selection. He tried on several during which his wife said nothing. Finally the choice lay between two and he addressed her for the first time. 'Which one do you like, lass?' Hesitantly, she pointed. 'I think I... er... I like that one, Jack.' 'Right,' he replied. Then to me: 'Wrap t'other wun up, lad.'

Much later I found I'd missed my chance at Hunters. Mr Fernlea had died – only five years after I'd left.

## Child-Rearing in Hard Times

By the late forties and throughout the fifties, Mam was too ill to work, and though Dad was a craftsman at the top of his trade, it was a dying trade. As a sample presser of specimen garments for the firm's salesmen to hawk around the stores, his job was becoming eroded by the Hoffman steam press that was making hand pressers redundant. He was earning less and less. As he listlessly moped, we all became more concerned at the constant struggle to keep off creditors. Times were hard. Just how hard I only appreciated later. Hardship has its own anaesthetic – it numbs through routine and insulation – but at that time I had no basis for comparison; when hardship is the norm it encourages its own routines.

One of my errands each week was to go to the nearby fish shop and ask the owner, Mrs Kemp, for 'bits for the cat'. She must have thought that if we did have a cat – which we didn't – then it must have been the northern hemisphere's hungriest moggy ever. Luckily Mrs Kemp was generous.[7] Her weekly offerings, chopped by Mam in the mincer and supplemented with matzo meal, onions and carrots, provided the family

---

7    The use of children to solicit favours on behalf of their families has been noted in many cultures. The practice permits favours to be asked when refusal to an adult might well be socially disruptive or involve too weighted an obligation.

with the week's gefilte fish. My other visit – to the bakers – was to collect stale bread at a discount (a taste I still prefer). Dad, somehow uninvolved, sailed above all this. Mam's meat balls with gravy – made entirely from porridge with added Bisto – was one of his favourites and fooled him for years. And twice a week we enjoyed lentil soup made from marrow-bone stock. By these means, and with a chicken provided each weekend through the goodwill of the local Jewish charity, by Mam's periodic entrepreneurial ventures, with all 'the Brothers' working at odd part-time jobs and pooling earnings, and by serial borrowing, we got by – just. But it could not go on. We needed more income. Finally, with the building society about to foreclose (again!) on the mortgage, something desperate was obviously due.

In 1949 I was 15. I could help but to do so needed a job. Having just failed the School Certificate[8] I could not be choosy. It would have been good to return to school for a retake, but obviously this was not on. Work beckoned.

A friend of mine, when told later of this period of my life, was surprised I was willing to work – in part to keep my brothers at the grammar school but in essence just to keep the family afloat. 'Wasn't there any feeling of resentment?' she asked. 'Didn't you feel you shouldn't have had to make sacrifices for your brothers?'

I had to think out why resentment and rivalry had – and still has – no place in our family, and why 'the Brothers' still relish each other's successes and are collectively cast down by our failures. The answer is simple: our Mam was a clever woman who had seen the effects of jealous rivalry in her own childhood and was determined to avoid it with her own children.

Mam's techniques were simple but effective. I remember Auntie Daisy, a long-term family friend, 'honorary aunt' and a devout Christian who was visiting one day when my brother Mel arrived from school. Mam told him there was a piece of a sweet for him on the mantelpiece. It was usual for scarce items like sweets to be cut into four– one for each brother. Auntie Daisy was startled. 'Surely it isn't worth bothering about – when there's so little?' 'That's *exactly* why it *is* worth bothering about – because *it is* so little,' – was Mam's unanswerable answer.

Another time, when my two youngest brothers, Mike and Mel aged about five and eight, were squabbling, blaming each other and whining to Mam for justice, they received short shrift and a good telling off. In

---

8    The precursor of today's GCE – except that one needed to pass in six subjects simultaneously. A pernicious system: several of my friends obtained only five and had nothing to show for their efforts.

Mam's view, they were old enough to sort out their own problems. And sorting out our own problems became the norm. There were never arguments about doing household chores – such as washing up after meals: who did them was decided randomly by tossing coins or drawing cards. We still have no sense of rivalry and continue to enjoy each other's company – nearly a lifetime later.

When later I fell among psychologists, I was surprised to find how entrenched was this idea of sibling rivalry as an instinctive – even a healthy – trait. Of course, as any first-year anthropologist realises, this view is ethnocentric – that is, culturally determined. Mam had effectively 'structured out' sibling rivalry.

With this ethic of collective solidarity then, the question of personal interests versus family interests was not in debate: I had to get a job.

## Factory Life: 'Just stick at it – you'll get used to it'

To get a job in Blackpool in the summer was easy: cafés and hotels always needed staff, but a firm called the Zonex Optical Company always had year-round vacancies. They made cheap Bakelite telescopes and were known to pay well. But they were known also to be lousy employers. Work there however, would lighten the family's plight. So, on a sunny Monday morning in September, I called at their offices that, with its factory, were set in a large Victorian house and its garden on Talbot Road. I was to learn what work was like in a Dickensian factory.

The Zonex reception area in black and chrome, contained a young woman receptionist, seemingly camouflaged in a black suit with silver earrings, a silver necklace and black, rigidly lacquered hair. She was too busy reading the *Daily Mirror* to notice me. After a while however, she put it aside and, indifferently raising her eyebrows, asked what I wanted. I said I wanted a job, and asked what they paid. She dismissively murmured that only jobs in the factory were available. When pressed, she grudgingly told me the pay was £3-10s a week – more than a pound over shop work. Immediately I said, 'I'll take it.' Sighing, she pushed away her paper, languidly reached for a card, took down my details, then picked up a phone. A few lethargic words later she went back to her paper. I waited. Eventually a sallow, middle-aged man in a brown overall appeared and nodded at me to follow him.

He opened a door and we walked through – to be hit by the scorched smell of hot oil. Ahead was the factory: a large shed, cheap and quickly thrown up as an extension to the original house. Over a hundred feet long, its walls had at one time been roughly whitewashed. Now, soiled and smeared, its cladding showed through irregular holes and fractures. Down half its length, a rattling and obviously mal-maintained conveyor belt whirred and grated as it swept incomplete telescopes past automatons who snatched them up, clipped on attachments, then flung them back.

The factory teemed with people and the noise of machinery. Few people talked – they were too busy with what they were doing. Some sat at small tables, bent over boxes of partially complete telescopes, or sorted components and collected or delivered boxes. Others, heads down, wrote in large ledgers. Between them moved men in brown overalls, the foremen.

I was passed to one of these. Pale, in his forties, he distractedly looked over my shoulder, then suddenly, looking closely at me, he barked: 'Can you pack parcels?' Assuming that nobody couldn't, I answered, 'Yes.' He took me to a table with rolls of sticky tape, a large ball of string, piles of vouchers and nearby, boxes of differently sized telescopes. On the adjacent wall hung a giant roll of brown paper. I was briefly shown what to do – then left to carry on.

I enjoyed that job. Later I found that packing jobs are apparently ideal for people with IQs of around 80. Packing allowed me to dream while I worked, and it was satisfying to create well-shaped parcels with neat symmetrical corners out of oddly shaped contents. It was a job that suited me but it was lonely work, though not – as I later found – the loneliest Zonex could offer.

At lunch time, the foreman came to check on progress. He glanced at my pile of parcels and he wasn't pleased. He winced, then sucked on his teeth. 'Is that all you've done?' I confessed it was. He snorted. 'Then you'll never make a packer. You'll be better off on the guillotine.' He did not explain what work on the guillotine meant. I was scheduled to start work with it after lunch.

The factory had no canteen, nor even the means to make tea. But during lunch-break, over sandwiches and flasks, I talked to other workers. They confirmed that most people did not stay long, and that the firm broke every employment law in the book. It seemed Zonex's safety record was one reason it could not keep its staff.

'You watch out for that guillotine,' I was warned.

'But the pay's good, isn't it?'

'Aye,' replied one old hand 'It's because folk would leave in summer, that's why.'

It seemed that Zonex had to pay above the going rate, not only because it competed with the holiday trades for labour, but because Zonex was a fiddle-free zone in a fiddle-active town. But though Zonex paid more, it promised to be pay for which you risked your life. Or at least your limbs.

After lunch I was taken to the guillotine – a weighted razor-sharp knife set in a frame with a vertical fall of about four feet. The same foreman gave me a brisk, few seconds induction, proudly explained how this guillotine could cut through heavy cardboard sheets – which it did 'as if they was butter' – then he left me to it. I did not know that guillotines should have guards. But after twice nearly cutting off my hand, I knew this one was dangerous. I sought out the foreman. 'I want a different job.'

He shook his head as though he couldn't believe what he'd heard. Again he winced, and again he sucked on his teeth. Then came the phrase that embodied Zonex's staff relations: 'Stick at it. You'll get used to it.' 'You just need to stick at it.'

But, pre-warned, and well knowing my clumsiness, I was adamant. I knew that guillotine could cost me dear. 'No,' I said, 'I'm sorry but I don't want to stick at it. I want a different job.' He flushed and seemed set to shout when his expression suddenly lightened. 'Do you want to learn how to make lenses?' That sounded skilled and interesting. And who knew to where it might lead? 'Yes,' I said. 'Yes. I'd really fancy that.'

He took me to past where the conveyor's clamour was at its loudest, to an enclave at the end of the shed. Here lenses were prepared for grinding and the air was full of the heavy smell of an all-pervading vapour that rose from caldrons and crucibles of bubbling pitch. And here I was introduced to George, my instructor.

George was about eighteen, tall, thin and with spots. He was affable and friendly with a welcoming grin, and though not quite my idea of a skilled craftsman/instructor, he was keen to teach me all he knew. He was slick and efficient. First, with a flourish, he ladled hot pitch from a large heated iron cauldron into a crucible sitting on a gas ring. When the pitch in its crucible started to bubble, he then showed me how to press a smaller crucible into it so the pitch overflowed. When it did, it left a lining on its inner surface. Alongside, heating up on another gas ring was a steel hotplate, and on it flat glass discs. George, with rapid swoops, then started to pick them up and to deftly place them in concentric circles in the pitch-lined crucible. When full of discs it went off somewhere to a polishing machine. As I watched George complete his display, I could see, inevitably, that I would pour boiling pitch over myself. Then it was, 'Now you do it' time.

With hands shaking, I just avoided spilling the bubbling pitch and even managed to control the overflow from its crucible. Then I picked up a glass disc. It was so hot I yelped, dropped it and jumped back. George had been waiting for that. He grinned. 'You'll get used to it,' he said. 'But they're practically red hot,' I protested.' In fact some *are* red hot.' 'Oh, you'll soon get used to it,' he insisted. 'You just need to stick at it. Look...' He stretched out his hands with the fingers extended. His hands were webbed: there was a triangle of raw, rough, scar tissue between his fingers.

Again I sought out the foreman. He might have been expecting me. As I approached he uttered a quiet moan. But I told him nonetheless: 'I want to give up making lenses. Wasn't there something else – anything else – I could do?' Then, that phrase again. 'But you've not even tried getting used to it. You've got to stick at it.' I insisted this was one job I wasn't going to stick at. I wasn't prepared to burn my fingers until they were webbed: I wanted a change.

'Well then,' he snapped, 'You can go on the belt.' It seemed 'the belt' of all available jobs, was the end of the line. Except that for me, it wasn't. The belt was not as noisy as others I have met with since – but it kept erupting with periodic grinding and screeching noises – making it difficult to think let alone talk. Along it men and women of all ages sat on each side. As it swept past they snatched up partly assembled telescopes and either screwed or clipped on a component from a box at their side. Because of the noise and the belt's speed, the job demanded constant attention.

I was led to the belt's controller, another brown-coated foreman. A fat sweaty man in his fifties, his job seemed to involve making quick sudden darts to different parts of the belt to replenish an operator's components when they signalled for more. I waited until he was free. He was eventually able to stop darting about just long enough to arrange a place for me. Between interruptions, he told me what my new job involved. Pointing to a box of components he explained, in three different ways and by slowly emphasising each syllable, how I was to screw component F from the box at my side onto assembled components A to E as they coursed by. 'Was I sure I had got that?' I thought I had. 'And don't you wait until you've run out of F's before you call for more.' That would involve stopping the belt. Stopping the belt he explained, reduced output. The boss 'Mr John' or his son 'Mr Harold' 'would go apoplectic' if the belt were ever to stop. I never saw either of them: they were furies held in reserve.

The two fastest workers in the world sat at the beginning of the belt, briskly snapping together the first two components of the telescopes then passing them down the line. Both middle-aged, bosomy, head-scarved women, they looked like sisters. Their rate, plus the speed of the belt set the pace for everyone else. It was work that involved coordination and dexterity – at a speed I feared, that was well beyond me. And it was. I fell more and more behind as uncompleted A's to E's sailed past without their F's. At first I needed to stretch to retrieve them; then to leave my seat and finally to run alongside the belt to grab at fugitive telescopes. Even then it wasn't possible to get them all. This amused my immediate co-workers enormously, but not the belt's foreman. He looked at my antics in silence, glared, and then stonily he stopped the belt. This was a welcome break: along the belt's length, the dexterous robots came to life and began to chat together.

But like a dog allowed only one bite, I was allowed only one stoppage. When, twenty minutes later, the foreman had to stop the belt a second time, he was breathing hard and evidently about to choke. He ground out slow and loud that in his, this foreman's, highly experienced opinion, I was utterly unemployable. 'Twenty years I've done this job and I've never met anyone like you. You must be some sort of fuckin' idiot. You've had four fuckin' jobs in one fuckin' day and you've been no fuckin' good at any of 'em'. He pronounced that I would obviously be unsuited for any responsible work. 'Ever.'

'You know what you are? You're fuckin' unemployable – that's what you are!' I thought he might have a point – one can be fairly suggestible at fifteen – and I waited with some pleasure to be sacked. But no. After his tantrum he became calmer and began to breathe more easily. Was there to be a reprieve? 'This is your last chance,' he announced. 'You can fill scent bottles.'

It was a job, I later found, wanted by nobody, but one I might, apparently, just manage. After my public shaming, I was passed to a new foreman, my third of the day. Aloof, middle-aged and in brown overalls like his predecessors, he looked at me impassively before indicating that I should come with him. Before we moved off, one of the motherly pace-setters at the start of the belt, leaned out of her seat and nodding at Mr Sweaty, shouted to me: 'You take no notice of him, Love. He's just an ignorant shit.'

My new Foreman marched me away. Stiff, silent, he strode briskly without comment through the factory, past workers at different tables who, it seemed to me, looked up to stare at this degraded, scarcely employable wretch. I followed him into what had been the garden where, randomly scattered, were five or so small wooden sheds. We stopped at one containing a chair, a table, a large box of small bottles shaped as Blackpool towers, and two giant carboys of bright yellow liquid that looked very like piss. But unlike piss, this liquid gave off a sickly chemical odour. I had seen these scent-bottles before. They were almost worthless – free consolation prizes given by stall gamesters on the Golden Mile.

Again there were detailed and repeated instructions: 'This is how you pour; this is how you fill; this is how you fix the stoppers. Do you understand?' 'Yes,' I said, finally, 'I think I do.' Again I was left to myself. After a couple of hours a bell rang to mark the end of the day. Reeking of the world's cheapest scent – there were no washing facilities – I gratefully headed for the bus and home. My fellow passengers soon indicated what they thought of me. They were not tactful: they sniffed – looked at each other – then moved as far away as they could get.

When I reached home the family was appalled at the stench I brought in. Zonex was obviously awful – but was anything else much better? Mam, who in our house made the decisions, decided. Our being hard up was now so bad she said, that even if I stayed at Zonex it would make little difference. I would return to school and retake the School Certificate - and there would always be the chance of summer work. When Mam made a decision it was settled. And somehow we did manage to stagger on and deflect our foreclosure.

The next morning, as light as air, I sought out the camouflage queen at reception. She went through the same routine. When she finally did put down her *Daily Mirror*, stopped sighing and ceased puckering her eyebrows, I was delighted to tell her I wanted my cards; that I was leaving. She remained indifferent.

I had difficulty getting paid – a not uncommon experience in Blackpool. But who cared? Some months later I was unsurprised to hear that 'Mr John' and 'Mr Harold' had developed a variation of traditional industrial relations practice. Their way of dealing with a troublemaker had been to beat him up. If I had 'stuck at it' and stayed longer it would very likely have been me.

Sometime later I was trying to interview a workman in a shed as big as an aircraft hangar and full of noisy machinery. He had worked there for over twenty years. The noise was so loud, conversation was impossible and I had to shout. He indicated I shout even louder. I bellowed – then asked how he tolerated this appalling noise? 'Oh!' he shouted in reply, 'It's a lot easier now. You see, I've gone a bit deaf.' And then, that phrase again: 'If you stick at it, you get used to it.'

It is only fair to point out there was little *evident* gangsterdom in Blackpool at this time (though criminal gangs, strong-arm methods and their link to councillors did exist). Nor was there organised – or at least, visible – prostitution. In this period Blackpool was marketed as a family resort and took pains to maintain a wholesome public image.

## Looking Back

This then, is an account of how I experienced war-time Manchester and of Blackpool as it was from the end of World War II to its peak in the sixties. The sixties marked the start of the town's quick decline into shabby penury – a situation that now appears entrenched. This was mainly, but not entirely, due to the introduction of cheap package holidays to Spain's Costa del Sol which were scarcely dearer than the cost of a Blackpool holiday. Droves of visitors who had loyally returned to Blackpool every year now flocked to Spain where constant sunshine was guaranteed. The drive of its entrepreneurs, so marked a feature of the town, and the buoyant prosperity that resulted, melted like snow in spring.

These changes also coincided with a growth in car ownership that allowed visitors to spend a day by the seaside rather than a week. Blackpool's previous peak – seven million visitors a year – has since risen to over twenty millions but in not lodging in the town they offer it little benefit.

At the same time there was a shift in the ideologies of many of Blackpool's clientele. As we saw in Manchester, a potential fragmentation in the working class was evident before the war – with growing home ownership, personal aspiration and the first signs of competitive consumerism aided by hire purchase: all were primed for a post-war take-off. Many who had identified themselves as part of a solidaristic working class, later saw themselves having more in common with the aspirant middle classes they had previously despised. This shift in ideology contributed to holidaying in Spain rather than Blackpool: collective expression was being replaced by competitive individualism.[9]

My time in Blackpool was interrupted by three months as a Civil Service clerk in London followed by two years' National Service in the RAF. I noted that Hilaire Belloc had written somewhere: 'Men who have never served in an army feel perpetually deprived.' I couldn't wait.

---

9   As foreseen and discussed in Hoggart (1957)

# PART II:

# YET ANOTHER CULTURE:
# THE ROYAL AIR FORCE

CHAPTER SEVEN

# 'YOU MAY 'AVE BROKE YOUR MOTHER'S 'EART – BUT YOU WON'T BREAK MINE'

We had expected much worse. This was the Initial Entry Unit for National Servicemen at RAF Padgate, near Warrington. There were fifty of us, mostly eighteen-year-olds, all compulsorily called to serve our country. It was the November of 1951, one of the coldest in a decade.

Yet officers and NCOs could not have been more helpful, attentive even. They met us with hot tea and biscuits as we dribbled in from our different towns and then apologised that things were a little disorganised. We began to relax.

They smiled and introduced themselves with their ranks but ranks didn't seem to matter. They showed us films about the Air Force and its command structure, then more tea and biscuits with plenty of time to chat and ask questions. We had lectures on equivalent ranks of the three armed forces and what our training would involve. It was all very calming. We began to get to know each other.

My friend Leon Weinberg, who had been 'called up' for the Army three months earlier, told how his army NCOs had behaved during his 'basic training'. He had endured a particularly sadistic sergeant and been punished every day for seven weeks. He would not agree with the Sergeant's daily assertion: 'Weinberg, you've got a face like a chicken's arsehole. 'Aven't you? Weinberg? WEINBERG?'

After seven weeks, he finally broke and admitted that, perhaps after all, he did share this resemblance. But his persecution continued – because he still marched 'like a fuckin' duck'. Our intake swapped similar second-hand information. We had all heard that some recruits had actually killed themselves. But then, that was the Army and we thanked God we had had the utter good luck to be called up to the RAF, and to Padgate, an obviously soft option. It was my first introduction to calculated organisational deceit (CODS).

On day two we were given our service numbers. By day three we had been kitted out and uniformed. Then, a motley rabble in our new, ill-fitting uniforms, we awaited the coaches with two attendant corporals, to take us to the 6th School of Recruit Training at Credenhill, near Hereford.

Chattering, we clattered aboard. But something was not quite right. These corporals seemed a different breed from the chatty, NCOs at Padgate. Their boots and brass glittered. Their uniforms were so excessively well-pressed that the creases stood up. And they stared ahead, immobile, expressionless, mute. They nodded dismissively for us to clear out of the seats at the rear of the bus then sat there together – upright, rigid, as if with steel spines. It took about ten seconds for our conversations to falter, wither and die. But no move from the silent robots.

Crises tend to brings forth heroes. Ours was Shrimp, a short, spiky-haired outgoing cockney, the epitome of the bouncy extravert, he thought no-one could be unresponsive if treated as a friend. He broke the silence. Taking out a packet of cigarettes he put one in his mouth and offered the packet: 'Cigarette, Corporal?'

We were startled that a single short reply could embody so much menace. A voice rasped, metallic, a full-stop punctuating each word: 'AIRMAN! PUT. THAT. CIGARETTE. OUT!' This was only half the message: our corporal then extracted his own packet. We watched as he offered it to his fellow robot – then slowly he took a cigarette himself. They both lit up. The message was complete. These men were dangerous.

What followed was eight weeks of 'basic training' – mostly drill and rifle practice with obsolete World War I. Lee Enfield 303s dating from 1895. Rifle practice seemed designed to get you and your kit filthy by making you lie in mud. Drill of course, aimed to break down individualism, to weld us into a cohesive, disciplined whole so that we learned to march like a single giant centipede with legs and arms swinging in unison. Not everyone quite managed it. Some were worse than others: I apparently, was worse than everyone. On our second day, this was brought to public attention.

'Flight Halt! Right Turn!' We halted and turned. The drill sergeant asked my name, repeated it, twice, then snarled that it would be better for me if he did not remember it. This seemed altogether unlikely. After suggesting that I marched 'like a double-ruptured, fuckin' earwig', he then announced that the whole Flight would do two hours' evening fatigues (extra duties) 'because of that fuckin' nignog, Mars'.

This exposure did not make me popular in the billet. Nor was it designed to: the idea of basic training was to enhance group feeling – and to do so, it seemed, by deflecting the antagonism of the group from the NCOs to what they saw as its weakest member. That was me. I was in a spot. After a day's hard drill followed by two hours' fatigues, feelings were running high. Luckily everyone was too exhausted to more than mutter about it all being my fault. But winter was now starting to bite and that day was the coldest we had had. The weather was to prove a lifeline.

Next day on the parade ground, our corporal's memory proved as sound as the sergeant's. After a series of routine commands, he bellowed a non-routine one: 'All the Flight... Wait for it!... Wait for it!... All the Flight – EXCEPT MARS – change step!' I was so confused, I changed step with the rest. He ignited. 'Flight Halt! Right Turn.' Still 'a nignog', I was now 'the sloppiest airman in the whole history of the RAF', and worse, 'a disgrace to G-Flight', our new collective entity. We gained another two hours' fatigues.

After drill and fatigues, tired and chilled, we returned to our freezing billet with its two small stoves, both on the point of going out because we had used nearly all the miserly coke allowance. Feelings were bitter about the Air Force and me in particular. And they were becoming dangerously specific:

'You got us another two hours' fatigues, you fuckin' nignog.'

'You should be hung by the bollocks, you stupid bastard.'

'We'll have to teach you a lesson – cuntface!'

Inspiration at the level I needed it, came for once, just in time. 'Look,' I said 'I know where we can get some coke. There's one place that's sure to have it.' They listened – and three of us set out. The officers' mess had no coke but did have a six-foot mound of coal. And a wheelbarrow with two shovels. Our raiding party returned with a full load, to a welcome that was ecstatic. We were heroes. It was a shared triumph, the wheelbarrow a trophy of war. We stacked the stoves with coal until they glowed red hot. 'We've shown the cunts! They can't treat us like fuckin' cattle!'

Never mind that coke is designed for lower temperature stoves; that by using coal we nearly burned down the hut. We just managed, by frenzied fire-fighting, to stop the stove's red-hot chimneys setting fire to the roof.

That raiding party changed everything and not just my place in the Flight. The rest of the evening was spent around the stoves, subverting newly amenable comrades in conversations that lasted until the small hours. These ranged over how our training was organised, to the strategies of NCOs, how they avoided the Flight's aggression and fixed it on scapegoats. It became accepted that fatigues as a collective punishment was a lie, a plot to deceive us: cleaning the cookhouse, peeling potatoes, polishing the floors of the sergeants' mess – these tasks had to be done – whether or not Mars was 'a fuckin' nignog'. It was a different Flight that paraded the next morning: more of a cohesive group but not quite the cohesion envisaged by our NCOs. We now knew something they didn't.

Two days later, on a cold grey morning under a pale wintery sun, we paraded for rifle practice with our World War I 303s. We marched to the butts (the targets), and in batches of eight were chosen to lie in the semi-frozen mud, rifles at the ready. There is only one sensible way to lie in the mud with a rifle and it wasn't the way they tried to teach us. To avoid the worst of the mud, you must lie facing the line of targets at a twisted angle with your body slightly raised on knees and elbows. Then you have to hunch your right shoulder to avoid the rifle's recoil. Do it this way and you'll probably miss the target. But do it their way and though you might hit the target you'll be covered in mud and likely to get a bruise not lightly forgotten.

Our batch of eight lay prone, poised for the order to fire. It never came. A shadow blocked the sky. The corporal towered over me. His boot pressed me firmly into the mud.

'Don't move! Don't you dare move an inch you 'orrible, 'orrible man.'

'G-Flight,' came the order. 'Gather round. Look at this 'orrible abortion of a fuckin' nignog.'

G-Flight gathered round – and looked. 'Look at 'is disgraceful, 'orrible position! Look at 'im. Look at the way this nignog is 'olding 'is rifle!' He began to shriek, 'Look at the 'ole obnoxious posture of 'im!'

They looked, and thanked the gods it wasn't them in the mud.

''Ow can 'ee ever 'it a target, like that?' he screamed. ''Ow can a fuckin' earwig like this take a proper sighting? Don't you move, you disgrace to the 'uman race.'

I stayed – firmly pinned by his boot as he ranted on. 'You may 'ave broke your mother's 'eart – BUT YOU WON'T BREAK MINE. When I give you the order to fire, you'll fire: One, two, three – FIRE.'

I prayed – and fired. There was a slight delay until the butts communicated the result: 'A bull for target number five.' There was a longer delay, then silence. The boot lifted. Then came the order: 'G-FLIGHT. FORM THREES. QUICK MARCH. AT THE DOUBLE. LEFT–RIGHT–LEFT.'

Rifle training was over for the day. No-one told the corporal I had been aiming at target number four… It might 'ave broke 'is 'eart.

Three weeks later, after succumbing to 'jab-fever' from a faulty immunisation injection, I found myself in the unit hospital. In the next bed was another of our corporals. We talked and, to my surprise, I found he spoke eloquently without a single expletive and with less than the broad accent he had previously. He proved civilised, fluent and knowledgeable on a wide range of topics and told me how much he was looking forward to his imminent demob. He was about to take up a scholarship - at Oxford.

Even in hospital however, the RAF still managed to hit lunatic heights. The ward had a 'ward corporal'. One of his jobs was to prepare us for visits by the MO – an officer and therefore, close to a god. 'When the medical officer makes his rounds you don't just lie around: you lie at fuckin' attention. Right?' He explained that 'lying at fuckin' attention' meant lying on our backs, rigidly stiff, with our toes pointing upwards. We dutifully mimicked the statuary on crusader tombs in country churches.

## 'Total Institutions' and Scapegoat Selection[1]

Later, when teaching sociology, I found the School of Recruit Training at Hereford was the perfect example of a 'total institution' – 'a place of residence and work where a large number of like-situated individuals, cut off from the wider society for an appreciable period of time, together lead an enclosed, formally administered life' – as in monasteries, asylums, prisons – and 'basic training' units of the armed forces.

Because total institutions operate 'round the clock' in a single setting, emotions cannot easily be dissipated: accordingly there is a 'heating up of relationships'. And where control is maintained by an elite, this 'heating up 'can be mobilised and focused so that control over the lives of ordinary members can be intense – even coercive.[2]

Schools of recruit training are run on coercion – base level members have minimal power and co-operate through duress, as *in extremis* they do in concentration camps and to a lesser degree, prisons. New recruits are first indoctrinated until a simple message is accepted – 'This is where the power lies.' Recruit training in the armed forces incorporates them into a collective that transcends their individualism.[3] When internalised, this will be carried to any subsequent unit they join.

There is a potential flaw in this process: the trainees' growing collectivism can mount a serious threat to the elite's authority. This threat was diminished by the NCOs responsible for our training. As we saw, they adopted a technique common to training units. They identified its weakest recruit – someone like me who was least responsive to the training regimen. I could never learn to march in any coordinated way, but any divergent characteristic will do. The elite then projects the group's antagonism by imposing or threatening collective punishments – the blame

---

1   For the definitive account of total institutions see Goffman (1961, p. 11).
2   I have here combined insights from Etzioni (1961) and Goffman (1961).
3   See Lawrence (1955) for a personal account of the destruction of individuality involved in basic training in the British army post World War I.

for which can be attributed to the selected scapegoat. This is how armies are built.

## Resistance from Below

Basic Training was thankfully followed by the much softer option of 'Trade Training'. Without recognisable talents, experience or qualifications, most of our entry, after primitive IQ tests, was sorted into levels – the basis of allocation to the trades we were to follow during our time in the RAF. The top of the IQ heap went for training as wireless operators. The rest of our intake were destined to be storemen.

After training as a Storeman (Tech) I was posted to RAF Stafford. Here the NCOs were mostly career family men, humane and resigned at having to do the best they could with unenthusiastic, conscript labour.

Many of the quicker-witted and more malevolent of the lowerarchy had a field day during National Service. Their tactics aimed to reduce the respect on which all authority depends. To do it they ran a guerrilla campaign against the hierarchy. Its weakest members were cruelly picked off; their blunders and faults recorded with care; their responses circulated with relish – all to make them appear ridiculous. A friend, orderly to a notoriously authoritarian Warrant Officer, circulated with delight how he had talked about buying his daughter 'an encyclophobia'. Another, inveigled into a discussion about Keats, admitted he 'didn't know what a keat was'. A third related how a storeman was rebuked by his corporal for desultorily kicking a box containing a valve. ''Ere! You! Can't you see what it's got written on there? See – it's got "FRAY-GILE" on it...'

The storeman acted dumb. 'Fray-gile, Corp? What's that Corp?'

'What's that?' echoed the corporal. 'It means you don't kick it abaht, that's what it means – or you'll fuckin' soon break it – and then you'll be on a fuckin' fizzer [a disciplinary charge].'

The storeman still pretended puzzlement. 'Fray-gile, Corp? I don't understand, Corp. Do you mean "Fragile" Corp?'

Flustered, the corporal examined the box, pronouncing the word first one way, then another. 'Fraygile?'Fradgile?... Don't be stupid. Where's the fuckin' D?'

Circulating these stories underpinned an outrageous snobbery. But it also helped modify the power imbalance that so weighed against us. This even extended to subverting RAF police dogs. One of us discovered an Alsatian that was amenable to bribery. Normally as unfriendly as his corporal handler, we found after a week feeding it meat scraps that it would roll over on its back to have its stomach tickled – to the chagrin of its handler. He threatened to charge any offending airmen he caught but could not stop his dog rolling over every time it faced a held out hand. The poor animal had to be sent away for retraining. We corrupted a series of dogs until the corporal too was posted for retraining.

The power difference offered a potential source of insurrection but the RAF recognised and diffused the threat by various stratagems and rituals besides its use of scapegoats. In an apparent reversal of power, for instance, as in most armed services, on Christmas Day the officers traditionally serve Christmas dinner to the men. As I later learned, such 'rites of reversal'[4] are not uncommon in cultures with marked imbalances of power. In certain Greek mountain villages, the women once a year traditionally 'take over' the village; men stay indoors while the women move to the tavern to drink, tell obscene stories and dance to the tunes of a blindfold fiddler.[5] Nearer home we have our own staff Christmas parties where intimacies between levels are dissolved. Rites of reversal do not weaken an existing power imbalance, they reinforce it by contrast: what is permitted on one day a year marks out the exceptional – and confirms what is definitely *not* the norm on the other 364.

## National Service and Social Mobility

There were few bullying NCOs at Stafford and fewer stereotypical NCO insults – the insults were instead refreshingly original. Once, when painting a hanger wall, twenty feet up a ladder, I dropped the paint pot. Half a gallon of blue-grey paint spiralled down – just missing the Tech. Stores sergeant walking below. Sgt Ashton leapt aside, looked up, listened to my stammered apology – and then, in a phrase to be cherished, muttered: 'By Christ, Mars, if you learn from your mistakes – you should end up a fuckin' genius.'

Some of us, if not geniuses, did end up markedly different from our pre-call-up selves. Now we could compare ourselves against our whole generational cohort. With only a few selected as National Service officers, it was possible to share a barrack hut that in my case included the scion of a business empire, a couple of public school boys due to go to university and a graduate – few it seemed, were any brighter than many of us.

When this kind of comparison is made obvious, people start asking questions, a process wartime conscription started and post-war National Service continued. As a result, many of us rumbled the great Eleven Plus

4    Melville, K. (1973) and Turner (1967)
5    Unverified communication of a witness

con-trick that divided the allegedly clever from the irredeemably stupid. The pressure for comprehensives, at least in part, started with National Service, just as the welfare state followed wartime conscription.

One friend, a sharp, loud Lancastrian, Peter Hindle, was like me from a family without higher education, and both of us were due to return to the Civil Service as Clerical Officers. Nodding at a member of our barrack hut who had a place at university after demob, he announced: 'If he can get to university, then I'm bloody sure I can.'

We both decided to aim for university and enrolled for A-levels at the camp's education classes. But they were hopeless – uncoordinated, inconsistent with unspecialised staff and frequent cancellations. University entrance was to prove a real challenge. In the early fifties only two percent of university entrants were from working-class backgrounds. It took Peter three years after demob, and me six, before we made it.

Bill Walsh, in civvy street a politically astute lorry driver and the hero of the 'fraygile' story, also came from a family without higher education. After demob we kept in touch. Six years later when I was at university, Bill, without even a single GCE O-level, also decided that if I could do it, then he certainly could. He enrolled at night-classes for three Ordinary levels but in error was enrolled for three Advanced's. At the same time he married and gave up driving lorries to sell insurance. Nine months later he passed all three A's and was top salesman of the year. He ended up with an MA from a prestigious university and a lecturing post in a college of further education. He then wrote during his lunch breaks, and in three years published four novels.

National Service changed many of us. Living in 'a total institution' with a cohort of our age group taught us not to blindly accept our pre-assigned stations, nor to uncritically accept constraints from our alleged superiors. It taught us the frailty of authority and that we could control our own fates. It also taught not only how this type of organisation 'worked' but how, like all organisations, it used ritual to serve its ends. Many of us learned to recognise the difference between organisational rhetoric and organisational reality and how flexible manipulation from below could 'bend' even the most apparently rigid organisation. National Service helped produce the core of a sceptically educated generation. And when later as an applied anthropologist I came to study organisations, to work in them and act as a consultant to them, I found I had a number of useful tools I could call upon.

# PART III:

# ESCAPE ATTEMPTS: AT HOME AND ABROAD

CHAPTER EIGHT

ESCAPE ATTEMPTS

## Being 'Proud to be British'
## in Attempting to Serve Kenya

After the RAF it was back to the Civil Service in London, to a clerical job on the sixth floor of a faceless ministry office block, St George's Court in New Oxford Street. Following the flexibility and friendships of the RAF, I hated being tied to a Civil Service desk – it wasn't too satisfactory for the service either. Any job, anywhere I thought, must be better than 'working under well-defined instructions' – as the demeaning job description for Clerical Officers then put it. So, desperate for travel and adventure, and buoyed by youthful immortality, I planned my escape: I would search for a job abroad and defer my RAF dreams of university to later.

Previous attempts to see the world had been notably unsuccessful. The RAF had even turned down my crazy request to serve in Korea. On the all-purpose form: 'Application for a Medical Examination', my cynical, world-weary Flight Sergeant had written under 'Symptoms' the all-too-rational 'Volunteer for Overseas Service'. Later I accepted an internal ministry job in Cairo and was set to go when it was cancelled. Being a Jew and with the Arab/Israeli conflict at one of its peaks, they belatedly thought to save themselves a possible 'remains returned home' incident.

And then a job turned up – in Kenya – with prospects of adventure, life in the sun and a chance to experience expatriate life – all on full pay. This was the fifties, and Kenya was in the news. Mau Mau terrorists, as we called them, or 'freedom fighters' as they did, were running a bloody campaign to rid themselves of the British – as bloody as the British were waging to rid themselves of the Mau Mau. But the advertisement for 'Administrative Assistants' made no mention of the troubles. They were trawling for 'clericals'. The pay was lavish, everything was 'found' – and all you needed was a School Certificate (the equivalent of six GCE O-levels), be over 21 and fit. Here was I, well qualified on all counts, except possibly the fit bit. Two of us applied from the same South Kensington hostel. My co-applicant, at six foot three, a sports-loving

blond giant, was also twenty-one. Though not the most reflective of men
he was an excellent rugby player. And like me, was youthfully eager to
experience the world while it was still there. He was an obvious
embryonic colonist. Was I?

Mr Breeze, my section's Higher Executive Officer, called me in. Five
feet four with a white toothbrush moustache, he was a peppery but well
intentioned paternalist. 'I hear you've applied for a post in Kenya? Then
let me give you a piece of advice. Before you go into that interview,
you're to repeat to yourself twelve times: "I'm proud to be British. I'm
proud to be British. I'm proud to be British." Got that?' 'Yes, Sir'. 'Good.
And good luck.' End of interview.

Armed with this tip from the top, I determined to make this application
succeed. To be sure, they would want awareness of the troubles and for me
to offer the appropriate 1950s imperialist mantra. I could easily do that.
'Native peoples throughout the empire are increasingly aiming for
independence. It should be given them – but only when they prove capable
of taking on its responsibilities.' With the 'Be proud to be British' jingle,
that meant two conventional verities. I could just about live with two.

The morning of the interview was wet and dismal, The Kenyan
Protectorate's offices were also dismal, its walls dominated by dark
panelling embellished with darker oil paintings of solemn Victorian
empire-builders. The decor to me emanated established surety with a
musty whiff of 'white man's burden'. I was ushered to an anteroom but
then immediately called to interview. There was no time to rehearse the
mantra.

Facing me was a panel of four 'burden-bearers', lean, interrogative,
middle-aged men with mahogany faces. 'Mr Mars, do sit down.' I sat.
Straight in, first question: 'Tell us, Mars, what do you know of the present
position in Kennyah?' The tone was superior, interrogatory, crystal. And
utterly confident. My prepared specialism! There is, however, a law about
interviews that needs wider exposure: 'You can swan through most
interviews with a degree of truth. But outright lies *must* be thoroughly
rehearsed.'

With measured deliberation, seemingly thinking it out as I went, I
confidently moved in: 'Native peoples throughout the empire are aiming
for self-government...' Pause for careful thought (good so far: now a
longer more reflective pause). 'I think it should be given them...' (a very
long pause here, before the *fait accompli* about independence and
responsibility) – 'but only when...'

This last pause however, was just a little too long. One of the panel
took it for a full stop. He could not be restrained. 'Are you really

saying...? You can't mean... You surely don't mean...' His colleagues on
the board waded in and brayed their support. 'You can't possibly...' Their
few remaining questions were more pointed, and my answers not as
carefully restrained – though the panel did not appear interested in
answers. Luckily the process did not, as interviews go, last for long.

My co-applicant was successful. He wrote me a letter that took some
time to arrive. The boat trip to Mombasa had been fabulous, straight out of
Somerset Maugham. Adventure had followed adventure. The morning
after arrival he had reported to his briefing address and was immediately
taught how to fire a Smith & Wesson. Then a crash course in how to drive
a Land Rover. After lunch it was map-reading and another crash course, in
law. Finally, the following morning, he had to drive to 'his territory' some
two hundred miles away. Here he would be the only white man. Before he
left he was sworn in as a magistrate and warned he had sentencing powers
of up to twelve years – but could only recommend, not order, the death
penalty. He was settling in well. He liked the responsibility: not many jobs
gave such opportunities to a twenty-one-year-old with just a School
Certificate. But after some weeks he found he was 'drinking a bit – a
bottle of whisky a day'. And, he wrote, he was 'shooting at shadows'.

So this wasn't a clerical post in the sun after all, more an inglorious
pointer to the painful demise of colonialism and the supremely misplaced
confidence of the colonialists. [1]And like the RAF Entry Unit at Padgate, it
was yet another case of 'calculated organisational deceit' – (CODS).

These attempts to escape from my constrained position in the Civil
Service were all attempts to escape the restrictions of strong classification
which have always intrigued me.

## Mixing with Police

After the Kenyan experience, it seemed I might be destined never to unroll
much of life's rich tapestry. With each week the work in my section
became more mind-crunching. A rule-based constancy overlay each long
day. Rules prescribed all possible actions: even exceptions to normal rules
were prescribed by conventions. One insisted that males wear a suit, collar
and tie to the office – but on Saturday mornings we were 'allowed' to wear
sports jackets – and custom prescribed it. Rules and conventions together
looked set to enmesh me for the next forty years. True, there were
intriguing interludes – like the unscheduled visits of a half mad fifty-odd

---

1    See Thiong'O (2011) for an account of the demise of colonialism from the
     Kenyan standpoint.

year old Senior Executive Officer. She would occasionally stride into the office, fling open the windows, shout, 'This room stinks of men,' – then exit. But though her visits were relished, they weren't enough.

The agony of routine was made tolerable by an increasing involvement with the Civil Service trade union (I was chairman of the building committee), and by attendance at WEA night classes. And then a different vision offered itself: the police.

'The Metropolitan Police Needs You,' shouted the poster in Kitchener mode. Amazingly close to my grey concrete workplace, around the corner in Gray's Inn Road, was a different world – varied, dynamic, with badges, ranks, uniforms and boundaries that separated the virtuous 'us' from the sinful 'them'. And of course: excitement. Part-time mixing with police as a 'Special' might offer new insights on the world. I joined the Specials and have been academically interested in police and policing ever since.

Our training at Holborn Police Station was run by a tubby inspector known, but not to his face, as 'Podge'. Coasting his way comfortably to retirement, he took us for classes two nights a week for a month. 'If during the course of these classes you 'ear bumps and bangs from the next room, don't worry. Heh heh! It's just the CID – taking a voluntary statement. Ho ho!' Disappointingly, we never did hear any bumps or bangs. Still, our training did promise excitement.

'If in the course of your beat duty you are called into an underground railway station because some unfortunate 'as flung themselves under a train, what do you do? It is your duty, as a police officer, to request a sack from the station officer in charge. And you then will place the pieces therein. 'Ave you got that?' Thankfully, this eventuality never happened either. Nor did the apparently frequent likelihood of 'being involved in a domestic' – which meant *not* being involved in a domestic dispute. 'The Golden Rule' insisted Podge, 'is you always stay out of it. Never get involved in it. Believe me, as like as not they'll both have a go at you. And the women are always the worst.' The contrast of Podge's mid-1950s approach with that of the twenty-first century's official attitude to domestic violence is startling and the police have to a degree, had to adapt.

If being a Special Constable gave no exciting contact with criminals, suicides or 'domestics', at least there was the *possibility* of variety and adventure. There was none at all in the ministry's Contract Sales Department (4B).

After a month's classroom training we were let out on four-hour patrols, each with a regular PC. Mine was Edgar, a tall, broad, country-complexioned, 'boy-policeman'. Edgar was solemn, uncommunicative and relatively new to the police He had been to a very minor public school. I hadn't met many of these.

Why had he chosen the police? What was it like? What did he hope to achieve? How did he see his world? But Edgar did not have much to say. Nor was he easily amused. There did not seem much to learn from him except that his school 'had concentrated on forming character rather than book learning'. He 'didn't believe in politics'. he hadn't read anything, been anywhere or done much – except work in the police – and nothing much had happened there. His school hadn't encouraged debate or conversation, or curiosity or enthusiasm – though he did like rugger.

Edgar's world, it emerged, was simple and predictable. Criminals came in three types: 'mad', 'bad' and 'greedy', while respectable folk like us, were 'sane', 'good' and 'reasonable'. This gave him an enviable confidence: he always knew how to judge situations, assess people and how to act. But his dependence on rules, rank and classification and his strong respect for authority seemed to preclude all spontaneity, levity or verve. He was dull. Then, by chance I hit on his experience of National Service. And he shone!

'I suppose you were an officer, then?'

'Oh no! But I was the next best.'

'The next best?' What on earth could this be? Surely – not a National Service Warrant Officer? 'What did you do, then?'

'I was a batman.'

'Hmm. Why was this next best to being an officer?'

'Oh – as a batman you do wonderful things. I did things as a batman I never could have done in civvy street'. He savoured the memory. 'Never!'

'Really? Tell me, what kind of things?'

'Well,' he replied, 'Do you know, I was as close as I am to you now – to – the – Duke of Edinburgh. Twice.' And at the memory, he smiled.

His was a world derived from total experience in hierarchic organisations – public school, the Army, and now, the police – all with strong boundaries and finite classifications. He fitted in well.

Hierarchic worlds may dress you in their uniforms but still exclude you. I learned that I could only peer into this one through a very dark glass indeed. Years later, I peered into it again when supervising the academic work of Ralph, a part-time post-grad. A bright police inspector of thirty plus, he was destined for quick promotion. More ebullient and intelligent than Edgar, he wanted to make things happen rather than just respond to events. But he too was a great respecter of classification. At that time he had few doubts about right and wrong actions – and right and wrong people.

One day there was an evening lecture on his thesis topic at the London School of Economics. I suggested we both go. He came in civvies and afterwards we went to a nearby pub. The Old White Horse was crowded with staff and students, and picking his way towards us came an obvious 'do-gooding' student. Pale, earnest and shaking a charity box for a worthy cause, he arrived at our table and it was then, that sitting on my shoulder, I heard this fatuously pompous, and embarrassing Hampstead intellectual, drivel away about his 'not being against charitable giving as such, being personally inclined, indeed, being as much in favour of this specific charity as he was. Yes indeed. But objecting rather, to the nature of a spontaneous call for emotional giving, if he may say so, in a milieu such as this.' I congratulated myself on the firmness of my stand. 'I hoped he took my point?' 'Oh yes. Most certainly. He had himself to admit...'

After about a minute and a half of this, my student, a policeman and action-man to the core, could bear this over-polite logjam of inaction not a second more. Groping in his pocket he whipped out his warrant card and waved it. 'Police! Now fuck off – or you're nicked!' Our earnest do-gooding collector scuttled off – as if Lucifer himself had waved his warrant card.

Sometime later, my wife Valerie, working with me on a study of household cultures, interviewed an extremely hierarchical couple, the Stanwicks. The husband was a long-retired policeman whose father had in his turn, also been a policeman. As with hierarchs generally, they have a tendency to regard the past as having been a better place than the present. There people were seen as committed respecters of rules and classifications that were unambiguous. In discussing the nature of policing, he commented: 'Look at the police nowadays, they've got hair on their collars, they wear glasses, they get off the pavement to let people pass – that's not policing.' His views on criminals echoed Edgar's and were similarly unambiguous: 'Police-work deals with people who have overwhelming urges. Sex and greed, that's what police work is about – except for the mad murderers. And it's hands on collars that counts. You don't bother about what the magistracy does.'

People like Mr Stanwick, Edgar and Ralph greatly respect fixed categories and are at home in bureaucracies, though Ralph proved the condition is not fixed, that if intelligent and flexible – and if the condition is caught early enough – then they may still be saved, as indeed he was.

# The Setting of Targets

Respect for fixed categories goes with the over-valuation of measurement that is inherent to many hierarchic organisations and that lie behind pressures to set targets. When later I worked with a very senior, retired policeman, I found him adamant: 'If you can't measure it, it doesn't exist.' In vain I pointed out that emotions, satisfactions or zeal, for instance, cannot be measured – and that if you try, you would be likely to be measuring something very different, And further, you would be likely to damage the morale of any workforce and seriously reduce an organisation's effectiveness – and what you try to measure would still escape you. He wasn't convinced.

I became sharply aware of the distortions that accrue from target-setting when I lectured at Bramshill, the senior police college. My audience were deputy chief constables in line for promotion to chief constable with a scattering of equivalent ranks from around the world. After the lecture we adjourned for dinner, and the conversation mellowed and relaxed. Discussion ranged widely then focused on different rates of clear-up. Someone asked an Indian policeman what the clear-up rate for murder was in his city? Without hesitation he replied: 'It's one hundred percent'. 'Aw, come on – no-one has a hundred percent clear-up. Even the Mounties – who claim to "always get their man" – even they never claim a hundred per cent.' 'Oh, yes,' came the quick response, 'I didn't say we get *the* man – but we always get *a* man!' Laughter exploded. Everyone knew about pressures to maintain targets and the creativity that bypasses them.

The lure of measurement has to do with power and target-setting – with making subordinates conform to top-down directives. It emphasises the gulf between controllers and controlled – the one often concerned with quantitative, the other more often with qualitative values. This gulf widens when the controlled are professionals who emphasise quality provision over the longer term, so often difficult to measure against short-term *ad hoc* targeting that can lead to pushing targets at all costs – particularly if an organisation is liable to ill-informed pressure from distant political controllers. This inevitably then leads to falsifying target levels and a distortion of the organisation's real aims. In the UK it is repetitively revealed in the police, schools, universities, and the NHS – all victims of political drives for top-down control and managerial acquiescence to target-setting – and the short-termism and negation of professional standards that goes with it.

The police and their political controllers offer classic examples. They publicly laud the role of Community Liaison Officers in preventing crime – but keep their status in the force relatively low. They have limited resources, few senior ranks, and often are not regarded as 'real police' – being dismissed as 'more like bloody social workers'. Detectives on the other hand have the highest prestige and score on all the criteria that CLO's lack: in solving crimes their clear-up rates can readily be measured (as in the Indian's example). It is not as easy to measure crimes that have been prevented.

## Breaching Official Secrets: 'You don't need to know that'

> Where did these secret envelopes come from?
> Where were the coded addresses they went to?
> And most of all – what did they have in them?

Reluctantly, in 1956 I had to leave London, my growing involvement with the Civil Service trade union, the friends I had made, the Specials, a WEA class and a promising liaison with a bright, pretty and amusing lab technician, Betty. But at home money was desperately tight. Dad was earning less than ever and three younger brothers, now all at grammar school, were proving expensive to keep. Mam could not work. Once again my wages were needed at home. I persuaded the Civil Service to transfer me north to any job in travelling reach of Blackpool. A bonus was that any job anywhere would likely be better than work in C Sales (4B). I was lucky to get a transfer to a Royal Ordnance Factory not too far from Blackpool.

Arriving at Preston station to change trains for Blackpool, I was surprised to see Peter Hindle, my old hut-mate from the RAF with whom I had attended the RAF's abortive A-level classes. Had he given up his clerical job to be a railway porter? 'No,' he told me, he was filling in time until the following October when he would take up his place at Manchester University. While I had been doing all sorts of odd things in London he had been steadily studying at night-classes for his A-levels. I enrolled that same evening at St Anne's College of Further Education for A-level English Literature, a one-year night class.[2]

From my first day, the new job promised excitement. Guarded by its own corps of armed police, it had its own closed railway station – and secret passes to get in and out. The ROF was, I surmised, perhaps making

---

2   I was lucky to have Roger Venables, the poet, as my teacher for A-level English, and later a brilliant teacher of economics, 'Taffy' Jones of Blackpool Grammar School who taught A-level Economics at another one year's night-class.

atomic bombs? In World War II, and for quite a while later, ROFs were identified only as being 'somewhere in England', and its workers were subject to the Official Secrets Acts. I gather I still am: the gag apparently lasts for life. All very exciting for a twenty-three-year-old in search of drama.

Nobody, of course, mentioned we might be making atomic bombs. And what we did make was never talked about and, it was intimated, our individual little parts of it must never be talked about either. Not to each other, to anyone, ever. So it has been – until now.

I was given a job as Dispatch Clerk, dealing with secret plans. Plans came in three grades: Secret, Top Secret, Most Secret, and a pile of them was delivered to my desk every morning. Each plan was securely sealed in a large brown envelope with its classification in red block letters stamped on the outside together with a mass of coded numbers and symbols. But what was inside these envelopes? What were these plans, plans of? When I thrillingly mused about this to my supervisor, Mr Needling, an ascetic bird-like, no-nonsense career clerk, I was briskly dispatched with the official 'need to know' mantra: 'You don't need to know that, Mars!' It was intoxicating though, to know that 'need to know' now applied to me: I must be really close to the core of 'state affairs'!

My job was to complete vouchers in ten copies for each plan and send them on to nine separate consignees. The original voucher, with its unopened envelope and its precious plan, were then dispatched to its secret coded destination – somewhere else in England. And even if I did not know what was in the envelopes, I could muse.

It was not an onerous job but it was getting in the way of my 'real work', swotting for my GCEs. You could swing this in the fifties when much of England was vastly over-manned – and the Civil Service more so than most. A colleague of mine worked every day for five years. pulling pints in a pub from 12 noon to 3 p.m. Another, obsessed by everything Italian, including his wife, spent most of his days translating Italian poetry or on the phone to her. A third continuously wrote very good doggerel. The waste of time, energy and talent was immense.

After some months, dispatching secret plans was becoming intrusive, especially with exams only two months off. I was falling behind in economics. There was no chance of extra help. (Mr Needling positively screeched at the suggestion.) And the 'need to know' principle was no longer satisfying as an administrative canon – it was becoming a personal obsession. Where did these secret envelopes come from? Where were the coded addresses they went to? And most of all – what did they have in them? I had my own 'need to know'.

And then one morning I noticed that one of the envelopes was partly open... its seal undone: its contents could be examined... The plan was understandable, even to a layman like me. It was etched in blue, and its title was 'Shell Filling'. It was the drawing of an extremely ordinary looking shell. The only interesting thing about it was the date: 'November 26th 1914'. Nervously, I opened a second envelope: 'Shell Filling, 26th April 1915'. Then a third. They were all the same: all Shell Fillings. The most recent, dated 1917, were over forty years old!

So I wasn't close to the core of state affairs after all – and never had been. My work was part of a meaningless charade. I never opened any more envelopes. Just sent them to their main consignees, ignored the preparation of nine copies of each and got on with the A-levels. As I suspected, there was no come-back. No outraged or worried consignees sent frantic telegrams. No armed security police burst into the office and bore me off to interrogation – or worse. Maybe there was a secret overseer? Perhaps his department knew all about my misdeeds but was too embarrassed to do anything? Or perhaps nobody knew anything because, quite simply, nobody cared – or needed to know?

With A- and O-levels safely passed, I was ready to leave the ROF for a transfer closer to home, to the final onslaught on the last hurdle, persuading a university to take me. Then I could take my official secret with me. So I did. It has stayed safe and secure – until now. Occasionally I wonder if those secret plans aren't still being dispatched with their satellite vouchers to nine other clerks in nine other ROFs, 'somewhere in England'? Does my fifth-generation replacement not have a need to know?

Bureaucracies tend to restrict information, a process operating to differing degrees in nearly all of them. In part this supports the authority of different levels. But it reaches its peak in government departments involved with national security where they strictly formalise the 'need to know' principle: 'If you don't need to know you don't need to be told.' But of course 'need to know', if carried to excess is liable to prevent the scrutiny of *anything* – with resultant in-built rigidities and waste. Where 'need to know' operates, few people get to see any administrative process as a whole – they only know about their own mini piece of it. And without sequential scrutiny, all sorts of idiocies can prevail. This is the lesson I learned from a surreal involvement with secret plans.

# Rites of Passage: Two Interviews

## The State Scholarship Board

Interviews have an unappreciated but central role in our culture. They are 'rites of passage', the most common filters that pass us from one status to another – or not. And the more important they are, the more stressful. Interviews are often not impartial to the interviewed. Interviewees are alone, whilst interviewers are likely to work in series, and by knowing the process are invariably more experienced and secure than interviewees. It is not easy to disconcert them. Not easy – but not impossible. I learned this at my interview for a Mature Student's State Scholarship.

For two years Mrs Hall, who lived on the corner of our avenue, knew I had been studying at night-school for A-levels with the aim of entering university, and she had mentioned this to her son Peter, then a lecturer in London. Peter suggested I apply for a Mature Student's State Scholarship. I'd never heard of them. But up to thirty, though usually fewer, were awarded annually to people who had been 'deprived of a formal education'. You had to get references, and those who made it to a shortlist were then asked to submit a 5,000-word dissertation. Over three hundred applied annually, about a third were interviewed, and of the successful twenty to thirty most went to Oxford, Cambridge and London universities. Many later did research and became academics.

By this time I had read some sociology, anthropology and economics and knew these branches of the social sciences could offer what I needed to help explain questions about society that puzzled me. For my dissertation I wrote a study of Blackpool's Golden Mile where I had worked as a spieler (barker). By the time I had finished it I knew this kind of research was the work I wanted in life. It was typed by a kind lady across the road and sent off to London – to its fate and mine. The fates were kind and I was summoned to interview.

Then panic! What to expect? What kind of an interview would this be? I had no experience at all of academic interviews. My record with job interviews had been unprepossessing at best. Some, like the Kenya interview, verged on the bizarre; others, like my RAF commissioning interview, had been absurd. The RAF has a series of graded interviews to select officers – with the first to ensure merely that your knuckles didn't scrape the ground. But my first interview was also my last. It was taken by an overweight, choleric squadron leader.

'Tell me, Mars, were you a membah of any clubs or societies in civilian life?' 'Oh yes, Sir,' I replied, stupidly naïve and keen to demonstrate an active public awareness, 'Clapham Labour Party, League of Youth.' His response was Batemanesque.[3] He seemed about to burst. A few more gabbled questions for the form of it – and that was the end of my prospects of a commission.

I now had to find out about this Ministry of Education interview. Mrs Hall again came to the rescue. She had asked Peter about it. 'He'll know.' But helpful as he was, he did not know. He had no idea and hadn't been able to find out. But he thought, 'It will probably be a board of three –two university lecturers and a chairman. The chairman would most likely be a medium level civil servant, probably a principal.' To be forewarned was to be foredoomed.

On the train down I rehearsed every possible question they could ask and assessed numerous varieties of answer. I was feeling apprehensive but confident that I was on top of my subject and uniquely so. There was after all no-one who had researched the Golden Mile as I had. And it was exhilarating to be back in London again and alight at Euston station with its massively familiar and welcoming Doric Arch.[4]

London was bright and sunny. I easily found the Ministry of Education building, spoke to a remote receptionist and was sent to another on the fourth floor. She directed me to an anteroom. I was quickly called to interview.

Years later the shock is still palpable. I had expected a board of three. But on one side of a long green baize-covered table sat a board of ten – all male, all austere, none seemingly under fifty. At the centre, opposite the chairman was a single vacant chair. I was directed to it. The chairman then read all the board members affiliations and titles. This reassured me not at all. Three were professors, two, senior inspectors of education. The chairman was an Assistant Secretary. My time as a Civil Service clerk told me just how high powered he and this board were. Ten sledgehammers – to crush one tiny nut!

I needed a cigarette, urgently. To my hesitant 'Do you mind if I smoke?' the response was a not quite firm negative.

---

3   H.M. Bateman (1887-1970) a satirical cartoonist, lampooned the establishment and those attempting to relate to it. Noted for his 'The Man Who…' series of cartoons, featuring comically outraged reactions to minor social gaffes, such as 'The Man Who Lit His Cigar Before the Loyal Toast' and 'The Man Who Threw a Snowball at St Moritz'.

4   Destroyed and broken up in 1961 in an act of official vandalism when Euston Station was rebuilt. Appeals were mounted to the level of Prime Minister MacMillan but he refused to intervene. Happily there is a current campaign to restore the arch which might possibly succeed.

I rolled my own at that time and had one ready. So I fished it out, lit up and inhaled. Then – unaccountably – it exploded. Flaming tobacco sprayed over the green baize, over the chairman and over two adjacent board members. They were surprisingly athletic. Leaping up, they dusted themselves down, brushed away the burning debris, and then with reduced dignity, reclaimed their seats. The interview continued – though less awesomely than it had started.

I had anticipated only some questions. There were probes to ensure I had written the dissertation. 'What difficulties did you find in carrying out the study?' This was a good chance to score since I was aware of and could argue for the advantages of participant observation. After all – I had actually worked on the Mile.

Then a grilling to explore intellectual range. 'Are there other aspects of Blackpool worth studying?' When I replied with a range of venues and was then asked how I might go about studying them, one asked: 'And what might such a collected study be called?' And he chortled as he answered himself: 'What about "In Darkest Blackpool?" Ho ho.' The board was amused. So far so good. It had gone reasonably well.

Finally they dug for intellectual depth – mostly by having me discuss the books listed in my bibliography. One of my sources was *The British Worker* by Ferdinand Zweig,[5] a Czech refugee sociologist who interviewed workers and their families in the North of England. He then wrote insightful accounts of their way of life showing how they viewed their worlds. One professor at the far end of the table, small, dark, Welsh and intense, seemed to have a fixation about Zweig.

He strained sideways to face me. Interrogatively and, rather loudly, he asked up the table. 'Could you be a Zweig?'

Not quite sure what he meant but assuming it had to do with Zweig's methods, I answered; 'Yes I think so.'

'No,' he said, even louder and with seeming irritation. 'Do you think *you* could be a Zweig?' He emphasised the 'you'.

This was beginning to sound dangerous: I called a retreat. 'I'm not quite sure I follow. But yes I think I can do that kind of work.'

This too was the wrong answer. 'No. No. No.' By now he was becoming shrill. 'Do you think *you* could be a Zweig? You, a *Zweig*?' On the emphasis '*Zweig*' it emerged gutturally as '*Zzweighggg*'.

There was nothing for it but surrender. 'I'm sorry,' I said, 'I don't know what you mean.'

---

5   Zweig (1953)

By now he was almost out of his seat. I noted, in a sideways glance, that other board members were becoming as concerned as I was. 'What I mean,' he rasped, 'is whether or not *you* could be a *Zweig*.'

A pause. I looked at him blankly. Then slowly he ground out: 'A *Zweig*! What I want to know is whether *you* could be a *Zweig* – could you, like a *Zweig*, go round pubs and clubs asking people about their sex lives?'

We were still not on the same circuit and no nearer a conclusion. Then it hit me. 'Are you saying, that, since Zweig is a foreigner, he finds it easier to get people to talk to him?'

'Yes,' he said, subsiding. Then in a masterpiece of mis-statement, 'that's exactly what I'm asking. Can *you* be a *Zweig*?'

'Well then, yes,' I said, 'Even though I'm not a foreigner. Yes, I can get people to talk to me. Yes, I can be a Zweig.'

'Good,' he replied. 'That was all I wanted to know.'

After this ordeal came a googly. One of the inspectors, who had said nothing until then, leaned forward and with a silken smile and a very elevated accent, asked. 'Tell me, did you enjoy doing this study of the Golden Mile?'

'Yes,' I said, 'yes, it was very enjoyable.'

And then, more softly, he returned. 'Good. Good. Would you say it was the most enjoyable thing you have ever done?'

Alert! RED ALERT! This was no academic question! It was a sincerity test! I did not think he really wanted a comparison of satisfactions – social research versus, say, memorable meals or erotic encounters. 'I would just say, it was very enjoyable.'

Another silken smile. 'Thank you.'

The interview had lasted nearly an hour when the chairman to my relief, said, 'That concludes the interview, Mr Mars. But let me give you some advice.'

'Yes?' I said, by this time hyper alert.

'If I were you,' and he spoke slowly, solemnly, stressing each word. 'If I were you, and if I were ever to appear before any other boards – say university boards – then I would never, ever, make that kind of request again.'

'I'm sorry?' I said, not understanding him at all. 'What request was that?'

At that point, his control went. 'That!' he snapped, stabbing furiously at some still scattered ashes of my cigarette, 'and that, and that.'

The next stage in this rite of passage was the letter telling me they had awarded me a State Scholarship.[6] Now I had to be accepted by a university.

## How Not to Manage an Oxbridge Interview

'I look forward to seeing you on Tuesday 6th June 1959 at 11:30 a.m. Please ask for me at the Porter's Lodge.' It was signed 'W. A. Camps, Tutor for Admissions', Pembroke College, Cambridge.

The porter, who could have been perfectly cast as a senior NCO,[7] called me 'Sir', directed me through the court – a series of buildings positioned around a meticulous lawn – and I felt watched me warily as I went. Pembroke College's Old Court seemed very old indeed, and it was crowded. Here and throughout the grounds, men in dinner jackets and women in ball gowns chatted in posh accents and laughed together. I had seen people wearing evening dress but only in films and newspapers. So this was how they lived then? Lolling about and dressed up in the mornings. The interview was awful.

Mr Camps' room, set in a stone-clad building, was approached through a Gothic arch. A month before, Auntie Daisy, a friend of the family, had insisted on reading my fortune in the tea-leaves. Reluctantly, I had agreed. Looking at the leaves she pronounced. 'Your life will completely change. It will all start with an interview. It will take place after you've passed through an arch. And it will lead you to having a title.'

The room beyond the arch was crammed full of sofas, books and pictures; it was comfortable, and utterly civilised. Mr Camps, late fortyish, tall, spectacled, very thin, seemed determined to put me at my ease. He stretched out a bony hand, smiled austerely, waved me to a soft sofa and asked with a slight stutter if I would care for a sherry? Nobody had done that before. Then he sat at the side of his desk and opened my file.

'Ah, so you are Gerald Mars, then?'

I admitted it.

---

6   I may be biased in believing this method of deciding university entrance has merits over the orthodox O and A - level route. It could however, run alongside the orthodox route. Similar, in fact stronger, 'empirical' considerations apply to applicants for postgraduate research which normally depend on first degree results. Where I have selected postgraduate students on other criteria but not necessarily with a first degree, they have been highly successful.

7   Which, I later found, he had been. Tom Sharpe (1974), the novelist was an alumnus of Pembroke College and his novel *Porterhouse Blue* satirises the college and particularly the head porter as its real controlling authority.

'Good, good.' Shuffle of the papers. 'And I see… ah, I see that you've come all the way from er… Blackpool, to see us?'

'Yes, I have.'

'Good, very good.' It was obvious he did not relish interviewing and had not read the file. He had, however, a prepared sequence. 'Looking at your CV, I see your A-levels… are… Oh! You have only two A-levels?'

'Yes, but I got them at night school.'

'Of course. Yes. Night school.' Back to the file. 'But according to your list here, you, er… you don't appear to have mathematics?'

'No. I didn't take it.'

'Didn't take it ?'

'No – not after the mock'.[8]

'I see. Did not take it after the mock. But you don't seem to have Latin either? Did you, er… not take Latin?'

'That's right. We didn't do Latin at my school.'

'Really! Did not do Latin at your school? But what about Greek?'

'No. We didn't do Greek.'

A pause. 'Then you have neither Latin nor Greek?'

'No.'

It was time I explained. 'You see, under the scheme I've applied for, I don't need Latin or Greek. I have a Mature Student's State Scholarship.'

Mr Camps had obviously not heard of this scheme – one for the educationally deprived – if not quite the outright illiterate and that leap-frogged normal entrance requirements. 'Ah yes. Of course. You must have some other languages though? Surely? French perhaps?'

'No'.

'I see. They didn't take French at your school?'

'Yes, they did.'

'Ah?'

'But I gave it up. In the third form.'

'Gave it up? Why did you do that?'

'I gave it up for Art.'

Mr Camps glimpsed a lifeline. 'Aha! Art. And how did you do in Art?'

'I failed Art.'

Realising this CV would be no guide in the Kingdom of the Blind, Mr Camps firmly closed the file and moved it to the far edge of his desk. He leaned back, managed a smile, and made a new start. 'Tell me, have you any outrageous opinions?' Mr Camps allowed me to tutor him on the

---

8   For anyone interested, I still remember the marks: Geometry – the best – 27%; arithmetic, the next best – 3%; Algebra – the worst, 0%. I have since managed to work out that this aggregate equals 10% overall.

essential and urgent need to close down the public schools, abolish the monarchy and redistribute wealth. Then he glanced at his watch and with evident relief sent me to see a Dr Robinson.

Dr Robinson was young, chatty and on the phone. His room was sparse and utilitarian; a room for effective working rather than cultivated living. He waved me to a seat while he talked. 'OK. Fine. Don't worry. Yes, I'm sure. Certainly. Leave it to me.' Replacing the phone, he greeted me: 'Hello. You've just seen Mr Camps? How did you get on?'

The only possible answer was the truth: 'Awful. It was a disaster.'

'Come now. It can't have been as bad as that.'

'Oh yes it can!'

Dr Robinson's session allowed a general discourse on personal experiences and the state of the world but with searching questions whenever I strayed into polemic. But there was an attempt at allowing me to pick up the pieces. And I did learn that undergraduates at Cambridge did not perpetually wander about in evening dress – except in May Week when the colleges held their annual all-night balls (which are always held in June!).

I could however, recognise a disastrous interview when I had had one. Leaving the college, I wended past the chattering socialites, determined that if I did not get a place this year, then I'd bloody well try a different college for the next.

Next morning, a letter from Mr Camps, with a cheque for five pounds. He hoped I 'would accept this contribution towards my fares'. An unheard-of indulgence. And he thanked me for coming to see them! And then, amazingly.... 'We'll be very pleased to see you at the beginning of the Michaelmas term.'

William 'Tony' Camps was a classicist whose shrewdness and humanity, despite his shyness, was evident in his later occupancy of the mastership of Pembroke College. When I came to know him better I found him one of the most humane, and – though he hated interviews and wasn't good at them – one of the kindest of men. The title never materialised – unless you count academic titles.

# PART IV:

# CAMBRIDGE

CHAPTER NINE

# A STRANGE LAND WITH STRANGE RITUALS

Adapting to Cambridge and its inhabitants meant learning to navigate in a new and strange land. I had never known people like them; they had rarely met anyone like me. I soon understood that my previous experiences had been relatively narrow and unbalanced – and then, later, that so was everyone else's.

There was a lot to learn. The university abounded with rituals that most people seemed to understand and appreciate but that to me seemed incomprehensible. This was especially clear in rituals to do with food and food-taking – universal keys to understanding social organisation. In some Cambridge colleges the dons literally dined at a higher level than the undergraduates: they ate on a raised dais – sometimes only a few inches higher than the basic floor level – but higher nonetheless. And at dinner everyone had to wear an appropriate academic gown. The dons' 'top table' was sited at the end of the dining hall nearest the college chapel ('nearer to my God than thee'). Another ritual permitted only dons to walk on the lawns in college courts (called quads at Oxford and by outsiders), while the wearing of uniforms – different kinds of academic gown – marked out different ranks as clearly as in any military unit, with sanctions for non-observance. These peculiar practices were understandable only when one learned how the overall system worked.[1]

The town's respect granted to students amazed me. On Bonfire Night in my first term I was in the Market Square, dressed, as the rules then required, in my newly acquired undergraduate gown. It seemed all hell was breaking loose as fireworks were thrown, and drunken undergraduates rocked a series of lampposts back and forth, leaving them drooping at an angle of some forty-five degrees. I watched at some distance from this

---

1   Anthropologists distinguish two functions of rituals – manifest and latent. For example, the manifest function of the ban forbidding undergraduates from walking on the lawns, and the one given to enquirers, is that it is necessary to maintain the lawns. The latent function has more to with the maintenance of social differences.

mayhem. Nearby two policemen, an inspector and a sergeant also watched.

Something was odd here. Why were these policemen so passive? Police had never been so inactive in my experience. Why weren't they rushing in and making arrests? 'Aren't you going to stop them?' I asked. 'Stop them, Sir?' asked the inspector. It took me a moment to realise that in 1959 Cambridge, being a 'Sir' extended beyond the insulated world of the college and its servants. 'Oh no, Sir. It's not as if they're hooligans from the town. Those, Sir, are gentlemen. They're the future leaders of the country.' I could detect no irony.

This attitude, quite untenable nowadays, emphasised how authority, hierarchy and classification were inherent to the culture of those who used the 'Sir' tag – and believed in it.

## On Naïveté – Mine and Others'

'Can you tell me, Gerald – is it true that you Jews don't celebrate Easter?' When first I arrived in Cambridge I was sensitive about my lack of polish and ignorance of 'culture'. I had read a certain amount but not conversed, and so mispronounced words in educated use. One friend from those days still ribs me for pronouncing 'naïveté' as 'nay-vette'. But in compensation I found my fellow students showed a startling ignorance of my world; there was a lack of 'street wisdom'. They too in their way, were as naïve as I was. Most of my peers were kinder to me for my ignorance than I was to some of them for theirs.

One resident on my staircase, Michael, an earnest, upper-class Christian Scientist, continually astonished me. A serious, enquiring soul he had the mien of a perpetually puzzled middle-aged clergyman. Michael would constantly quiz me, not only because, it appeared, he had never before met anyone who wasn't from Social Class I – except possibly servants – but also because I was the first Jew he had ever met. He genuinely wanted to learn, and continually raised questions.

One day Michael came to my room, his brow creased with yet a new query. 'Gerald,' he began, 'I wonder if you can help me with a question that's been bothering me?'

'Certainly, I can try,' I said, putting aside the spanner I was using to tune up a bicycle. I was buying, repairing and selling second-hand bicycles at that time. 'Now, what's the problem?'

'Well, Gerald…' he paused, as if to pronounce a profound conundrum.

'Yes?'

'Well. Can you tell me, Gerald, is it true that you Jews don't celebrate Easter?'

I could not resist. 'No,' I said with certainty. 'It's not true.'

For some reason this left him immensely relieved. He smiled. 'Oh, I'm so glad, so glad. Thank you.' He headed for the door.

'Wait.'

He paused. 'Yes?'

'But only the Friday.'

Michael's lack of experience hadn't been helped by his missing out on National Service. But though it is said to have benefitted nearly everyone who did it, it appeared to have less impact on those who became officers.[2] In my first year of anthropology I was asked to give a seminar paper on the organisation of the Golden Mile, the fairground on which I had based my scholarship dissertation.

We had been studying the Nuer of East Africa, an egalitarian tribe noted in anthropology because they have no leaders nor formal political structures.[3] Lacking more usual ways of arbitrating disputes – and being wary of the schisms that could follow if they tried [4] – they accumulated their grievances until a stranger passed through their land. Then they would corral him as an independent outsider, shroud him in a leopard skin as a badge of office and make him act as an arbitrator. I had given my paper and explained how the Mile 'worked' when an upper-class undergraduate, recently demobbed from a smart regiment, drawled: 'Tell me, when you worked on the Golden Mile, did you find they used you to arbitrate their disputes?' He was serious.

Nearer home, egalitarian groups, characteristically reluctant to allocate authority to arbitrators (or to anyone else) find themselves particularly prone to schism. This is often the case with communes, co-operatives and radical reformist groups[5] where dissidents typically form break-away groupings.

---

2    Also recounted by Shindler (2012)

3    Evans-Pritchard (1940)

4    The inability of egalitarian groups to legitimise arbitrators is a cause of ongoing instability in these groupings which make them prone to repetitive schism.

5    A variety of examples is to be found in Flanagan & Rayner (1988). See also Chapter 21 (where egalitarian groups are referred to as 'Enclaves', p.206).

# Cambridge Women

Some culture clashes were not easily bridged and could be troublesome – but others were fun. Women undergraduates were a revelation. Sexually, they were more liberated than women I had known in the North. I could relate to them. They would share, discuss and argue: real friendships were possible. They were less single-minded in pursuit and in being pursued, and less calculating than women I had known. In the North, for the most part the sex war was explicit and make-up was commonly referred to as 'war paint'. In Cambridge the sex war was more akin to negotiated co-operation. There was no question of 'not until we're engaged'.

Though mostly virgins and naïve on arrival, Cambridge women were unlikely to be either on graduation. These after all were women who had often sacrificed their pre-university social lives to ensure their places at Cambridge. Many had attended girls-only schools and were keen to catch up. There was little promiscuity – they tended to search out a man and then stick with him. At Cambridge in the early sixties, with one woman to ten men, they had a wide choice.

Instead of regarding me as a rough Philistine, many women wanted to know more of this odd creature from a strange land who had won a scholarship, apparently for spieling on a fairground. But this background offered valuable social capital. Even my skill as an ex-weight guesser was in demand. At tea-parties I was required to talk about a life that was different and – as a party trick – to guess people's weights. A license to ostentatiously size up girls' figures, ponder their measurements and feel their arm and leg muscles, proved the perfect ice-breaker.

By the early sixties the colleges were hesitantly beginning to acknowledge an encircling sexual revolution. But they still acted *in loco parentis* and it took some time before liberal policies took hold. It wasn't long since women undergraduates could only entertain men in their rooms if the door was wedged open. Men still had to have their girlfriends out of college by 10 p.m. There had been recent cases of undergraduates sent down for breaking these rules. Pembroke however, was relatively liberal. In conversation with one don, I asked what it was that could be done before ten o'clock that couldn't be done afterwards? 'It's not a question of what can be done before or after. It's to stop you doing it again.'

Because of the imbalance in numbers, many undergraduates imported girlfriends from outside the university. Cambridge women acted as the core of networks to introduce their out-of-town friends to university men they didn't want for themselves. This was how I met Marian, the friend of an unresponsive (at least to me) but helpful Newnhamite. 'No, I'm fully booked, Gerry,' she insisted firmly, as she again repulsed my attempts to know her better. 'But my friend Marian is between boyfriends. She's coming up next weekend. You'll like her.' She came up. We took to each other immediately; to me she epitomised this new world of clever, educated women.

Marian was twenty-one, dark-haired and tall. Her hair in fashionable beehive style raised her height close to a statuesque six feet. Able to complete the *Times* crossword, usually in five minutes, she could also speed-read – in both Latin and Greek. When she took the tough written Civil Service executive examination, she topped the country. After an oral interview when both marks were consolidated, she was still top. But she wore her brilliance lightly, was dismissive about her talents and insisted: 'it's all technique'. Of a national radio quiz when she knew most of the answers, she remarked in exasperation, 'Oh – it's not do you know – it's do you care!' She later came out to Newfoundland when I was doing fieldwork – though this was a relationship destined not to last.

Cambridge offered the chance to observe life as an experiment. There was a tolerance of behaviours that to me verged on the certifiable. Among the women, eccentricity was sometimes pronounced. One outstandingly clever Newnham undergraduate painstakingly fed the mice in her digs, morning and evening, until her landlady finally located the source of the plague that engulfed the whole building and evicted her without notice. I had never met anyone quite like another Newnham woman who has since achieved fame as an actor. She was – and still is – an ostentatious breaker of taboos. 'I won't ask you in, Gerry. There are used sanitary towels all about the place – it's not a pretty sight!'

My State Scholarship was extremely generous and paid more than my salary had been, but even with vacation earnings, money was still needed at home. Since I had always made extra from part-time earnings, I exploited a gap in the market for bikes – since everyone in Cambridge needed one. The nearby market town, Cherry Hinton, was a good place to buy second-hand bikes, and each week I would cycle there, buy one and ride the two bikes back. Many, I suspected later, had probably been stolen earlier in the week. Being reasonably adept mechanically, I cleaned, oiled and repaired them as necessary.

My room sometimes looked more like a workshop than a study. Inner-tubes hung from the mantelpiece; in one corner cycle-chains were soaking in pans of paraffin; another had warped wheels waiting to be trued. This activity might have stopped if the college had discovered it. The college servant who cleaned my room and made my bed each morning (called a 'bedder') was the fat and jolly Mrs Kitson. Her secondary job, so we believed, was that like all bedders she acted for the college to report untoward behaviours – like bike repairing and women staying overnight. But she was generally tolerant towards 'her gentlemen', and this was ensured with a liberal tip at each term's end.

Buying and selling bikes led to another surprise. Though Cambridge men were often unworldly, the commercial sense of many Cambridge women, admittedly to generalise, seemed quite defective. I usually put up two postcards – side by side – on various college notice-boards. Written in different handwriting one would say:

For Sale – Bike
In perfect order
Guaranteed for a year
£5
Mars, Q6, Pembroke College

The adjacent card would read:

Bicycle for Sale
Fair runner but needs some attention
£6
M. Johnson, Trinity College

Trinity was by far the biggest Cambridge college, and the absence of a room number, I hoped, would make it difficult to chase up the imaginary Johnson. The number of women (but never men) who said they had spent time searching for Johnson as their first call, amazes me still. And they had no idea of haggling.

## Living with 'Lord Leigh'

After two years' living in college, Pembroke undergraduates were cast out to find digs in the town. Town rooms were scarce and dear. They also tended to be squalid and hedged with restrictions particularly limiting visits by women. One friend, innocently giving tea to his girlfriend, had his door opened by his landlady. Reeling in disbelief at sight of this pair of tea-drinking devils, she shrieked at her husband. 'He's only got a young woman in there with him!' Her 'heavy' lumbered up and loyally threatened that if he dared do that again, he would 'be out'. With this and similar accounts in mind I was apprehensive about the lodgings market.

Together with Geoffrey Leigh, an earnest final-year economist, I started our search for digs. Geoffrey, whose father worked the markets of poor Lancashire towns, was a clever, militant Marxist, sent to Earth to bring about a workers' paradise. But despite his economics – or because of it – he was unrealistic about rents. After he had vetoed a number of prospective flats, we were still without accommodation when term began. Then, reduced to scouring shop ads, a scruffy notice in a tobacconist's led us to Mrs Paderewski: 'Rooms to let, suit students,' it read. 'Suit students' was ominous and should have sounded a warning. We went to see Mrs Paderewski in her small house in Tenison Road.

A stooped, bony woman of about fifty opened a shabby front door to release a stale smell of dust and cabbage. She looked us over and obviously did not like what she saw. She did though offer us two small bedrooms with two tiny desks and a minute and musty sitting-room facing an enclosed yard, just visible through a small dirty window. The room had a strip of grimy carpet, a worn, greasy armchair, and little else. Mrs Paderewski's *pièce de résistance* however, was the shared bathroom/lavatory/kitchen/dining room. It combined its functions through a single washbasin/sink and had a chipped bath that, when covered by a board, doubled as a dining-table. A scruffy lavatory nestled in one corner – next to a grease-encrusted stove.

We had no alternative. Geoffrey haggled hard, buoyed by all the injustices endured by all the working peoples of the world. Mrs Paderewski however, would not be moved. But at least her rooms were cheap – and she hadn't mentioned women. Eventually, after mammoth haggling, she agreed, grudgingly, to replace the filthy armchair and get us a new strip of carpet. We moved in – me with my cycle parts and Geoffrey with his twenty or so pairs of shoes – he seemed never to have thrown any out since pre-adolescence.

Paderewski himself made few appearances. A tall ultra-thin, gloomy Pole with little English, he kept odd hours and led an erratic working life – possibly, we conjectured, as a cat-burglar. Unlike his wife, he never bothered us. Mrs Paderewski however, was totally occupied in silently noting our entrances and exits, our guests and our callers. Tight-lipped, uncommunicative, she hardly spoke. On the very odd occasion she did, it was to boast about the more illustrious tenants she had had in the past. We were obviously a come-down: 'her previous gentlemen' had included a baronet's brother, a lord and a hon. They must have been dreadfully down on their luck.

Each morning when the post arrived, Mrs Paderewski became enervated. At first rattle of the letterbox she would leap to the front door to intercept the mail. Scooping it up, she examined each letter in turn before unwillingly surrendering any that were ours.

We had to bear with Mrs Paderewski and her awful rooms. As the weeks passed it became more depressing to spend time in such a dismal place. And after a month there was still no appearance of the replacement chair or the new piece of carpet – despite Geoffrey becoming more assertive by the day.

For Geoffrey, our squalor became a cause, a spearhead battle in his war against landlords and world capitalism. He was starting to lecture anyone who would listen on the theory of rent and the need to overthrow the parasitic rentier class of which he now had direct experience. After yet a further onslaught against the unresponsive Mrs Paderewski who had failed to supply the items she had promised, I realised something should be done. Then I had a brainwave.

I bought a large impressive envelope, scrounged use of a college typewriter and addressed it to 'Viscount, The Lord Leigh of Layton, 28 Tenison Road, Cambridge'. Sealed with purple sealing wax and stamped with an imposing seal borrowed from a tolerant antique dealer, I posted it – and waited.

Next morning Mrs Paderewski, as always, beat me to the post. She swept up the mail – then stiffened as she stared at the envelope with its impressive purple seal. Turning it one way, then the other, she actually stroked the wax. Speech seemed beyond her.

'Any mail for us?' I asked.

She turned slowly, then reading from the envelope, croaked: 'Visscunt. The Lord Leigh [pause] of Layton. Him a Visscunt – is he?'

'Yes,' I said 'Yes, that's Geoffrey.'

'Ahah! – Yes. I always knew he was something special. I said it – I did. A Visscunt eh? Yes. I knew. All them shoes.' And with that she reluctantly surrendered the envelope.

When we returned that afternoon, we found a new and bigger strip of carpet and the worn, greasy easy chair replaced by a moderately acceptable second-hand one.

## The Cambridge University Expedition to Ceylon[6]

Until the early sixties, students in general, but Oxbridge students in particular, were considered a rarefied elite. This was naturally exploited. Students planning an adventurous summer would have notepaper printed with the heading 'The Cambridge University Expedition to… Wherever'. They would then shamelessly petition generous, perhaps gullible, commercial firms for support. To my amazement many firms responded: they would be offered everything from vehicles to toilet rolls. It was too good a bandwagon to miss. I decided to organise an expedition. With two

---

6   Ceylon changed its name to Sri Lanka when it became a republic in 1972.

other first-year 'anthropologists' we very loosely 'planned' an expedition to Ceylon. We would study 'some tribes.'

That year however, the university felt it needed to limit such blatant scrounging. It instituted a vetting system: to claim the title 'Cambridge University Expedition to...', applications had to be assessed by a specialist don. Our application was allocated to Edmund Leach, apparently an expert on Ceylon. We had hardly heard of him when we assembled at his rooms in King's College.

Leach, a tall, gangling man in his early fifties, ushered the three of us into his untidy, dusty room packed full of pictures, anthropological artefacts and tottering piles of books. He sat us down, crossed and uncrossed his legs, and in a slow drawl asked us a few straightforward questions. As the instigator of the proposal and the oldest, the talking was left to me. Leach seemed genuinely interested in our plan. Responding to the points I made, he was unthreatening and appeared not too alert. This was fine by us – we had expected vague, general, waffley questions about our expedition. In explaining our intentions, I offered him some first-year anthropology and this too he took in his stride and nodded encouragingly.

We were doing rather well, I thought. Then...

'Tell me,' he asked conversationally, 'how do you plan to get from the mainland [of India] to Ceylon?'

I was prepared for this. 'By the bridge,' I answered, being almost tempted to add 'of course!'

Leach looked thoughtful and a little hesitant. 'I...er... I don't recall there having been a bridge in my day. Which bridge is that?'

Obviously this was not going to be a testing test. 'Oh,' I replied, having boned up on that one, 'it's called Adam's Bridge.'

'Adam's Bridge. I see. Have you a map?'

Certainly I had a map – I took it out and spread it. 'There it is, Adam's Bridge.' I pointed to it. And there it was – clearly named – two dotted parallel lines, linking mainland India to the coast of Ceylon.

Leach looked even more thoughtful. 'I think,' he said, slowly unwinding his legs, 'that you'll find Adam's Bridge to be a subterranean layer of rock. It is six hundred fathoms down.'

He rose and thanked us for coming. We thanked him for seeing us. Leach, we later found, was an immensely distinguished anthropologist and certainly the world's top expert on the peoples of Ceylon – though that level of expertise had been largely untapped in his dealings with us. He was later knighted becoming professor of anthropology and a radically reforming provost of King's. It was he who opened King's (and eventually all the men's colleges) to women – the first college to do so. We never made it to Ceylon. But failing to get there was the start of what might be called, a 'vertical learning curve'.

## Lateral Thinking

I found many dons a puzzle. I'd met nobody quite like them. Some appeared to short-circuit problems – like the anthropologist Reo Fortune, author of a well-known work on sorcery. A benign man, he often gave students tea at his home, and one afternoon one of us, glancing at the ceiling, noticed a neat circular hole by the light fitting, some three inches in diameter. 'Excuse me, Sir, but why do you have that hole in your ceiling?' 'Oh, that?' he replied, glancing up. 'Every night when I was nicely settled in bed, my wife would turn to me and say, "Reo! Reo! Are you sure you turned the light out?"'

Other dons would skirt around a problem if it would avoid confrontation. They would nonetheless invariably be successful in their manipulations. They were the polar opposite of more direct North-Country types I had grown up with who tended to be more confrontational. One subtle 'skirter' was Meredith Dewey, the dean (chaplain) of Pembroke. Meredith, a small relaxed bachelor in his sixties, was, I felt, a bit of a concealed radical. I describe him here because he was like nobody I'd met before and yet was not so different from many Cambridge dons.

Meredith had a way of half smiling and would hold his head sideways as he mischievously shared a confidence. Yet on reflection you realised that invariably he learned a great deal more than he revealed. His manner was appealing, and yet not quite graspable. He was certainly not the stereotypical priest. Extremely generous in the time he gave to undergraduates, he was probably the guardian of more secrets than the rest of the fellowship combined. My room was close to his, and during my first year our paths often crossed. He had wide experience of the world, including time in the Navy, and had worked in a slum parish – so I felt we had some things in common despite differences of religion and age. I later found many undergraduates held this view, whatever their backgrounds.

Each landing of four or so undergraduates shared a small kitchen called a 'gyp-room'. As I was fond of cooking stews, made with a strong fried onion base, I sometimes took to cooking one or two a week. So when Meredith met me one day and I told him I was about to make a stew, he said he too was fond of stews. So I made a little extra and left it on his doorstep. He was very grateful and I included a regular portion for him whenever I made a stew. And then, towards the end of term, I found a notice pinned to the gyp-room door.

GENTLEMEN ARE REMINDED OF THE
COLLEGE RULE THAT FORBIDS
THE FRYING OF ONIONS
ON ACCOUNT OF THE MESS AND
SMELL INEVITABLY OCCASIONED

This was worrying. But I realised the duplicated notice must have been pinned to every gyp-room door in the college. There were over thirty gyp-rooms so I reasoned that a single transgression would hardly be noticed. I kept making my stews, and Meredith remained a grateful recipient.

It took time before I found there was no college rule about frying onions, that indeed the notice emanated from Meredith and that, though he may well have liked stews, he loathed the smell of onions, but was too kind to say so. I was learning that this was Cambridge, where direct confrontation was avoided and signals were more subtle than I could guess.

Meredith was scheduled, it was said, to be the next Bishop of Ely but preferred instead to stay at Pembroke which allowed him to follow his main love – cultivating the magnificent college gardens. He confided that he had secretly arranged his own anarchic memorial – a slow-growing but mammoth Eucalyptus tree that he said would eventually grow to over two hundred feet. But, he insisted, the college would certainly veto this proposal if it got out. His secret was safe with me – and probably with countless others. But it seems the secret did get out – or that it was Meredith's idea of a hoax. Fifty years later there is no sign of his memorial. But his memory does live on: returning to the college years later, I found his prohibition about onions had been formally incorporated in college rules.

It is toleration of the dons' independence that is so valuable to the university as a whole. One don in my own college, Pembroke, had for over twenty years allowed a stream of young men with criminal records and no formal entry qualifications but with high IQs to enter the college. Similar creativity operated at Oxford. The tutor of an Oxford college, responsible for admissions for over thirty years, told me how he too had amended the entrance procedures. 'I look out for applications from men whose headmaster's references say: "Under no circumstances should you take this man: he is a scallywag." I've been taking three of them every year.' When I asked how they had turned out, like the don in my own college, he said he'd noticed no difference between their results and subsequent careers and those of the normal intake.

# Weighing-Up

Looking back over an eventful and life-changing three years, I still have to pinch myself to realise how privileged I had been to go to Cambridge. The training in economics and anthropology was good, and the contacts and friendships were memorable. Some later opened useful doors. Despite initial concerns about class barriers I was surprised how this came to matter little as friendships soon crossed class boundaries. Eventually they determined the most significant relationship of my life – how I met my wife, Valerie, at a wedding. I was a friend of the bride, Valerie a friend of the groom.

One benefit of Cambridge was to learn something of how an extremely singular organisation works and, like all hierarchies, how it uses ritual to assert and support its structures. But the governance of the university is so complex with its thirty-one self-governing and independent colleges, one hundred and fifty departments and faculties and its six schools, that it needs involvement over years to penetrate its mysteries. Nonetheless, it has successfully evolved and adapted over seven hundred years. How it has done so is in part a lesson in devolving and balancing autonomy and control.

The university demonstrates how a complex hierarchy which could so easily fossilise instead adapts by accommodating to its many individualists. It does so by giving its dons opportunities for autonomy and innovation. It is this essential alliance of hierarchy and Individualism (as discussed in Chapter 21) that permits cautious adaptation to change. It was this same flexibility that lay behind the lack of direct confrontation between people not only on the same but at different levels. And the adaptable organisation that results contrasts markedly with the tyrannous university organisation I describe in Chapter 14, with its confrontational management style.

One advantage of Cambridge to me was the experience of being a participant observer in what was an extraordinarily alien culture – one with its own taken-for-granted values, its singular system of ranking, its unique sanctions and rituals. There was also the important lesson that *everyone's* way of life was limited by a relative lack of experience. Just as I had arrived at Cambridge with an awareness of the yawning chasms of my own ignorance and experience, so too this was mirrored by many of my fellow-students and their ignorance of the world. This limitation also applied to many of the dons.

With formal coursework in anthropology and economics now behind me and varied experience of cultures as different as The Avenues, Blackpool and the RAF, I was now ready for systematic fieldwork. The next step to becoming an anthropologist was the successful completion of a doctorate based on fieldwork.

# PART V:

# ON THE WAY TO BECOMING...

I soon found that to become an anthropologist was to prove expensive.

Mam's eldest brother Uncle George, a widower, cantankerous, opinionated and eccentric had squabbled with both his sons and most of his siblings. Our part of the family however, humoured him, believing family idiocy, indeed most idiocies, should be tolerated and that his advice if not his support might be useful – given he was the only family member ever to have made any money. But there was never any support – and though insistent with advice, none of it was ever useful. He was adamant, for instance, that we four brothers should wear rupture trusses. 'Now, do it now – while you're still young. Don't make the mistake I made. You have to wear a truss *before* you get a rupture – not after.'

When he heard I had got a university place he declared this 'a good thing' and proposed to make me his heir. He came round to the house during my first term to tie up the details.

'And what is Gerald doing at university? he asked Mam.

'Social anthropology,' she told him.

'What's that about?'

'Well I don't know really. He says it's a kind of sociology.'

The effect, she said, was dramatic. 'What's that, you say? Sociology? That's socialism! I don't know much – but I know this! I won't leave my money to any socialist.'

Nor did he – it was the end of my great expectations. Contact ceased. Later life as an anthropologist was to show that further sacrifice, even danger, was inherent to the job.

126

CHAPTER TEN

FIELDWORK IN NEWFOUNDLAND

By the end of my course I was determined to do research, but in the early
sixties there was little funding. I decided to take a job in an African school
and use this as the basis of fieldwork, when my tutor, Jack Goody, told me
that Memorial University in Newfoundland wanted an anthropologist. The
project was to research industrial relations in the port of St John's. He said
he would support my application and, if appointed, suggested I register for
a PhD at Manchester: 'The best place for industrial anthropology.' 'But
who's funding it?' I wanted to know – a matter of concern in a
disputatious arena like industrial relations. Goody was reassuring. He
believed it was the Canadian government.

Preliminary enquiries however proved far from reassuring. I had
envisaged researching an exotic culture in the sun but there was nothing
else on offer, and this research suited my experience. Newfoundland
however, was Canada's poorest province by far. With its truly awful
climate dominated by an annual fifty-five inches of rain, snow and fog –
over twice the London average – it negatively bottomed or topped all the
wrong statistical lists – from least education and income per head to most
poverty, the shortest life spans and the highest percentage of unemployed.
With no manufactures, and acid soils that precluded agriculture, all
consumer goods – including most of its food – had to be imported, mainly
through the port of St John's. The island's only resources were codfish,
moose, logging and the Canadian state's family allowance – the 'baby
bonus'. This though was a sizeable asset since Newfoundland's population
growth, at over 30 per 1000 per annum, matched that of many developing
countries.

Newfoundland had been Britain's oldest colony, and most of its
population was descended half from English Protestants and half Irish
Catholics (though the overall accent sounded Irish). There were a few non-
conformist churches, the biggest being the Salvation Army. There had
been a history of discord. Orange Day marches had ceased only a few
years previously, and the island was now politically stable though
industrial disputes were common.

Despite this depressing picture I applied, was awarded a Research Fellowship, and went out to The Memorial University of Newfoundland and the adventures of fieldwork. I landed at St John's airport in a torrential downpour to be welcomed by Ian Whitaker, an Englishman, the professor of sociology and anthropology. As we drove through the town along streets of picturesque Victorian clapboard houses, he was full of buoyant reassurance about the province, the project and even the weather. I enjoyed a short and pleasant two-day stay with him and his wife while the wind howled and the rain poured. Despite his optimism, what he had discovered about prospects for doing the project were not reassuring.

The port was in decline. Disputes were frequent, with longshore jobs eroding as trade shifted to the railway. It was known that the employers, with government backing, were planning to drastically cut the size of work-gangs. Unsurprisingly, the union's membership, with a reputation for being insular and suspicious of outsiders, was not inclined to welcome a prying stranger – even if this one *had* been an active trade unionist. The union's President, while not directly refusing to let me speak to his members insisted that he 'couldn't guarantee their co-operation'. Indeed, they weren't at all welcoming. I have done a lot of fieldwork since but this project was the toughest I've faced.

I found many tensions on the island were kept at bay because fiefs were strictly allocated according to religion. As the Prof. only half joked, even university deanships were shared out on this basis, and for him to be promoted (to Dean) he would have to join the Salvation Army –"the next sized religious group without its Dean". I later learned there was a Catholic/Protestant divide in the union: all executive members being Catholics, all gang foremen, Protestants. These divisions seemed roughly to reflect the balance of power in the island as well as the union.

On my second day in the province, with rain now only intermittent, I made my way through the oldest part of town to the harbour. Its wooden houses looked well past their prime with rotting boards, and peeling paint. The harbour was spectacular but contained few ships. The Union Hall close by was large and must once have been impressive. Now it looked as shabby as the houses around it and it too could have done with a lick of paint. Men I took to be longshoremen chatted in groups on the quay.

When I hesitantly entered the hall I found a cavernous open space filled by men sitting at small tables. All wore overalls and cloth caps and all appeared to be over fifty – I later found the union, which ran a 'closed shop' had stopped recruitment some years previously. Now the survivors were hanging around waiting for work – when there was obviously little work to wait for. They did not seem pleased to see me.

I tried to introduce myself but they already knew who I was. None would talk; most ignored me; one or two suggested – in what seemed an authentic Irish brogue – that I should 'fuck off'. It seemed, as I later realised, that I'd already been slotted into at least one of their two most feared categories: I was either 'Joey's stool' – a spy for the 'anti-labour' Prime Minister, Joey Smallwood (who claimed credit for establishing the university). Or being a 'Limey' from London, I had been sent by Lloyds of London Insurance to investigate pilferage. After half an hour of getting nowhere, I left. Later I found St John's had the highest pilferage rate of any Canadian port and, with its large gang sizes, the highest labour costs for each cargo-ton unloaded. No wonder they were worried about clamp-downs on pilferage, the threat of anti-labour politicians and anxiety over impending redundancies. It was hardly surprising that they were apprehensive about a prying stranger. But at least I had learned something of their principal fears.

The union, reasonably enough, would not allow me to work on the dock when there was little work for its members – and when I tried lodging with a longshore family, no-one would take me in. So I moved into a retired office-workers' home. I had just moved in when my landlady said: 'I don't suppose your family will be missing you at all?' 'Why not?' I wanted to know. 'Well you're from England, aren't you? You know, a nation of fisher-folk?' Many Newfoundlanders had similarly insular views, while the rest of Canada had the same denigrating 'Newfie jokes' as in Ireland (where they have the same 'Kerry jokes').

In those early months I learned that though most longshoremen had 'sent me to Coventry', a few were prepared to talk. These were the 'outside men'. With no regular gang affiliation, they filled in for regular gang members when the occasional vacancy occurred. Most outside men got little work and with no representation on the executive had what seemed valid grudges against the union. They were pleased to find in me a willing audience. I later learned that often a society's marginal members are initially the most available informants. But their views are likely to be unrepresentative and occasionally distorted – while their cooperation tends to 'contaminate' relationships with a society's core members – as it did in this case. Through them, however, I began to glimpse a fascinating world – albeit one hard to enter or understand. I was puzzled, for instance, by their continual dismissal of foremen as 'straw men' – as having no power – despite that they did the hiring. They asserted that regular gang members controlled who worked in the gangs though they did not or could not explain how.

Though engaging with regular longshoremen was difficult I could still watch what was happening on the quay, and 'keep my eyes and ears open'. So I kept watch on the hiring process – 'the shape-up'.[1] When a ship is to be unloaded, the foreman stands on deck looking down at a huddle of forty or more men who 'shape up' in a rough horseshoe shape on the quay beneath. Only twenty-six men out of the forty or so present were picked for each gang. When they were given a nod they climbed a gangway to the deck and given a small brass disc – their later claim to pay. Nothing it seemed could more readily demonstrate the imbalance in power between foremen and their men.

Yet if I were to believe my 'outside men' informants – that the foremen were 'straw-men' without power, that it was gang members who determined who were hired and who excluded them – then why did forty or more men assemble at a shape-up if only a known twenty-six would be hired? Were the foremen really 'straw men'? It seemed unlikely. Would I get the chance to crack these puzzles? I would – but it would prove a long haul. Meanwhile I stored this data for retrieval later. It was more than a year before I uncovered how a gang's constituency was determined – which depended on a complex of how kinship operated in the port, how pilferage was organised, whether men were teetotal where they worked, how they were regarded as work-mates – all of which affected who was and who was not hired.

If being seen with outside men made for difficulties relating to regular men, then being seen visiting employers did not help either. They too were reluctant to talk. No-one apparently, understood the nature of research or that research could be impartial. This was proving a much tougher project than expected: it seemed impossible to talk to either side. So I mooched about the dock and was largely ignored. I decided to spend little time in the Union Hall and more in the taverns that longshoremen favoured.

## Drinking among Longshoremen

Drinking by longshoremen was taken seriously[2] and appeared the main focus of their leisure. It bonded workmate relationships where, as I later found, the support of workmates was indeed vital in obtaining and maintaining a place in a gang. Men who did not drink were regarded with

---

1    'Shape-ups' are the traditional way of hiring dockworkers when the work is casualised: when work is decasualised, vacancies are equitably rotated on a roster Larrowe, (1956).

2    Mars (1988, ch. 4, pp. 91-101)

considerable suspicion and had less chance of securing employment. As one informant later put it when gesturing toward an 'outside man': 'I don't trust him. He's a loner.'

'Why's that?'

'Because he doesn't drink, that's why.'

It was a commonly expressed view. But few men were teetotallers so other factors also appeared important.

Early in fieldwork when exploring longshore drinking I was to have a narrow escape from what promised to be a serious physical assault. The Dragon, a large square drinking den shrouded in cigarette smoke, was the main after-work venue of men working at the Furness Withy wharf, one of the largest in the port. That evening it was noisy and crowded since, exceptionally, several ships were in port. I sat in a corner having a quiet drink with a couple of outside men' I'd invited. Like most longshoremen, they were small and wiry, few being much above five feet six inches. One of the more outspoken to my presence in the port, however, was an exception. Joe Quinlan, dark and glowering, was well over six feet. I glimpsed him in the opposite far corner, drinking quietly at a table for four.

That evening my luck was in. After a depressing couple of months gaining little data, I found after a few relaxing drinks that my 'outside men' companions were more keen to share what they knew. They proved insightful informants – though of course what they said had later to be carefully cross-checked. I learned that the shape-up was a form of drama – that most of those who attended knew they stood no chance of selection but what they gained was insight into the shifts of politics reflected by even small changes to the gang's membership. It was a bit like deciphering political shifts by studying the line-ups at the Soviet Union's May Day celebrations. And it was from them that I learned more about what made some longshoremen outside-men while others were regular gang members. Bachelors, older longshoremen and teetotallers it seemed were invariably outside men, which raised questions about values, stigma, the power within families, changes in the life-cycle and the role of drinking. There was however, still more to learn about the constituency of gangs.

Collective drinking prevents the accumulation of disparities in wealth[3] which would otherwise create divisive inequalities where solidarity against employers is considered important – hence the opposition to teetotallers. This basis for the destruction of capital through drinking has been noted elsewhere in collectivised labour forces, particularly among miners and

---

3    Dennis *et al* (1969)

shipbuilders (where in the UK it is colloquially known as 'pissing it up against the wall').

I felt I was beginning to learn about this community, and my hopes started to rise. Perhaps this project might be feasible after all? As the evening passed our bonhomie grew, I mused at what an interesting life I had got myself. Despite all the difficulties, here I was with the chance to do research – and, by then I had even negotiated beer money from the university to do it with! Then the spell broke. Through the hubbub came a clamour of raised voices. Chairs scattered, a table overturned, there was a crash of broken glass, and I made out a couple of longshoremen struggling to restrain a third. He was a furious, and by then very drunk, Joe Quinlan. Roaring curses he broke free and started to make his way across the tavern. He was heading for me.

The tavern's benign conversational buzz ceased. The only sound came from Quinlan. He began to bellow as, weaving across the floor, he explained how he was 'finally, once and for all, going to settle this fuckin' Limey!' Swaying nearer to my table he elaborated on his methods. Luckily I had drunk just a little too much to be sensible – a state not usually advised for those facing imminent assault. A crazed idea came to me. I stayed seated. 'Hello Joe.' Breathing hard and sweating heavily, he stopped to focus. But buoyed by drink – and folly – I followed through. 'You wouldn't be thinking of doing anything silly, Joe? Joe glared and started to reach for me over the table. 'Stop Joe. You wouldn't want to be dealing with a red-belt judoka. Would you, Joe?' Joe looked me over then, to my intense relief, dropped his hands, and delivered merely a tongue lashing. With a final snarl he swayed away then tottered back to his seat. I could breathe again.

It wasn't politic to tell anyone. Though I was indeed a red-belt judoka, red belts are worn only by tyros. They warn more experienced judoka not to throw them: being absolute beginners, red-belts do not even know how to fall!

## The Breakthrough to Acceptance

Despite this braggadocio and the degree of respect it gained, there was no breakthrough in getting acceptance with the union's core membership. My optimism began to fade as weeks extended to months. Then one day the local paper, the *Telegraph*, printed a letter that caused much resentment – and that opened a door. The writer objected that longshoremen were hanging around the waterfront, drinking, urinating and being a nuisance on the street rather than being at work. He asserted that longshoremen should not get relief unless they qualified for it – and that qualification should be subject to something called the 'Elberfeld System of Relief'. He did not elaborate. Luckily I knew about the Elberfeld system. It involved middle-class families overseeing social security claimants and their families and assessing them on their overall respectability.

I wrote a reply on university paper saying what good hardworking fellows longshoremen were, how they could not work if work wasn't available, that they were mostly decent family men, and like the rest of us 'only trying to earn an honest dollar'. Then I explained how the Elberfeld system worked and finally, as a *coup de grâce*, that it had reached its peak in Germany post-1933 – under the Nazis. This correspondence dominated discussion in the Union Hall. Longshoremen started to see me as someone who perhaps was not so antagonistic after all and who might even be an ally. More of them were willing to talk. A few days later an excessively laudatory letter appeared in the *Telegraph*:

> How fortunate are we in Newfoundland to be able to attract scholars of the stature of Gerald Mars. His letter to the *Telegraph* should be compulsory reading for every official and every politician in the province.
> (signed) Nimshi Carewe

Never had I received such unqualified praise (and never would again!). Who was this new-found fan? I sought out a Newfoundlander who knew everyone and asked him: 'Who is Nimshi Carewe?' 'Oh! Nimshi?' he answered, 'Is he out again?' Out of prison? Out of a mental hospital? Deflated, I went to see Nimshi – fans were scarce and needed cherishing. I found a slightly manic man of about fifty. In Newfoundland the churches picked out exceptionally bright orphans for adoption by the island's richest families. Nimshi had been one of the selected. Unfortunately he suffered severe and periodic breakdowns but in between was charming, erudite and, I was reassured to see, lucid, though he had some strong enthusiasms. We discussed unemployment and he offered useful data and insight.

After my letter to the *Telegraph*, acceptance by the union's executive gradually became easier, particularly with the union secretary, Wilf Atkinson, who eventually became a good friend. I found he was ignorant about alternative ways of hiring and decasualising dock labour and was very keen to learn. Short, intense and very bright, he was kept on a tight rein by his wife who worried about his periodic drinking benders. She allowed him time with 'The Professor' however, as she and Wilf called me, the most junior of researchers – because she wrongly thought professors to be soberly respectable. Wilf became an invaluable informant.[4] It was hard keeping us both sober but well worth the effort. And with the union secretary vouching for me, my acceptance by the body of men gradually eased.

## Learning from Jokes

Now I could begin to spend more time with the men, chatting, listening and learning – the basis of fieldwork. One day I joined a group of four in the union hall, all aged about fifty. They were baiting an older man, Bill Courtney in his mid-seventies, about his lack of sexual vigour.

'You can tell us, Joe,' said one, you're past it now, aren't you?'

'No, I'm not past it,' rejoined Joe with spirit.

'Well,' replied another with a wink at his fellows, 'I bet it takes you a long time?'

Joe's answer was immediate. 'Ah well,' he replied, 'but you see, I don't begrudge the time.'

This witty exchange typified the gap in prestige between younger men able to work and older men who could not. It led me to trace the connections between family, organisation and employment status. In an occupation where strength was important and access to work was valued, old men like Joe were treated with scorn. They were baited, termed 'derelicts' and their status in the family and the community diminished with age. Lacking Joe's sharp wit and ready response, most older men were, not surprisingly, bad-tempered and disconsolate. They were usually on bad terms with their sons who did have access to earnings but gave any surpluses to their mothers whose prestige rose as they became older. Not so their fathers, whose prestige fell, thus exposing a structural split at the core of longshore families. Men's natural allies in the family were their

---

4   Whyte (1955) in his Appendix offers a celebrated account of his relationship with a key informant he calls 'Doc'. Doc occupied a similarly significant position in his community as did Wilf in his. Other anthropologists have reported similar good fortune. The appendix to the 6th and subsequent editions also offers a classic guide to doing fieldwork in urban settings and the details of his relationship to Doc. It is as valid now as when it was written.

daughters, but younger women, on the whole, controlled few resources.[5]
As the power and prestige of men waned with age therefore, the influence
and power of their wives waxed. As well as benefiting from receipt of
funds from their sons they usually embraced a positive role as
grandmothers – whereas older men could only become derelicts.

It is by listening to and recording jokes, by noting which categories of
person are typically joked with and by whom and whether equal status
responses are or are not typically expected, that one can gain valuable
insights into a culture and how relationships, including power
relationships, work.[6]

---

5    The usual pattern of inheritance in Newfoundland is for men to inherit capital
     goods – houses, fishing boats – and for women to inherit movable goods such
     as dishes and tableware. A structural split is therefore evident in the nuclear
     family between fathers and daughters against mothers and sons over the
     perceived passage of goods to daughters during the father's lifetime. The split
     is exacerbated by sons donating earnings to their mothers. Problems over
     inheritance and similar tensions within the nuclear family are recorded among
     the Tallensi of Northern Ghana, though there the wedges between father and
     son develop from the age of about five rather than at working age (Fortes,
     1974).
6    The first definitive reference to 'joking relationships' in anthropology is
     Radcliffe-Brown (1940). Later developments are discussed by Freedman
     (1977). Subsequent discussions are summarised in *The Britannica Concise
     Encyclopaedia* (2006, p. 298).

Chapter Eleven

# Gangs: Their Organisation of Pilferage and Their Role in Industrial Relations

As fieldwork extended, I was slowly becoming aware how membership in a gang occupied a pivotal place in the life of longshoremen and in industrial relations. Later fieldwork showed how the gang, besides offering income, acted as a source of illicit income from pilferage and from welfare in a country where government welfare provision is relatively low. Gang members collectively paid for the medical treatment of sick or injured members – one gang during fieldwork supplying several pints of blood for transfusion to a fellow gang member. The gangs also offered support in crises such as house fires – frequent in St John's where most houses are made of wood – and they collected funds in cases of sickness and injury. In this respect the gangs stood alongside the churches as primary dispensers of charity. We saw too how the gangs were a focus of leisure – their members drank together – but they were also central in providing support in disputes with management. It is no wonder there was massive opposition to management's attempts to reduce the size of gangs.

It was much later in fieldwork that I found how the gang was integral in organizing the theft of cargo – with twenty-four of the gangs' twenty-six occupational roles – winchmen, signallers, holdsmen and shed staff – each possessing a parallel role in the illicit and complex division of labour by which their functions were reassigned to coordinate the furtherance of pilferage.[1]

Understanding how the gangs worked and how pilferage was organised alerted me in subsequent fieldwork to explore how the deployment of power in any organisation cannot be understood without considering its underlying deviance. And often indeed in understanding everyday work in the majority of organisations.

---

1   Mars (1974)

# The Morality that Underlies Dock Theft

I called on the manager of a wharf to talk about manager/worker relationships. Red-faced, angry, he told me he was 'outraged'. 'What,' I asked, 'had outraged him?' 'It's the constant, blatant thieving that goes on – almost under my eyes.' I asked for an example and heatedly, he told how that very week a cargo of portable *(sic)* Telefunken radios had been pilfered. 'They cleared the whole lot; never left a single one.'

I already knew of this theft from the men. Here was a chance to learn a manager's view. 'How can you be sure it was done in St John's?' I asked. 'How do you know they weren't lifted between Hamburg and St John's? They could have been lifted in London? Couldn't they?' With mounting anger he explained just why he was so sure. 'Oh, yes! It *was* taken here. We found packaging on the dock. But can we catch them? Never! Why? Because they stick together with their damned lies. That's why.'

Discussing this case later with a trusted informant whom I knew had been involved in this theft, I was amused to find him equally outraged. 'That bastard...!' He explained how he had sold one of the radios to that same manager. And he too had corroborative detail. I later found this manager was furious because the *whole* cargo had been lifted, instead of the theft being kept within mutually accepted limits. It became 'theft' only when people took too much. I recalled the Blackpool hotel manager who had been similarly outraged by the theft of a whole smoked salmon (page 62). He too had been annoyed, not so much at the *idea* of theft but at the *level* that broke unstated agreements about permitted amounts.

The whole issue of cargo theft raised questions about morality, limits and ethnocentricity. To the town's middle-class traders, longshoremen were undisciplined, lawless thieves. One trader warned me. 'Don't trust them an inch. Never hang your coat up on the dock or they'll have it. And never, ever, lend them money. They're just out-and-out crooks.'

The reverse was true: they had an unyielding morality: it was just a very different morality – a quantitative morality – rather than the qualitative morality of middle-class society. It was a morality sustained by gang-imposed sanctions against those breaking limits or stealing passengers' luggage – and on occasion men have refused to work with such deviants.

## 'Working the value of the boat': the formula that determines pilferage levels

Longshoremen operated a system of tolerated limits on amounts they could take. Here they based it on a formula – what they called 'working the value of the boat'. If a boat was 'good for four hours' work at $4 an hour, the permitted 'take' was $16 worth of cargo per man. The formula was necessary to equalise takings throughout the different insulated sections of a gang – distributed as they were in the vessel, on the deck, the rigging and in the sheds – so there could be no ambiguity about the agreed level. If anyone took more, sanctions were savage – and if a culprit proved recidivist, the men might well refuse to work with him. These levels were unofficially acceptable to the employers and imposed stability in an otherwise unstable context.[2] Not unlike much of what I had found in Blackpool.

I have since found similarly established – and colluded in – limits in a wide variety of industries.[3] And where a group has to coordinate the different functions of its members to facilitate its fiddles, it invariably imposes controls and sanctions against its own deviants. Occupational theft is normally bound by rules, especially so when it involves groups – and then it is rarely anarchic as outsiders tend to claim.

## Learning from a 'Trouble Case': the Case of the Two Drunks

Early in fieldwork, when very few longshoremen would talk to me, I found it was becoming possible, just by hanging around, to at least scrape the surface of fieldwork. One day on the dock I heard raised voices. Approaching, I saw two drunken men shouting abuse at a foreman who, I gathered, had just sacked them. Nothing startling here – except that I had heard it was more common for gang members the worse for drink to be hidden under tarpaulins while their work was done by their mates. I noted

---

2   Since I would not reveal confidential data that might work against the interests of my informants, it was ten years before I could publish how dock theft was organised in the port. By then the technology of cargo handling had altered through the use of side- and end-loading vessels, and the union gave me clearance to publish.

3   See Mars (1982). It was relatively easy for Newfoundland longshoremen to calculate the value of cargo taken because in St John's, cargo was predominantly 'general cargo', items found in shops whose value was common knowledge.

the details, found the names of the sacked men, who were brothers, and stored them for future enquiry.

I remembered a teaching of Max Gluckman[4] – that 'trouble cases' could prove invaluable in pointing up the realities of social situations and highlighting aspects of social structures not otherwise evident.[5] It was a year before this trouble case bore fruit, helped by a growing insight into the role of foremen as 'straw men': men without the power that their office assumed. It was to provide a bountiful harvest and made me grateful to have maintained a diary.

Much later I found the two sacked men were the foreman's sons. Earlier I had rashly assumed that kinship preferment in the Newfoundland docks would be similar to that in the UK, so that men in St John's would help their relatives find work and they would work in the same gangs – as they did in London and Manchester.[6] Not so. It seemed that fathers and sons in Newfoundland were strongly rivalrous, and rarely worked in the same gangs. The gangs, it later emerged, operated as self-sustaining collectives, and their power was considerable. Gang members would object if the foreman gave a preferred job to someone the gang did not like, or sacked someone they did. If either happened they would threaten sanctions – from organised slow-ups to a withdrawal of labour. As I had been told, the foremen really were 'straw-men'. Despite their apparent power to hire and fire, they were, as my outside men had insisted, relatively powerless.

But there was one exception I appreciated only later in fieldwork – the minimal claims of kinship were allowed by the gang if a foreman's sons worked in his gangs' least desired positions, on the quay in full view of passers-by, thus precluding their access to pilfered cargo.

This foreman therefore faced a dilemma.[7] He had been told by his manager to reduce drunkenness on the dock and maintain discipline when his power to do either was minimal. His answer was to wait until his sons were drunk – and then fire them – the only men he could discipline with impunity since they would get no support from fellow gang members.

---

4   Gluckman (1967)
5   Using a 'trouble case' to maximise and highlight aspects of social structure benefitted from a rhyme I use as a checklist: 'I keep six honest serving-men, They taught me all I knew; Their names are What and Why and When And How and Where and Who.' (Kipling, 1902). I have added a non rhythmical seventh man, 'With'.
6   Young & Wilmott (2007); Simey (1956)
7   A common structural position of foremen arising from their intermediate role between management and men: see Whyte & Gardner (1945).

This 'trouble case' indicated how authority and prestige in the workplace is not necessarily as it seems, as it appears, or as it is presented. It is figuring out this kind of paradox that makes occupational/organisational anthropology so satisfying. In Blackpool for instance, as here, a job holder's prestige was frequently related not to the title the job carried but whether it offered or failed to offer fiddled earnings or had the ability to allocate them.

## Accepted by the Men and a Pariah to the Employers

Because employers were worried about my impartiality they decided to ban me from their meetings – and even from management/union meetings. This proved the final breakthrough to my acceptance by the men. If the bosses banned me, then I *must* be 'a union man'. I still hoped however, to mend my bridges with the employers.

When I had been in the field a year, the contract was due for renewal and negotiations with employers were reaching deadlock – a reduction of gang size being high on their agenda. The gangs' welfare, social, economic and insurance functions all ensured that the men would vigorously reject any attempt to reduce the size of gangs. But impatient for a showdown, the employers began to organise a lockout. An intransigent confrontation was inevitable – especially as union meetings to discuss contract negotiations coincided in the same period with union elections. These favoured a new and relatively inexperienced batch of militant negotiators who used the general meetings to discuss contract renewal as an oppositional platform for election to the executive.[8]

The employers called their lockout. The union answered with a general meeting, at which a packed and euphoric membership, disastrously voted overwhelmingly for a countervailing strike. Member after member jumped on stage and praised the backing they had been promised. 'Give thanks to the teamsters for their wonderful help and support.' 'The body' roared its approbation to wild and wilder applause, cheers and stamps. 'Give thanks to the railwaymen...' And so it went on. Then, just as things were calming down, one of the Union's activists jumped on stage. 'And we mustn't forget Gerry Mars – without him this strike would never have been possible in the first place.'

What brought this on I had no idea, but the audience, whipped to a new frenzy, stamped their feet and cheered louder than ever. Wilf sagely noted: 'That'll be back with the bosses in an hour.' It was – there being a known

---

8   Mars (1979)

'fifth column' in the membership. As a result, I moved from pariah status to folk hero with the men – and to firmer pariah status with the employers. Neither position is recommended to researchers. The 'method experts' insist that you must never appear be seen partial in disputes. But this is I found, practically impossible in an industrial conflict when the parties are about to be involved in a strike/lockout. After this meeting none of the senior bosses except one – Bill Crosby – would talk to me: attempts at being seen as impartial were doomed.

## The Strike/Lockout

The membership's euphoria was misplaced. The employers decided, in face of union intransigence, not to reduce gang size but to abolish gangs altogether. Instead they proposed to introduce the new technology of end- and side-loading vessels that were unloaded by cranes, the cargo then being handled by fork-lift trucks. With the abolition of gangs, the core building-blocks of the union would be eradicated and most longshoremen made perpetually redundant.

If the employers had initially attempted to negotiate a reduction in the size of gangs on the basis of say, seniority, or some other unambiguous base, then this might well have been accepted. Without such unambiguous criteria however, *all* twenty-six members of e*ach* gang felt they faced possible redundancy and, unsurprisingly, all were united in determined opposition. And the dispute might also perhaps have been avoided if the employers had brought forward or deferred negotiations so they did not coincide with the elections that mobilised hard-line union militants to discuss contracts as vehicles to further their election chances. In the event, the resulting and unnecessary year-long strike/lockout proved a bitter hardship for all concerned.

The dispute proved useful to me. I was able to unravel the role of churches as providers of charitable help during the strike and the food shops as providers of extended credit. I recalled the role of the Catholic Church in Manchester and, alerted by the comparison, noted how in Newfoundland this too was related to the level of piety able to be demonstrated by its recipients. The churches with their charity, and the shops – with their ongoing debt relationships – together made it possible for the union to stay out longer than they might otherwise have done, an area of enquiry I might well have missed unless alerted by the Manchester comparisons.(p.15, fn. 16).

The new capital-intensive technology not only cut out expensive man-handling of cargo but eradicated pilferage at a stroke. With containerisation, the longshoremen of St John's were one of the first to suffer the onslaught of globalisation as it affected shipping.

## 'Cross-Cutting Ties' between Men and Employers

There was only one employer, Bill Crosby, who exceptionally and from the beginning had been willing to discuss industrial relations with me. Bill Crosby, a big modest man in his forties, was that rare presence in Newfoundland (and elsewhere): a scholarly businessman who appreciated the social sciences. He belonged to the premier business dynasty of Newfoundland and I was impressed by his balanced views on industrial relations.

Bill Crosby had cultivated a close knowledge of longshoremen. One day when visiting 'Dirty Jack', the union's delegate (the UK equivalent of a shop steward) in hospital, I was surprised when Crosby arrived in the ward. And more surprised still to find he and Jack seemed the best of friends. Yet Jack, the roughest of diamonds, uncouth in language and appearance, was the *bête noire* of the employers. They found him difficult – and often, I suspected, far too clever – to deal with.

'I've brought you some grapes, Jack,' Crosby announced, producing a huge bunch. Jack was delighted and both chortled at some joke I did not see. Later I found Jack had a notorious weakness for grapes; he was known never to have left a consignment intact.

Their alliance surprised me but I was later to find that the most rancorous industrial conflicts are likely to have 'cross-cutting ties' between management and labour that can sometimes provide the route through a negotiating impasse. This reflects a common African expression: 'They are our enemies; we marry them.' Such potential links in the West are often ignored because they are informal and bureaucracies tend too often not to exploit them. They may well, however, provide a basis for settling conflicts.[9]

Fieldwork in Newfoundland taught me to look out for the unstated fears of informants, to record the jokes they made and to analyse their 'trouble cases'. It demonstrated the importance of holism – the anthropological truism that a line cannot be drawn around any one set of activities at any one time and that knowledge of one informs others – how kinship relations for instance, affect the workplace and vice versa; how leisure and work are connected, and how work, kinship and the life-cycle

---

9    See Zartman (2000, Introduction) on the wider applicability of cross-cutting ties in disputes; and Gluckman (1965) for African examples.

were all linked: these were benefits that would not have emerged with questionnaire research.

CHAPTER TWELVE

# THE MEMORIAL UNIVERSITY OF NEWFOUNDLAND

## High Drama: never drink with a homicidal maniac

'Look – we can bang him on the head and stun him... We can cut him into pieces – then burn him in the fire... And no-one would know.'

Newfoundland's Memorial University attracted eccentrics – for the same reasons many universities do and as I had found was so in Cambridge – because in universities, there are (or were!) less pressures to conformity than in other jobs and because individualist diversity is encouraged. Some of Memorial's faculty were lured by the island's austere beauty and pre-industrial lifestyles; others, like me, because of its research opportunities. A few were brilliant; others merely odd. And then – there were the mad.

One such was Otto, a short, square Austrian noted for his booming laugh and amusing, original conversation. None of us knew then that his originality also took in a singular approach to homicide.

The weather that Christmas was one of the worst on record. Most of the faculty had already left St John's to visit their families before the winter's weather finally closed the airport. Otto and I, both bachelors without women, were marooned to face a lonely Christmas. Luckily, a good friend had offered me his apartment while he was away – a welcome break from my mean and overcrowded longshore boarding house.

On Christmas Eve I moved thankfully into my borrowed apartment, four floors up in a wooden block. Close to the harbour, it directly faced winds from the North Pole. All that day heavy snow buffeted by howling winds enveloped the port as the old wooden building creaked and shifted. I lit a huge log fire in the open hearth then phoned Otto. Would he like to come round? I had some potent Aquavit; would he like to break a Christmas bottle? Otto finally found a taxi driver with wheel chains who was willing to brave the storm and who delivered him with his offering – a second bottle of Aquavit.

We were through the first and into the second when there was a knock at the door. Who could this possibly be? And on such a terrible night? On the doorstep, direct from a surreal fairy tale, stood a dwarf. With his long ginger beard, red coat and expectant smile, he gave a little bow, opened a red leather case full of trinkets, turned it into a tray and in a thin high pitched voice, began a sales spiel.

I could only stare with blurred astonishment. Then, aware that Otto was pulling at my sleeve, I half closed the door and turned to listen to his urgent whisper: 'Look – we can bang him on the head and stun him. We can cut him in pieces – then burn him in the fire. And no-one would know'. His voice rose. 'No-one would know. Don't you see? No-one would ever know! Except us.' He began to laugh; I instantly became sober.

I tried to shut the door with Otto, red-faced and increasingly frantic, still pulling at my sleeve. His voice rose as he began a mantra: 'No-one would know. Don't you see? No-one would know. No-one will ever know!'

Pushing Otto aside I turned to the unlikely salesman, still there, still smiling, still with his tray. I bundled him off – closed the door – then to deal with Otto, now no longer manic but sitting disconsolately by the fire. I insisted we had both had enough. There was trouble getting him a taxi but I finally found one prepared to face the storm. The driver and I escorted Otto down the stairs – and off.

Late next morning – the telephone's insistent bell. It was Otto.

'Listen carefully! Did anything happen last night?'

'No. Nothing happened.'

'But are you sure? You're absolutely sure nothing happened? Nothing happened. Did it?'

'Yes,' I was finally able to reassure him, 'nothing happened. Nothing at all. It could have – but it didn't. Everything's fine.'

'Oh! Thank God! Thank God for that!'

He later told me of several near-misses he had avoided by sheer good luck. The year before he had been driving in the early morning with a girlfriend through a desolate part of Manitoba. Passing through a small village, they had caught sight of what looked like an old lady in the headlights. Otto aimed the car directly at her. Luckily his girlfriend grabbed the wheel and swung the car off the road. Another time he had been carefully planning the death of a neighbour when the neighbour suddenly moved house. His accounts continued.

I lost touch with Otto but recently checked his name on the Internet. He's since had a distinguished academic career. When I look back I shiver to realise how close we were to a lifetime in gaol.

# Low Drama and Party-Going: where sherry isn't alcohol

The university faculty comprised people from a wide range of nationalities, disciplines and backgrounds, and what gave them unity, as is usual in expatriate communities, was to party and to gossip. Alcohol flowed freely but in Newfoundland there was a strong anti-drink lobby, and drink was obtainable only from a few licensed liquor stores. There were none close to the new university, so an *ad hoc* committee of thirsty academics lobbied for one. The Dean of Humanities and Professor of Philosophy, Carlton Whinnard, an austere, ascetic teetotaller then set up a counter committee in opposition. Carlton's committee was successful and the proposed new liquor store was shelved.

So, I was baffled shortly after rejection of the new store, to find Carlton at a faculty party, apparently drinking alcohol.

'What'll you have, Carlton?' he was asked.

'I'll have a dry sherry please,' answered the teetotaller.

I could not resist asking: 'But Carlton, I thought you were teetotal?'

'So I am.'

'Then why are you having a sherry?'

'Good heavens!' he replied, 'Sherry isn't alcohol!'

Two days later, in the staff common room, still bemused by his answer, I was getting myself a coffee when Carlton walked in. I called over: 'Can I get you a coffee, Carlton?' 'A coffee?' came the reply. 'Good heavens, no! I'm lecturing in an hour. Coffee is far too stimulating.' By switching categories and bending definitions, you can re-order the world – especially if you are a philosopher.

As in many expatriate communities, parties were frequent and eagerly attended. One professor's wife, a witty, attractive, clever and very bored housewife, entertained whole rooms of party-goers with much exaggerated accounts of the discussions she had allegedly had with her naïve Newfoundland psychotherapist. All chat would stop as, with rolling eyes and lascivious gestures, she acted out her sessions – with lurid accounts of the Freudian symbolism that allegedly worried her:

'So I told him about my latest weird dream. How I was trying to climb this huge red tower. But it was too slippery – and the more I climbed the higher it grew. And then the whole tower started to pulse and vibrate and I began to slip down. I was exhausted – so exhausted – and then whoosh – down and down I went – until I found myself in a massive cavern with rushing water and a whirlpool that swung me ever so round and round. And then I woke up – absolutely shattered'.

She would then recount the local psychotherapist's embarrassed responses and, looking round, wide eyed, ask: 'But what does it all mean?'

These serial accounts were eagerly awaited as she delivered them in polished sequences at one party after another. She amused everyone – except her poor husband who would stand at the edge of these gatherings, chewing his fingernails.

## Postscript on Newfoundland

Ten years later, on a trip back to St John's, and with the doctorate secured, I was chatting to Bill Crosby.

'Do you know who funded your study?' Bill asked.

'Oh yes, the Canada Council.'

'No, I don't think so,' he replied. 'In fact I know it wasn't.'

'Well that's what I've always understood – that it was a Canada Council Fellowship.'

'No,' he said. 'It wasn't. That's what you had to be told. I funded it. But I made the university keep it secret. It would have been impossible to get an impartial study done otherwise.'

Similar cases of altruistic and anonymous patronage are rare. Newfoundland could surprise me still.

## Yet Another Interview

At the end of 1963 and after a year in the field, it was necessary to return to the UK for an intermediate period of library research and preliminary assessment. There was however a problem with my registration at Manchester. They had changed their postgraduate policy and now wanted me to enrol and be examined for an MA degree before being allowed to proceed to the PhD. 'Even our own Firsts now have to do the MA,' said Professor Gluckman, possibly suggesting that Firsts from elsewhere were inferior. So where was I, without any sort of a First? However, the LSE had previously offered me the chance to bypass their MA if my fieldwork proved satisfactory. I had always hankered to return to London and here was the opportunity. It was no contest: I reapplied to the LSE.

I was interviewed by the patrician department head, Professor Sir Raymond Firth, a Grand Old Man of British social anthropology. After discussing anthropology in general and my research in particular, he leaned back and asked why I wanted to come to London? I decided, with innocent naïveté to be absolutely honest. 'Well,' I said, after explaining about the MA problem and the move to PhD... 'and of course, Manchester is Manchester – but London is London.' I was implying that the stimulus and attractions of the capital were naturally alluring to a young man. But I hadn't appreciated the rivalry between the two heads and their departments – or perhaps how Firth relished the chance to capture a PhD candidate from his rival. Fortuitously, Firth missed my point. 'Yes,' he said with quiet satisfaction. 'Yes, I suppose we do have something of a reputation here.'

So I moved registration to the LSE and was able to bypass the MA. I completed the doctorate part-time while working at Middlesex Polytechnic and – with Raymond Firth – benefitted from a superb supervisor.

# PART VI:

# USING ANTHROPOLOGY
# IN DIFFERENT FIELDS

CHAPTER THIRTEEN

# MIDDLESEX POLYTECHNIC

'Well,' I was advised by staff and fellow postgrads at the LSE, 'you'll never get a decent academic job if you do.'

I was at the LSE, writing up my Newfoundland fieldwork and had announced I was applying for jobs in the new polytechnics. In 1966 they were growing fast but were very much looked down on by staff in the universities. But married, broke, and with Valerie the same, I pressed on and applied regardless. For me it was no contest. My starting pay, exactly double when measured against that for a university assistant lectureship could bear no comparison. Luckily at the selection board I could argue that having done research in an industrial setting as an anthropologist gave me experience to teach industrial sociology. And equally lucky, there was a distinct shortage of academics to fill the expansion. Middlesex College of Technology, then aiming to be a polytechnic, was offering 100 percent mortgages in its bid for staff. I could always convert to finishing the PhD part-time – and if the Poly did not turn out, well, I could always leave and felt sure to get another job.

Of course, the snobbery factor exaggerated differences. As today, in 'the new universities', there are pockets of excellence, just as, in Oxbridge, there are (admittedly small) pockets of mediocrity. This most certainly applies to staff, but to a lesser extent also applies to students: the overlaps are greater than people suppose. What we had then in the poly's was enthusiasm and the chance of innovation. The flip side was that we learned as we went without any sustaining web of tradition or the guidance of senior scholars.

Two of my first tasks at Middlesex were to lecture on industrial sociology and industrial relations, and to be admissions tutor for the BA degree in business studies. I used the admission interviews to try to find just why applicants felt a degree in business studies might be useful and if they understood how abstract much of the teaching was.

Our students often had little idea what higher education involved. This caused problems not faced as sharply in the older universities. We were closer to our students – and less deference was paid to us. This was refreshing – but it needed subtlety to manage. I am told I am not noted for that. And humour without subtlety never helped anyone.

One of the courses I helped construct was a full-time release scheme for trade unionists on a year's course in industrial relations. I relished teaching on this course. It allowed me to build on both my Newfoundland work and experience in the Civil Service when I had founded a union branch and chaired it for some years. But my militancy seemed to be below the required standard: this was the ultra-militant late 1960s – the period of university occupations and lock-ins, and these trade unionists were extremely militant. They early set up a Students Representative Committee 'to present trade union students' views to the management'. Representation is laudable. But we were not 'management' – both sides of academe shared, or should have shared, the same *educational* aims and values: a polytechnic is not a factory – though ours looked like one. The committee, however, misunderstood the distinctions between managers and workers and students and tutors. But never be funny about this… and never, ever, use irony.

We gave tutorials – in those honeyed days, one-to-one teaching – and one day a trades union student arrived who had missed his previous week's tutorial. He was older than the average, in his forties, small – he had been a miner – and with a pinched face that spoke of hardship. 'What happened to you last week?' I mildly enquired – and was hit by a harangue. 'Well I had to work didn't I? I was short of cash, wasn't I? I don't live in a fuckin' big house in Hampstead, do I? I'm not a fuckin' senior lecturer. I'm not a fuckin' landlord either.'

His up-to-the-minute assessment of my resources surprised me. And there was an element of truth to all these injustices – though the house, a new acquisition, had most of its rooms let to pay the hefty mortgage. But this was 'Fair Exchange Ville'. 'Look,' I said, raising the tone of my accent a little. 'Hard up? Then why don't you just do what the rest of us have to do when we're hard up?'

His response was guarded, sullen. 'What's that then?'

I couldn't resist. 'Well, do what we all do – why don't you sell some shares?'

Up he jumped. He was out of the room like a jackrabbit. Within an hour a complaint had been tabled by the Students Representative Committee, with insistence that I be stopped from teaching on the course forthwith – 'because his ideology is not in conformity with trades union values'. The course head was able to diffuse the row – but only just. I was told 'to stop being funny. Because it's not funny, Gerry.' I disagreed, but by then was a marked man.

My next run-in, a week later, again occurred in a tutorial, this time with the committee secretary. We were to discuss 'the culture of poverty.' Or perhaps not. 'Have you read anything on the culture of poverty?' I asked, as I thought, innocuously. He moved straight in: 'Why are you taking this fuckin' tutorial?' he snarled. 'What the fuck do you know about the culture of fuckin' poverty? Eh? Eh??'

Whereas my previous antagonist had been small and pinched, this one was large, beefy and sweaty – and, it struck me, possibly dangerous. Actually I had probably had more experience of real poverty than he had. Try having a craftsman father in a redundant trade of a declining industry, a sick mother, and being the eldest of four brothers, all aspiring to higher education. I had also possibly had as much active trade unionism as he had. But now I decided to respond according to the role he expected. 'Look,' I said persuasively, 'I've probably read more books on the culture of poverty than you've had hot dinners.'

He did not hit me – but it came close. He was not placated. Nor was his committee who again pressed for my removal from the course. Nor indeed was the course head, though he successfully defended my position.

Later, and by looking back comparatively at the rise and fall of union militancy in Newfoundland, I noted that there the structures making for militancy in the longshore union were activated only when barriers to collective action were overcome (when union wide meetings to discuss contract renewals coincided with union-wide meetings to decide elections). Then turbulence either took the form of militants routing the executive, vigorously opposing the employers, or both.[1]

The students' committee had similarly been convulsed with a series of militant spasms. Looking back, I found in every second term of each new course year, the committee had run collective campaigns. Since each new entry of trades union students came from backgrounds that were widely disparate, it therefore took the first term to consolidate their relationships. Only by the second term could they overcome their differences enough to act in concert. And the nearest available common cause was to gang up on an ideologically suspect member of staff – the well-used 'select a scapegoat' technique – or alternatively, to oppose an aspect of polytechnic policy.

Relations with colleagues were also becoming problematic, again because of my propensity for 'smart-arse' responses. In the staff-room one

---

1    Explored more fully in Mars (1979, pp. 135-157)

day, one of my colleagues, an earnest Irish psychologist asked what I thought of the Jensen/Eysenck hypothesis[2] that relates IQ scores to race.

It was an explosive topic at the time. But it offered too much scope to be flippant.

'The Jensen/Eysenck hypothesis? Oh yes, they're absolutely on the ball, aren't they?'

He was astounded – and horrified. 'No – this is the theory that says race and IQ are directly related.'

'I know,' I said. 'Doesn't it say the Jews and the Chinese are at the top of the IQ ratings? – and the Irish and Blacks are at the bottom?'

'That's right. But surely you don't believe in that rubbish?'

'Oh yes,' I said. 'Look ! Even among us Jews, we well know that the stupidest Jews are the Irish Jews.'

Unfortunately, before I could remedy things with 'Joke! Joke!' I had been overheard by a colleague of the far left, and my faux observation was frequently repeated as my perceived truth. Which of course, served me right.

Teaching on a business course was especially high on the far left's contamination scale; it was 'consorting with the enemy'. A revolutionary left-wing friend of mine in another college had a more rational approach: he too taught sociology to business studies students – but as part of a planned strategy to subvert them.

All this was during the turbulent late sixties and early seventies when both sociology and sociologists were strongly politicised and many had close links with revolutionary socialist movements. They were well represented at Middlesex – and it was easy, in their binary style of thinking, to be branded a right-winger – or worse – a 'class traitor'.

And then Thatcher became minister of education and assiduously provoked every liberal she could. Higher education generally came to the boil with walk-outs and sit-ins. Thatcher herself came to Middlesex and was met by an organised riot. We had after all, forty-five sociologists at our peak – many of them militant members of the Socialist Workers Party. Our department was despairingly described by Alf Holt, the dean of social sciences, as 'One of the last of the great sheltered workshops'.

The trouble with this staff workshop, riven as it was with conflicting 'tendencies', was that it too needed scapegoats to hold it together. I admit to being largely self-selected – but having a talent to annoy was a great help. All in all it was an exciting job. I only moved into a 'decent' one eighteen years later; it was much less exciting.

---

2   Jensen & Eysenck (1982)

CHAPTER FOURTEEN

# THE UNIVERSITY BUSINESS SCHOOL: MORE BUSINESS THAN SCHOOL?

In 1984 I left Middlesex for a job with a university School of Policy Studies. I was offered leeway to design a MSc degree in 'Crime Risk Management' – a combination of criminology, management and anthropology. It was just what I was seeking: intellectually stimulating, innovative - and part-time which allowed for consultancy. It came with a professorship and was well-paid. Early on however, the school, with me and my course, were absorbed into the university's business school at the instigation of its expansionist Director. Entering the business school meant I had bypassed its normal selection process - normally in the director's control since he sat on every selection board and always took deciding decisions.

What followed proved a revelation, an insight into the fate later to overtake other universities (and other normative organisations) – their attempted corruption to become 'consumer-led', quasi-businesses. It led me to take an interest in the 'pathology' of organisations and what has been termed 'tyrannous organisations' where information and resources are strongly centralised.[1]

Insight began in my first week. I was invited to lunch with the Director – curious about his new acquisition. A kindly colleague took me aside. 'Look,' he warned, 'when you meet him – be careful. Don't mention 'ologies': they get him very bothered.'

Though warned off 'ologies' I unfortunately had not been warned off 'theory'. The director, a practical man, had little time for theory – he should have appreciated Kurt Lewin's observation: 'There is nothing more practical than a good theory.'[2]

The director, a short, brisk man with a self-assured confidence, soon made it obvious he was indeed bothered about both 'ologies' and 'theories'. But without them it wasn't easy to explain what the course was

---

1    Mars (2013, ch. 7, pp. 111-113)
2    K. Lewin, (1952, p. 169)

about. I tried but there was little common ground, and he quickly revealed his obvious exasperation. Theories in particular seemed to irritate him. This was not because of any intellectual blindness – though that was apparent – but because he wanted his staff to present a hands-on 'practical management' image of the school and its courses that he believed would maximise income.

He began to assert more and listen less - then made clear his management style, what he called 'running a tight ship'. 'The first thing I had to do here was abolish tenure. They hated me for that.' This had been followed by 'prunings' – sackings and early retirements. As lunch proceeded, neither of us, it appeared, was much impressed with the other. My position as an invalidated new arrival was becoming clearer – then was made explicit: 'If you don't like the way we play tennis here and prefer to do ballet – then I'd advise you to go where they do ballet...'

He was pleased to tell me the school provided a significant proportion of the parent university's overheads – which is why, I surmised, they were so lax in overseeing the quality of what was sold as their business school's 'products' – and why there were surprising variations from the quality standards that (then) were routinely found elsewhere.

The business school's financial underpinning in the heady 1980s and 90s was determined not just by fees for its flagship MBA course but for tailored short courses – close to £3,000 a head for weekend residential courses In the 1980s, consultancies were charged at £1,500 for a raw lecturer, and £2,500 or more a day for senior staff. With income this high, there were strong vested interests. Indeed the university, keen to cherish its milch cow, gave its director a free hand and rapidly promoted him– now titled 'Professor' – to be the university's deputy vice chancellor.

Much can be deduced about an organisation by looking at its procedures and rules – especially if considered comparatively. Universities, for instance, have rules about the length of PhD theses; these range from 70,000 to 100,000 words. This business school however, specified a maximum of 50,000 words – little more than normally required for a research master's degree. But understanding formal rules must be complemented by assessing *informal* procedures – particularly its deviance and rule-bending. These did not feature much in the school's teachings on 'organisation'.

The school excelled at bending procedures. Some staff paid for papers bearing their names for onward submission to the RAE (the Research Assessment Exercise that governed the level of government funding). Ever sensitive to the 'the market' they settled on a fee of £500 a paper. Rule-bending extended to student recruitment. I came across one application for the Master's degree who was given a place despite his blatantly fraudulent application. When I raised it I was told: 'We're too low on numbers to bother about that.'

Because of pressure on staff to do consultancy, the research rating of the business school, at Grade 3, was lower than that of many non-research oriented ex-polytechnics.[3] This lack was only partly overcome by recourse to incessant public relations and the school's revamped and much quoted 'mission statement'.[4]

Evidence mounted to reveal how far the school was selling its market short. I was told to prepare short courses and given a budget for outside speakers. I chose a distinguished anthropologist to talk on development and its problems. This was vetoed. 'She's over seventy. Students won't take her seriously if she's over seventy.'

I proposed a course on long-wave economic cycles – that helped forecast downturns if linked to mounting levels of credit [5] – that too was vetoed. 'We don't want to spread despondency with our courses.'

This corruption especially affected staff recruitment and promotions. The director, with his allergy to both 'ologies' and theories had been the marketing director[6] of a major multinational. Of minimal academic standing, he had been appointed ahead of a notable scholar who subsequently went on to revitalise a business school elsewhere. On appointment he quickly promoted as his deputy director a lecturer who, though not shining at research, was nonetheless a whizz at selling courses and drumming up consultancy.

As well as controlling information and selection; promotions and other rewards were similarly in the director's gift. He granted 'allowances' – additional increments to selected staff members. These were not made public but given to those with high consultancy earnings or extensive public relations impacts or who in other ways appealed to him. These

---

3   Of six levels of research ratings the business school was in the fourth level from the top. In a randomly selected monthly newsletter (Sept. 1992) a column headed 'Papers and Publications' listed 13 papers, only one of which had been published in a peer-reviewed journal – the rest had been presented at gatherings and conferences. There were no books.
4   Mission statements so often appear to be PR creations directed at the outside and used as justifications for political control of the inside.
5   Which later appeared in Mars (2013, ch. 9)
6   The same marketing provenance appears to apply to several of the CEOs of banks appointed in the period immediately prior to the 2007 credit crunch – including the Royal Bank of Scotland, the biggest defaulter of all UK banks.

differentials divided and polarised staff and precluded the growth of collegial collectivity.

## Using 'Ologies' and 'Theory' to Understand the Business School

Some hierarchical controls necessarily exist in all organisations. But for an organisation to be effective, its elite's power must be modified and alternative interests given their place within an overall system of checks and balances. Otherwise an elite's unmodified power will dominate and distort the allocation of resources, monopolise control of internal communication and cause the elite to lose contact with its lowerarchy. Lowerarchies are in wider contact with an organisation's environment, and the absence of information from this source means that the elite will progressively become out of touch with aspects of its environment. This will eventually reduce its effectiveness. Where these features occur, as in this business school, we find the subversion (and often negation) of a hierarchy's checks and balances that results in a 'tyrannous organisation'[7] – a category that organisation theory has little explored.

The director controlled information both up and down the organisation. Missives, commands, injunctions and interpretive views flowed from the top while collegiate forums able to present approaches that might support alternative policies were eroded or eradicated.

When individuals expressed dissatisfaction they were typically ignored or encouraged 'to do their ballet elsewhere'. Good scholars who researched and produced publications – but generated less funding than their consultancy-rich colleagues – were side-lined and left the school. In an academic variation of Gresham's Law, 'bad academics drove out good'.[8]

This account is not applicable to *all* business schools. When I gratefully left to take a similar post in another university business school it was to find an emphasis on high academic standards and an administration where both 'ologies' and theories were appreciated. The difference was

---

7   A concept originally devised by Mary Douglas (1992, pp. 104, 144). For a development and practical application see Mars (2008). For a satirical application to universities see Mars (2003).

8   c. 2000 years ago Plato had noted that 'A ship's crew which does not understand that the art of navigation demands a knowledge of the stars, will stigmatise a properly qualified pilot as a star-gazing idiot, and will prevent him from navigating.' (Quoted by Goodall, 2009)

that here, the director was a scholar with experience of business – rather than a businessman with little experience, or feeling, for scholarship.

If a business school is judged as a business, then more mercantile criteria have to be applied than to other university endeavours. But even in the most commercial of organisations the power of its elite *must* be modified if the organisation is not to become tyrannous and is effectively to mobilise its staff and relate effectively to its environment.

CHAPTER FIFTEEN

# RESEARCH IN THE USSR: A STUDY OF THE BLACK ECONOMY IN SOVIET GEORGIA, THE CIA AND THE KGB

It began like a lot of projects in our house, over breakfast. I had just sent a manuscript to the publishers on the culture of fiddling and the black economy,[1] when Valerie asked: 'Well, that's over. What's next?' 'Well,' I said, 'it should be a study of fiddles in the Soviet Union – they're the world's experts – but just imagine trying to get permission!' 'Well, why not study it by talking to Soviet migrants in Israel, or the USA?' Beautifully simple!

Two years later, after researching the topic, I was awarded a grant. It was 1984 and the Cold War at its height. The award was for 'An Anthropological Study of the Black Economy of the Soviet Republic of Georgia'. St Antony's College at Oxford was interested in the research and offered a Senior Research Associateship to help me pursue it.

Georgia was the most corrupt (or free enterprising?) of all the Soviet republics. An estimated 30 percent of its GNP was 'underground'. There was a large community of recent Georgian migrants in Israel, and I signed up an Israeli research assistant, Yochanan Altman, to train in anthropological methods and live with them. I spent some weeks in Israel. The material flowed in; good publications came out.

Next I arranged a visit to Soviet Georgia and obtained a place on the British Council's Senior Scholars Exchange Programme. At a briefing it was explained to a group of us that this scheme was highly regarded by the Soviets. It was always the last to be scrapped when relations froze. 'This is because we send them our scholars,' a Council official explained, 'and they send us their spies.'

A further briefing explained the dangers of *femmes fatales,* bugged bedrooms and especially *agents provocateurs* who might ask us to smuggle manuscripts to the west. This last, to the Soviets, was apparently

---

1   Mars (1982)

heinous. It all sounded exhilarating, particularly as we were entitled to stay in the best hotels, have the full-time services of a guide/interpreter and enjoy a generous stipend. 'And if you have any problems, just tell them you'll have to speak to the British Cultural Attaché. That'll bring them to heel!'

Arriving home after these meetings I faced searching debriefings from Valerie. She was becoming less enthusiastic by the day and even suggested aborting the trip. But as I explained, we senior scholars were especially privileged and therefore the risks were minimal! She was not easy to convince.

I applied for a visa and approval of a programme of visits – to restaurants, hospitals, docks, shops and factories – not overtly to deduce aspects of the black economy in these workplaces but to study *aspects* of the economy. This was no more than the 'economical truth'. I felt my antennae would be able to deduce black economy activity without having to be overt about it.

Americans who quickly picked up on my research were carrying out most of the work on the Soviet Union at that time. They were extremely supportive, perhaps too much so. There was talk of mega-grants to continue and develop this work with its obviously fruitful migrant database and its original research methodology. It was suggested that there could be all sorts of expanded research opportunities: cash for research assistants, secretarial support, travel. I was naïve enough to think that I might avoid direct involvement with the intelligence services. And then, before the visa was approved, came the first fruits:

'Come to Hawaii,' said the invitation, 'and give a paper to a conference of Soviet specialists. We will pay your expenses.'

Hawaii was everything I had expected of it – even to Valerie's forecast of a slice of pineapple on the steak. The hotel was magnificent and the paper went down wonderfully. During it I mentioned I was due to visit Georgia and one of the organisers later asked if I had a visa. 'Not yet,' I said, it's in process.'

'Well,' came the answer, 'I wouldn't bank on it.'

'Why not?'

'Because we can't guarantee the security of this conference.'

'What does that mean?'

'It means,' came the jaundiced reply, 'that they have their spies here. They'll report back on your research.'

A charming young woman with a beautiful smile, a Soviet scholar at a leading west coast university then sought me out. She had heard I planned to visit Georgia.

'If the Soviets give you a visa, could you do me a wonderful favour?'
'It would be a pleasure.'
'And deliver a message to a friend of mine, in Tbilisi?'
'No problem, really.'
'She badly needs medicines and they're only available from the States.'
'But of course, whatever I can do to help.'
'That would be marvellous. Thank you, thank you so much.'
She would write me before I left.

At my next debriefing from Valerie and before I had even begun to describe the appealing young woman and my errand of mercy, she was positive the visit should be aborted.

The visa did come through. So did the letter from my charming American together with a letter I was to recite to her friend. It was long and peculiarly complex.

'Dear Tamara,' it began reasonably and then followed complex technical data about medicines, their chemical names and quantities and, if these were unsuitable, a range of equally complex chemical alternatives. I was to learn all of this in detail by heart – it being 'better not to take this letter with you – indeed it would be 'better to destroy it'. The last paragraph contained instructions on how to use a Soviet phone box – it apparently being 'inadvisable to phone from the hotel'. It was now impossible to kid myself further – I was in it up to the ears.

I assured Valerie I wouldn't attempt to deliver the message and that the full might of the British Council was behind this visit. Nothing could happen to me. I was after all 'A Senior Scholar'. Oh hubris! And of course I would phone home. She proved harder to convince by the hour.

In Moscow, on route to Tbilisi, I had a few hours to spare before meeting the Cultural Attaché with whom I was initially to stay. I took a taxi and was amused (as someone who was supposed to know about fiddles) when the taxi driver gave me obsolete (and worthless) currency in exchange for a high value note. Taxi drivers of the world it seems, are united.

The British Council's briefing proved its worth. In an English-language bookshop there was an attempt at a chat-up and proposition. But it was not, after all, a *femme fatale* but an English-speaking youth. Perhaps the KGB was relying on stereotypical views of the English? Or of Cambridge? I would discuss this with the cultural attaché. He was sharp and alert. I had not been in his flat for two minutes however, when he waved me to silence.

'We're bugged, of course. Be careful what you say.'

But of course! It was a relief next morning to settle into his car.

'Talking of…' I began.

'Be careful. The car's bugged.'

It was only then that it fully struck me – this really wasn't a game. Thank goodness I was protected by the British Council's Senior Scholars Exchange Programme.

Tbilisi airport after midnight was cold and damp when I touched down. Another charming young woman awaited me.

She beamed a welcome. 'Dr Mars?'

'Yes,' I answered eagerly. 'You're my interpreter/guide?'

'No,' came the let-down. 'I'm taking you to two men who want to see you.'

The two were waiting in a sparse office on the far side of the airport. They were identically tall, broad, utterly uncommunicative and without even a spasm of facial mobility. They both had long dark coats. They beckoned me to a car. 'Where are we going?'

'We are taking you to your room,' was the reply.

A sick joke? Was my room to be a dungeon somewhere?

We travelled into the countryside for about eight miles – in silence – then drew up at a series of shabby huts that looked like and probably was an old army compound. It did not seem like a Georgian *Lubyanka* but it was not the best hotel in town either. It turned out to be a students' hostel but with few students. I was shown to a tiny room. Lit by bare light-bulbs, with unadorned, fly-blown walls, it had five beds – but only, it seemed, because they could not have quite managed a sixth. At least it wasn't a dungeon.

I protested vigorously. They were uninterested in the Senior Scholars Programme, my rights to the best hotel in town, my entitlement to an interpreter/guide, the British Council – even the threat of the Cultural Attaché.'

'Tomorrow!' was the reply to my every protest.

Around midday a recognisable human being, affable but wary, came to see me. This was Michael, a young academic with excellent English but in answering questions, as closed as a clam. He would be available as my contact but not all of the time – he had other duties. The university would act as my host. What then about my agreed programme? My hotel? My full-time guide? I insisted on speaking to the Cultural Attaché.

'Later, later. Calls to Moscow are very difficult.'

The next day I found it had not been possible to arrange any part of my agreed programme. I was, it seemed, destined only for a long series of uncommunicative non-conversations with a changing group of nervous academics. They were being rotated on 'duty watch' and had obviously been told I was dangerous. Meanwhile, lines to Moscow and the attaché were said to be constantly down. I booked a call to Valerie. Lines to London were down too, of course. I then insisted I wanted to abort the visit. I wanted the next flight back to Moscow, then to home – I wanted to get entirely out of it.

'All seats on planes to Moscow are booked.'

'Then I insist on phoning the British Council in London.'

'All lines to London are down.'

But the threat partly worked. Two days later, I was moved to a hotel – and though far from luxurious, it really was the best in town. Michael came to collect me but he was still clam-like. There was no contact with the attaché, no progress on the programme or any sign of the guide. I tried again to book a call home. Lines to London were still down.

Next morning, moving through the hotel lobby to breakfast, my way was barred by a shabby, bearded loiterer. Clutching a manuscript, he muttered quietly at me in Georgian, edged me to a corner, then pushed the manuscript at me. So the British Council really were on the ball! I recoiled and thrust it back. He did not seem to understand and tried again. He then addressed me in Russian. I side-stepped. So did he. He then started to speak in poor English. The more he tried to force the manuscript on me, the more vehemently I refused. We became engaged in a cross-cultural quadrille. Surprisingly, with each refusal, his English improved. Eventually however, he had to accept my outrageously pious: 'I can't possibly take your manuscript. I'm a guest of your government.' He moved off.

Perhaps because of this good behaviour, there was another breakthrough. That night at 3 a.m. I was shaken awake. My call to London was through and I was able to speak to a vastly relieved Valerie for twenty minutes. At 7 a.m. the 'landing babushka' [2] came to collect the cost – an extortionate 120 roubles – £120 sterling at the then exchange rate that took most of my allowance.

Later that morning, in my desultory group of wary academics, I was seated next to the professor of psychology. A large rotund fellow, he looked the type who might enjoy a drink and a joke. Now however, like the rest, he was solemn and brooding. Busy doodling on a sheet of paper, he then pushed it to me. I looked and recognised a famous diagram from managerial psychology – it was 'Likert's Linking Pin' diagram relating

2 Under the Soviet regime each floor of every hotel used by foreigners had an official who kept track of, and recorded, the activities of all the guests' movements. It was a job that seemed to be a sinecure for old grandmothers.

different levels of management to their staffs. Anthropologists learn some odd things!

'Oh,' I said, 'Likert's Linking Pin! Do you teach Likert here?' Likert after all was an American management specialist.

He stared. 'You recognise Likert's Pin?'

'Of course.'

He turned to the group with new enthusiasm. 'He knows Likert's Pin! He recognises it!'

This was my *rite de passage.* I instantly morphed from dangerous spy to validated fellow scholar (though of course, I could have been both). The conversation was transformed, became animated, exploratory: they wanted to know about the UK's educational system and especially the latest thinking in the social sciences. They wanted to know what life was like for an English academic. And they were having a picnic in the woods later that afternoon. Would I come? Tomorrow there was to be a feast. Could I manage that too?

At the next staff gathering I had a question.

'Tell me,' I said, 'are your international phone calls really as expensive as the rate they've just charged me?'

'How much did they charge you?'

'120 roubles.'

They gasped.

'For how long were you talking? Who were you talking to?'

I told them I had been speaking for twenty minutes to my wife. To my surprise the professor choked with laughter. He turned to the group and with a wink and a lavish gesture brought all the gathering into his joke: 'Aha! We charged him 120 roubles... And for twenty minutes,' he gurgled, 'he *thought* he was talking to his wife!' Their laughter erupted.

But though accepted by my new-found colleagues, I was still obviously a suspect and still not allowed to follow my programme, though I enjoyed being a guest at a variety of feasts. Nonetheless, it was with relief at the end of my scheduled stay that I set out for Moscow airport – where the next ratchet tightened.

'Papers, please.'

I passed them over.

'Wait here.'

I was taken from the queue to a cubicle. Other passengers came – and went. Departure time was getting close.

'Look!' I complained. 'Why is there this delay? I'm in danger of missing my plane.'

A shrug. Finally I was told: 'You have not clearance. Come this way please.'

And then through the cubicle's open doorway, summoned on my behalf by the Goddess of Serendipity, strode the cultural attaché on his way home on leave. Slipping my keeper I called him.

'I'm afraid you've not quite finished with me yet.'

The cultural attaché swung into action. A few authoritative phone calls was all it needed. And this time they really did come to heel! A huddle of Soviet officials conferred – and orders were given for my release. Thankfully I made my way to the waiting British Airways flight. And thanked God for the British Council – and the Cultural Attaché.

Postscript: I came home and wrote to my charming American that I hadn't, after all, transmitted her message. She never replied. But thereafter there were no more enthusiastic suggestions about grants for bigger and better research programmes. Eager prospective collaborators ceased to offer encouragement; or even retain contact; proposals in process went unfunded. Some months later, a good paper I had been encouraged to submit to an important academic journal in the States was rejected out of hand. What was surprising was not the rejection but its blatant content. The anonymous referee's assessment was, according to convention, sent to me. It read: 'I do not think we should accept this paper when *one of our own* [my emphasis] is due to come on stream in three months or so.'

It was pleasing finally to get a straight response – and a relief not to be thought one of 'their own'. And it was revealing to realise how the intelligence services penetrate academia. Not too difficult, I surmised, if other academics were as naïve as me.

In the event, though my visit to Soviet Georgia had not gone as planned, attendance at their feasts proved an invaluable source of information. I learned that in Georgian society which emphasises networking and feasting, feasts were in fact personal networks made manifest. They extended contacts, consolidated relationships, cemented the links between members of different organisations and facilitated deals – all functions necessary to the black economy.[3]

The overall research was highly successful in uncovering the working of that state's black economy. The breakthrough came as a result of my research assistant, Yochanan Altman, being able to live with members of one nearly complete community of Jews from the same Georgian town who had migrated in bulk to Israel. Through them we were able to

---

3   Elaborated in Mars & Altman (1983)

reconstruct the processes of production – from illicitly obtained raw materials through to final distribution.

We homed in on ex-workers from a single biscuit factory and, by cross-checking informant accounts, found how its management were able to distort their targeted plans; how this involved collusion with all levels of the workforce; how they obtained finance and raw materials; arranged the printing of counterfeit labels (where all printing was centrally controlled and even typewriters were licensed); showed who had to be bribed (including the police chief and his deputy[4]) and with how much, and – in a state where transportation and fuel were rigidly controlled – how they transported the final products with false documentation. We did the same to show how the stores too, coordinated a parallel distributive network – no mean feat when roads were patrolled by police continually checking vehicles in transit.

We were able to reconstruct the extent of Georgia's subterranean and parallel economy with detailed examples of each stage's operation. We showed in effect that the rigidities of a Soviet command economy could not operate without its symbiotic black economy and how this was underpinned and facilitated by Georgia's feasting and networking.[5]

There are pointers here to understand some of the emerging dilemmas facing managements in liberal economies. With growing globalisation and increasing competition, outputs and targets are often set by far away controllers, as in the Soviet Union. Managers at plant level will therefore increasingly be liable to use informal and deviant means to achieve targets.[6]

---

4    'Why both?' we queried.' Obviously both,' was the reply. 'What if the chief is away when there's about to be a purge?'
5    Mars & Altman (1988a; 1988b)
6    Mars & Altman (2008)

CHAPTER SIXTEEN

# MAGIC AND THE MULTINATIONAL

By the mid-seventies Valerie and I had two children, and since we had decided she would stay at home to look after them, I once again sought extra earnings. One well-paid part-time job was as a quasi-psychologist advising on the selection of fast-track graduate managers for a major multinational. Sitting on selection boards was valuable in learning how they worked – and not least – in how psychologists thought. But it also revealed how magic pervaded this aspect of life in the West that we think of as rational – as governed purely by objective science and (western) logic – when it is nothing of the sort.

The boards met at 8:30 and over coffee and biscuits members introduced ourselves and discussed the candidates. With a personnel specialist as chairman and a junior executive 'runabout', my role, as one of two consultant magicians was to advise four senior executives who made the final selections. They had seniority, power, prestige and imposing rooms. We supplied comforting divination, magical measurements and esoteric rituals – all disguised as the output of 'behavioural science consultants'.

We magicians were not surprised that selectors were often tense. To select a duff candidate could reflect adversely on them, perhaps for years. They therefore aimed for unanimity, especially on marginal cases. After all there is security in a group decision, even a daft one.[1]

Selection is particularly prone to insecurity: it deals with intrusions across the organisation's boundary from outsiders aiming to become insiders. Boundaries, both conceptual and physical, have long been noted as sources of danger. Anthropologists frequently observe how entering and leaving doorways and the doorways themselves are often marked by ritual,

---

1  This is a reference to 'Group Think' – a feature of groups – common to committees within organisations that exert a pressure to making consensus decisions without critical reasoning or assessment of consequences. Group think derives from a desire not to exhibit conflict and it negates creativity and individuality (Janis, 1972).

talismans and magic. So it should not surprise that underpinning the whole selection process was this belief in our magic: we were there to reduce uncertainty in an uncertain and dangerous world.

Accordingly, we magicians gave reassuring answers to questions the selectors raised. Yes, we asserted, it is certainly possible to select people rationally. And yes, we could advise whether a candidate would or would not 'fit' the company's culture – when no-one could define what a 'fit' involved or what that culture was about. And yes, we assured them, we could identify the elements that make a good manager and, even more, we would rate all candidates on a comparative scale and, if pressed, even suggest how they might develop over a lifetime.

To give selectors what they wanted, we used the latest psychometric tests and watched candidates perform group tasks. We calculated, appraised, graded and compared their intelligences; assessed their personalities and estimated and ranked their adaptability and creativity. We interviewed them – one-to-one and in pairs. We determined their maturity, diplomacy, tenacity and 'social skills' – anything indeed that might justify our assessments of whether they would make fast-track managers. And where we possibly could, we measured these attributes. We ignored of course that most were not measurable at all; we had the backing of our tests that provided objective, finite and comparative scores.[2]

It is emphasised that despite flaws, this system is more effective than many selection procedures that preceded it, which often amounted to 'selection by hunch.' And at least this method tries to avoid prejudice and partiality.

Further rationality was provided by the accumulated managerial experience of the four selectors. Though our tests provided some useful and objective insights, we were there primarily to supply a 'science-backed' magical confidence-boost where uncertainty was high, especially when assessing marginal candidates. But a weakness was evident at the core of the process. Nearly all the company's senior managers who acted as selectors had successfully passed through similar boards. Obviously therefore, the process was brilliant at selecting the very best: its very consistency confirmed its efficacy! It was sanctified; so sacred was it that nobody since it started had dared question, let alone subject it to rigorous assessment – to study say, the subsequent careers of in-post managers and

---

2   Such selection methods however, tend to use too limited a definition of intelligence - usually based solely on tests of logical deductive reasoning instead of also acknowledging other types of intelligence- especially intuitive emotional and streetwise intelligence. See Gardner (1999).

compare them to their selection performances. This day though, was to be different...

Our magician forebears who had designed the system and we, their successors who validated them for close to forty years, gave it further validity. One difference however, was that one day, among our selectors was 'a Very Senior Executive indeed.' A big, confident man, he had a chin that protruded like a shelf and he demonstrated his high rank with an over-loud voice.

We should have sensed the day was cursed. Mr Chin used his introduction to challenge the whole *raison d'être* that had brought us together. It was 8:45 when he announced his very own secret of selection. 'What I always look for,' he boomed, 'is the size of a man's chin. It never fails.'

He was telling us – not just that our complex and sacrosanct selection system was rubbish, our attendance and tests a nonsense, that our emperor had no clothes – but that he had a ready-made suit of his own that was easy to slip on and fitted perfectly. We were not reassured but there was no discussion, just an embarrassed shuffling of papers. He was after all a Very Senior Executive. I too kept quiet: my own chin made me far too vulnerable. I wondered though, whether he had a similarly simple formula that might be applied to women?

The rest of the morning was spent giving tests and observing group tasks but at last came lunch. Board lunches were often spirited and relaxed; today they were subdued. And during lunch, the board secretary, was called to the phone. He returned, hesitant. 'I'm afraid there's something serious I have to tell you.'

What he told us stunned the group. Three months before, the company had selected an outstanding Oxbridge student. I remembered him well – he had been the star of one of my boards – a handsome, confidant man with a stratospheric IQ. And he had worked brilliantly in groups, both as leader and follower. His analytic skills were highly refined. He had taken Firsts in his first two years, been awarded a Blue, been captain of the team and been president of a political club. At the board he easily surpassed other candidates on all the tests and in every exercise. Each year produced only one or two such stars. Here was one on whom indeed the gods had smiled.

Discussion was hardly necessary. That day's selectors vied to recruit him to their companies. Appointed by return, he accepted a coveted post and for three months fully justified his promise. And then the plot unravelled.

His application was a dazzling work of fiction – he had never been an Oxbridge student. He was a college servant – who had validly used the college address as his own. His superb academic record, sporting success, his chairmanship of a political club were all false. There was no suggestion that his brilliant and creative performance might permit him to stay. I thought his entrepreneurial selling of himself would alone have been worth harnessing? But no, he had been instantly sacked.

When they had digested this debacle the selectors sat silent. Yes, there would be blame though this fault was the responsibility of a different board. But worse than blame, much worse, was evidence that even senior executives could be utterly conned, even in unison, even with attendant magicians. If the company had asked for references, the fraud may have emerged but selectors were too secure in the perfection of their process. After all the majority of them had successfully come through it. Now, if finitely measurable calculations and years of executive experience backed by authoritative magic could no longer be trusted, what could? It takes only a lack of faith to undermine magic.

By late afternoon, after probing interviews, came final assessments. There was limited, muted discussion but at least the selectors had consensus and no-one stepped out of line. Seven of the eight candidates were quickly dealt with: none passed. The eight, however, like the college servant before him, appeared worryingly outstanding. His IQ and social skills were impeccable. As an undergraduate he had established a business for the sale of second-hand, high-performance, Italian sports cars. It extended over three counties. He was making a fortune. His very excellence raised doubts. Even his chin was impressive.

'Why,' asked a selector, 'is he prepared to sacrifice all this to be a management trainee?'

Large companies tend to give lip service to the idea of recruiting entrepreneurs but always find them difficult to cope with. Being individualists they tend not to work well in groups – 'a sure sign of immaturity' insisted the ever-supportive psychologist magicians. The success rate of entrepreneurs at the boards was low, which again of course only proved the rightness of the process. Further, they can be unpredictable and, worse, they tend not to respect authority. But how to justify not appointing this entrepreneur was going to be difficult. So discussion meandered and flowed without getting anywhere. The board needed unity and certainty and we magicians, being impotent, could give neither: our magic was flawed.

But magic can be surprisingly resistant: it survives because 'bypass loops' allow for the negation of unwelcome evidence. Quite unwittingly, I offered just such a loop.[3] 'Just imagine,' I mused aloud to break the tension, 'just imagine the dilemma if he were to park his Maserati beside the chairman's Jag?'

The image was ludicrous – but for the first time that long day, the selectors smiled. They began to chat. Without realising it, this magician had produced a new and effective spell: uncertainty was banished; this candidate could be failed. He so obviously would not fit into that capacious, all purpose, portmanteau: 'the company culture'. Voting was unanimous: the candidate failed. 'Group Think' had won again.

The board broke up – jovial and relaxed at a good day's work well done. And though we had just sunk that season's best candidate, no-one – certainly not the Very Senior Executive – had dared, even once, to mention his chin!

Bronislaw Malinowski, one of the founding fathers of modern anthropology first looked at the function of magic in dispersing uncertainty when participants otherwise lacked control of their environments. In studying the South Seas Trobriand Islanders,[4] he showed how they did two kinds of fishing – lagoon and open sea. The first was safe, predictable and secure; the second was extremely hazardous. Lagoon fishing involved no magic; sea fishing however, as with these selection boards, could not proceed without a whole range of ritualised magical procedures. The belief that magic removes uncertainty lies behind a lot of our own behaviours. Many of us, for example, own charms and amulets, swear by the use of 'lucky' pens at bingo sessions or have images of St Christopher hanging in our cars. But psychometric tests are so much more 'scientific' and 'rational'. Are they not?

---

3   This is another example of the 'bypass loop' discussed in footnote 11, p.45 by which magic survives because it allows for the negation of unwelcome evidence. See Evans-Pritchard, quoted in Gluckman (1955, p. 215).

4   Malinowski (1954, pp. 30-31).

CHAPTER SEVENTEEN

# LEARNING FROM NIGERIANS
# AND AVOIDING 'WA-WA'

Glancing out of the cabin as our plane dipped in descent over Lagos airport I was startled to see a crashed wreck at the side of the runway. My colleague Peter, with long experience throughout Africa and a trained pilot, leaned over unperturbed, and remarked, 'It's still there, then.' It had, it seemed, been there for several years.

Peter explained: the wreck offered a cheap, effective and beautifully simple way to deliver a crucial message. It was a low-tech warning to descending pilots to take especial care in landing at a difficult airport. There followed two weeks of privileged insight – and intense learning.

The two of us had been asked as consultants to advise a quasi-government institute in Nigeria on its management practices and organisation. But the assignment allowed me to appreciate how cross-cultural contacts so often involve misunderstanding and stress – and to learn how Nigerians solve problems in ways we could not contemplate. The visit offered sound lessons in negating ethnocentrism.

The appalling Lagos traffic soon provided another good example. This was the period of military rule in Nigeria and. in the absence of traffic signals, directing traffic at each major cross-roads depended on a gesticulating soldier with a whistle in one hand and a whip in the other. Drivers who ignored his whistles and gestures were liable to be ordered out of their cars and given a whipping. I never saw anyone whipped – but the traffic was certainly well disciplined and flowed smoothly.

We of course find the idea of arbitrary and severe punishment unsustainable: our ideas of punishment are based on Individualism and the value we place on individual variances. But in cultures derived from and sharing the values of small-scale, integrated, face-to-face communities, it is threats to the collective that are deemed extremely serious, and group power to control them is considerable. This is difficult to appreciate in cultures such as ours where groups, though plentiful, are not all-embracing or overly powerful, so that by our standards their punishments appear severe. Sanctions invoked under Sharia law, for example, provide myriad examples – from the stoning of adulterous women to the amputation of thieves' hands. The Individualist bias in Israel compared to the strong group bias in Arab states helps explain why the Israelis will exchange a thousand Arab prisoners for one Israeli. And why the one can equably countenance the use of suicide bombers that is anathema to the other (and also why there is no shortage of volunteer bombers who wish to serve the group).These differences are spelled out in Chapter 21.

We spent the next few days interviewing senior staff. But suddenly, on the third day, none were available. Why? I asked.

'They're sitting on a selection board?'

'All of them? Must be an important job?'

'Yes – it's for a new doorman.'

Why should the entire directorate be pulled out to select a doorman? The answer again was deceptively simple but not overt: the institute had a national mission and therefore had to represent all ethnic groups. But since employment was highly valued, anyone able to grant benefits was expected to give preferment to their kinsfolk first or at least to their own ethnic group. The strains on benefit-givers were massive since for every job there were usually about ten applicants – and nine rejections. But a selection board not only cut out partiality, it avoided responsibility. Each member could say in all truth: 'I did my best – but what could I do? I was only one of seven.' Yet another lesson.

Peter and I were treated with lavish respect. It was embarrassing to be regarded as such experts that our every word was listened to with what seemed like awe. Even the most senior staff seemed overly impressed that I was a doctor and used the title repetitively.

After yet another respectful interview discussing matters with the membership director responsible for recruitment, I broached the possibility of my own membership of the institute which normally required a basic qualification in management and some experience. I was startled therefore at a sudden contrast in his demeanour – from subordinate respect to inordinate control. He drew himself up – shot me a haughty glance – and barked interrogatively: 'And what are your qualifications?'

This sudden shift could have been interpreted in negative stereotypical terms – as say, the possibly expected response to a reversal of power and authority. But reflection offered a more convincing explanation. In cultures based on small, face-to-face communities people simultaneously hold a number of roles. Occasionally one role needs to be split off to give it especial emphasis.[1] This is typically achieved visually – by ritually painting the body, wearing a mask, special clothes or regalia. The same happens in our own culture. A mayor's chain of office, for example, separates a mayoral role from an incumbent's routine role as, say, 'Sam the butcher'. Here the membership director asserted differences in his roles through his bearing and demeanour – which was all he could mobilise at short notice.

Asserting a role is often achieved by wearing a uniform. And sometimes the very wearing of a uniform defines the role. I recall a journalist present at the filming of *Oh What a Lovely War* who noticed that in breaks between scenes those wearing the uniforms of other ranks would open their collars, loosen their ties and hunker down over mugs of tea. Those wearing officers' uniforms remained standing in a separate group, their collars and ties intact.

In our first week, collaboration went well. The institute's staff seemed enthusiastic, and together we prepared schedules, plans and projections that were popular, agreed-to and were well-received. And then... nothing: coordinated schedules remained uncoordinated; time-based arrangements we had all agreed to were left unarranged – or missed. Were the Nigerians rejecting everything we had agreed together?

And then it became clearer. We were operating on 'western industrial time', they on a developed form of 'pre-industrial African time'. We viewed time as linear – once gone it was gone forever: they viewed time pre-industrially, as infinite, as cyclical – as in agriculture, so that an opportunity once missed would re-present itself.[2] Once we understood this, we were reassured and work proceeded, albeit not as fast as we had planned.

It is in industrially-based societies that the coordination of people is primarily organised through time – time *is* money – and urgency is a constant. The greater the degree of linearity, the greater the urgency – which is why wristwatches are necessarily widespread in the West. And why in Africa, those who wish to demonstrate their affinity with development and thus with linear time, invariably wear a wristwatch – often an extra-large one. But there are variances of linearity. In most of the US the tolerated time allowed for a late appointment is about five minutes; in the UK, fifteen, in Greece an hour – and in most of North Africa – up to a day. When working in Soviet Georgia – a culture that shares many

---

1   Thus says Gluckman, these may be termed 'Multiplex' roles and ritual is
    usually necessary to stop one role being intruded upon by others. Gluckman
    (1962, pp. 70-71)
2   Allen (1994, pp. 503-526)

Mediterranean characteristics, I found its officials on visiting Moscow, were subject to metropolitan constraints. When they went there they wore watches they did not wear in Georgia.

I had planned whilst in Nigeria to explore the notoriously endemic problem of corruption as a hindrance to development. I raised it – tactfully I considered – with the organisation's director general. I thought we would have an obvious area of agreement. Not so: I received a sharp rebuke. 'A lot of what you call corruption', he insisted, 'I don't call corruption at all. Much of it I call 'redistribution. What I call 'corruption' is when money is salted away in Swiss bank accounts. That's real corruption. Redistribution is different – it's vital in spreading wealth'. Not perhaps an argument the World Bank might appreciate, but surely worth some understanding where poverty is extensive, the distribution of wealth is extremely unequal, where social welfare is minimal and obligations of reciprocity are more widespread and more extensive than in the West.

A closely related source of cultural misunderstanding comes through different cultures rating the priorities of others ethnocentrically. I recall a colleague's account[3] of the dilemma faced by World Bank officials in India who had agreed to fund the construction of a village irrigation scheme. When they returned after a year they found nothing had been done. Construction hadn't even started; instead the funds had been spent on building a rather splendid temple. When the officials protested, the village elders replied: 'But how could we possibly start building an irrigation scheme without first placating the gods?'

It is easy to sneer at alien practices when thinking ethnocentrically. And very easy to lack experience of the differential rating of priorities in different cultures. Ex-pats shake their heads at Nigerian ways and, when things don't go according to (their) plan, may be heard to resignedly mutter, 'WA-WA' (West Africa Wins Again). Yet ingenuity and intelligence often find solutions to problems we in the developed world do not now have to face – especially where there is a shortage of capital, inadequate infrastructure and absence of state social security. A wreck at the side of a runway or a controller of traffic with a whip can tell more than appears; much 'corruption' undoubtedly does satisfy important social needs, while the negation of punctuality often derives from different perceptions of time and a differing order of priorities.

The perceived savagery of punishments and disregard for individuals are not easy for members of western industrialised societies to understand whilst nepotism and partiality can well be the result of social pressures

---

3    Dr Michael Thompson, personal communication

impossible to ignore. Yet one does not necessarily condone alien practices by understanding them.

The big asset of anthropology is that it allows us to understand a culture by appreciating how its own people view it – not judge it through the distorting prism of one's own ethnocentricity. The five archetypal ways of categorising cultures outlined in Chapter 21 should prove of considerable help in this respect.

CHAPTER EIGHTEEN

# CHAMELEONS:
# THE RISE OF THE AUTARCHS

Anthropologists are always 'in play'; one cannot stop noticing and applying the tenets of one's craft. It was in the ordinary processes of living – hiring a gardener, attending an adult education class, chatting to friends – that I first came to recognise the common features and significance of what appears to be a newly-emerging social entity.

Though its members vary widely, they have similar values, attitudes and behaviours: they prefer to travel light in terms of both goods and relationships. They have a preference for part-time work and short-term contracts and have a sensitivity against being exploited – or of exploiting others. I call them Autarchs.[1]

Underpinning and justifying these characteristics is one dominating concern – their wish above all to be autonomous.[2]

## Richard: the Adaptable Gardener/Teacher/Photographer

Richard planned and planted our garden. He works every summer for a variety of different employers – 'so I'm not beholden to any one'. In winter he is a teacher of photography in a college of further education – 'but only part-time'.

We were impressed by Richard's expertise and honest costing when compared with other gardeners. He is a strategist: his effectiveness allows him to choose who he works for, when, and under what conditions.

Richard (42) and his partner Norma (37) have been together for seven years and have no children. They have followed typical Autarch careers.

---

1 Some aspects of this grouping were originally defined by Mike Thompson (1996) who termed them 'Hermits'.
2 In Cultural Theory terms – see Chapter 21 – they occupy the fifth solidarity in that they reject affiliation to any of the CT categories since involvement necessarily involves the acceptance of their characteristic constraints.

After abandoning a literature degree, Richard travelled for eight months in Africa. On his return he worked for eight years in the family language-teaching business, and in this period he married. After his divorce he completed an MA and enrolled for a PhD but could not get funding. Next he did a degree in photography and then he took up gardening: '...because I wanted to be flexible and be my own boss. And because it would allow me to do [freelance] photography. But you know how things develop – it took over. I certainly did not want to end up in an office working for some exploiting firm.'

Norma too was working on a PhD but never completed. She works for a charity and has done so full-time for two and a half years ('she has a very strong social conscience, firm beliefs'). At the time of writing, Norma planned to go to Nepal in two months to teach. After the end of Richard's current term at the FE college, and when he has saved enough, he says he will follow her. (And he did.) He's unsure how long for, or quite what he'll do in Nepal. 'I could teach or do admin – and I would like to do some photo-journalism – I've done a bit of that.'

Intelligent, adaptable and observant, Richard finds that types of garden give him a good insight into his customers' view of their worlds – and their garden preferences. He applies his insights to understand, anticipate and cater to their needs: a rarity where jobbing gardeners tend to offer 'packages' of their own preferences that often override those of their customers. His insights give him a competitive advantage in choosing or rejecting customers.

Richard finds marked distinctions between the gardens of well-organised hierarchic households and those of opportunist Entrepreneurs. The first adhere to convention, rules and precedents, preferring closely-defined layouts, firm boundaries, disciplined flowerbeds and well-clipped hedges. They want orthodox designs, and traditional plants.[3] Their owners draw inspiration from elite country-house gardens. He finds the gardens of Entrepreneurs are very different. They tend to reject classification and convention, often prefer a wild appearance, maximise display and push for the latest in gardening styles, plants and design – decking, fountains, statuary and the newest in unusual or exotic plants. 'Their gardens are for showing off,' says Richard.

As one might expect, collectively oriented households want their gardens sown with wild-flower seeds to be fertilised with natural compost. Richard's approach allows him to anticipate and cater to the needs of even

---

3    I have found these preferences particularly well represented in the gardens of established suburban households..

this relatively unusual preference: he tolerantly does what is requested, adapting to and making suggestions that mirror his customers' preferences. Richard's pragmatic adaptability emerges well in this account of how he treats his resources relative to consumption.

> I try to have a fund for reserve – but it fluctuates a lot. I try to avoid credit cards – I've a great suspicion of those. I rely on cash. I'm even a bit suspicious of cheques but I'm getting used to them. I don't like borrowing – unless I absolutely have to – and I borrow as little as possible. If there's something on the horizon then we'll batten down the hatches until it arrives. Otherwise I'll borrow if I have to. But first I'll extend the overdraft. I can go to the family. But that would be exceptional. I never borrow from friends. My aim is always to keep income and spending in a balance. We've room to cut down. But usually there's a chance to earn extra if we have to.

> I keep my involvement with tax minimal and don't go in for claiming expenses – and I don't claim benefits – I never have. I prefer to work – it's a question of avoidance.' [By this he means avoiding involvement with bureaucracies and their procedures – not avoidance of tax.]

> We've led a nomadic existence – moved around a lot. We've not kept contact with childhood friends. Neither of us has a big circle. Most [of my] leisure is spent with Norma – mostly the cinema or TV or with Norma's friends. We mostly go for walks with friends over the downs and we'll perhaps end up in a pub. Not otherwise though – we're not pub-goers. We've been involved in environmental things and we've helped clear some sites.

> With gardening, I taught myself – read up a fair amount. It's been the case that I've benefited from recommendations. I would like to continue gardening but not rely on it. It needs networking, and positive networking isn't something I'm particularly strong at.

Richard's friends are similar in ideology, occupation and behaviour – none wants a nine-to-five schedule; all prefer short-term contracts and eschew competitive achievement with its dependence on 'positive networking'; none maximise their income and none have children. All would rather avoid anything that involves, as they see it, exploiting others, and all object to 'exploitative employers'. 'I would be surprised to find an organisation that isn't trying to fleece you in some way.'

Two months after this was written Richard followed Norma to Nepal. He left no forwarding address and did not indicate a likely return date. Autarchs travel light; they 'cancel and move on'.[4] In social activities, as in

---

4   Strinberg (1900)

financial affairs, they avoid obligations and reciprocities that might limit their autonomy

## Mary: the Consultant Squatter

I met Mary when working on a project commissioned by a major multinational. In her mid-forties, Mary worked as a marketing consultant. Neatly coiffed, wearing a severe black business-type suit and a discreet pearl necklace, she sensitively related to all the executives we worked with and was well regarded by them. But don't be fooled! At the end of each day she packed her briefcase – and returned to her squat in North London.

Mary effectively straddles the worlds of bureaucracy and collectives. She is at home in hierarchic multinationals as a highly competitive professional and equally at home in her collective and egalitarian squat, whose members share their incomes, accommodation and way of life. But none of these command her central loyalty. Her involvement with them is subordinate to her central interest – to be autonomous. She is an archetypal Autarch, not least because at first glance she would be difficult to distinguish from denizens of the other worlds in which she mixes: she is indeed a chameleon who, in the short term, changes colour according to context.

## Elaine: Writer, Part-Time Teacher and Ex-Solicitor

Elaine teaches creative writing. We met when I joined her classes, and in getting to know something of her history noted how aspects of her background and interests closely paralleled those of other Autarchs that had crossed my path.

Elaine, also in her forties, was employed as a well-paid solicitor until she had a 'messy divorce' when she reappraised her life and decided to follow her hobby – writing. Her income is a fifth of what it was, but in five years she has published three books of poetry and a number of articles. Her basic but just adequate income mostly derives from part-time teaching in an adult education college.

Autarchs like Elaine and Mary may be engaged simultaneously with all of the other groupings they reject. But such involvements tend to be partial and periodic. In their moves from job to job and often from place to place, they may be thought shiftless – but this is not so: there is an overall strategy to further their aim – to be autonomous.

## James: Freelance Film Animator and Fork-Lift driver

James shares the same defining characteristics, attitudes and behaviours as Richard, Mary and Elaine. He works when he can as a nomadic film animator. But such work is based on short contracts so he readily travels the world to find work that suits him. The level of pay is a low priority. Nor is he constrained as are most of us by entanglements of residence: he ignores leases and mortgages – he lives on a canal boat. Like the others he takes pains not to become enmeshed in the constraints of financial dependency.

> I keep three bank accounts – in Europe, the US and the UK so my funds are independent of exchange rate fluctuations – and I aim to keep up a slush-fund, about three thousand pounds in all, so I can move around. And if I have to get work between jobs, then I'm a licensed fork-lift driver which is a skilled job. There's always a need for fork-lift drivers – they too are short contract (high turnover) jobs – so whenever I call at a factory I can usually get work.

## Overall

When one examines Autarch budgets we find an emphasis on balance between income and expenditure, ends and means. Comparisons with the budgeting of other lifestyles reveal basic differences. Competitive Entrepreneurs strive to expand their incomes to match expanding consumption while bureaucratised Hierarchs follow rules that keep both in unison at a level appropriate to their relative position. Egalitarian collectivists – such as those sharing Mary's squat – typically 'manage down' – they reduce their consumption as a first priority then accommodate it to their lower incomes.

Autarchs, in attempting to minimise the constraints of alliances, nonetheless need to engage with those of other solidarities. Of course, most people simultaneously engage with different groupings for different purposes but most people accommodate to them and accept the constraints involved. Autarchs however, limit their accommodations to minimise the constraints they involve. They especially abhor the pressures of competitive individualism with its insistent tension to expand and improve the 'quality' and usefulness of networks and the pressures to competitively display.

If the Autarch is not over-concerned to network – the mark of competitive Entrepreneurs – then neither are they 'group people'. They reject full-hearted involvements in collective groupings offered by the

Egalitarians since these too involve accepting constraints – in this case the conformity (and often demonstrated piety) that is inherent to collectivism. Nor are they happy to have a place in hierarchic bureaucracies with their constraining rules, procedures, precedents and ranks. Their involvements are minimised and calculated in the furtherance of autonomy.[5]

Autarchs may be thought of as holding collectivist moral values– often expressed as concern at the exploitation of under-dogs or of dangers to the environment. But they see organisations pursuing these aims, indeed all organisations, as essentially manipulative. They are therefore, 'non-joiners' or at least 'none-stayers'.

The jobs Autarchs do tend to involve a single unit of labour – their own. So we find them well represented among owner taxi drivers, tutors, artists, writers and as self-employed in craft-based industries, as consultant professionals in occupations such as furniture restorers, caners or as small-scale dealers or workers on smallholdings. They deal in antiques and collectables, work as jobbing gardeners or as self-employed jobbing tradesmen – they prefer having a variety of bosses, so long as none has undue control. They may have a number of part-time jobs or do different jobs at different seasons or move to work in different locations. To further their aims – as Richard puts it – they tend to be 'nomadic'.

Autarchs take satisfaction in having above-average expertise and being more conscientious and well regarded which – as with Richard, James, Mary and others – improves their range of job choices. The formal education of Autarchs appears to be higher than average. Many are graduates – but figures are not readily obtainable since they have as little as possible to do with official bodies.

Since rearing children inhibits autonomy, many do not have them – which perhaps explain why men seem to predominate in this grouping. The arrival of children often involves a change of life-style – at least for a time.

A personal feature Autarchs seem to share is to have suffered significant life crises – estrangement from parents, a divorce, redundancy, death of a partner or a marked shift in conditions of employment that involves their choosing a life-style that puts autonomy above earnings.

People embrace Autarchism in different degrees at different times of life. Autarchs range from the full-bloodied to the partial, from the differentially active to the latent – who may well wait years for the opportunity to embrace self-sufficiency. Where the employment of professionals is pronounced, as in public-sector organisations such as the

---

5  Dake & Thompson (1999)

British Health Service and in teaching, conflicts between the demands of the organisation and professional aims to autonomy are pronounced. This has been enhanced by the fashion for setting top-down targets and has led to a massive shift to Autarchy via early retirement and independent private practice.

Autarchs often cannot preclude working in organisations, though when they do they tend to prefer part-time work. Increasingly however, professionals find themselves having to work in them because their training rules out other forms of employment (teachers, doctors and medical auxiliaries are examples). Here they can be identified by a refusal to follow expected career paths or respond to usual managerially-set incentives. They do not readily take on extra tasks which are not central to their core interests (though they often compensate by performing extra tasks that do). Nor do they make strategic choices that would benefit their career prospects. They tend to refuse promotions that involve extra responsibilities, and – despite seniority – are liable to be found in their profession's basic grade.

Autarchs flourish in economic booms when there are more safe niches in which they can avoid the constraints of commerce and industry. And with the competitive pressures of globalism and its ratcheted targeting, we have a worldwide tightening of organisational controls that serves to produce more Autarchs. But with their adaptable approach to life, they are also well set to 'get by' in recessions. They are to be seen moving out of cities, converting their hobbies to generate income, and reducing their wants to match. It is not surprising that their numbers should grow as more people come to reject both consumerism and the constraints of orthodox employment. In their search for autonomy, Autarchs are the arch-pragmatists; when conditions shift – they adapt.

This small random sample does not claim that Autarchs are a statistically-based social entity. They have been selected because they all live within my own socially-limited milieu. But and others like them appear to share closely similar characteristics – values, attitudes, views of the world and behaviours – and because, once identified, examples constantly recur.

'Keeping one's eyes and ears open,' having sympathetic involvement with one's subjects while maintaining detached neutrality, making comparisons of characteristic behaviours – these, the key features of anthropological fieldwork, justify at least a preliminary recognition of a new estate's appearance on the social scene. And one that appears to be growing.

# PART VII:

# EPISODES

CHAPTER NINETEEN

# DEALINGS WITH DEATH

In our culture, taboos and accepted practices surrounding death do not mould behaviour as they do in most other cultures. Here, instead of well-understood bereavement and mourning procedures, death invariably causes dissonance and uncertainty.

## Cousin Gerald

Cousin Gerald died over thirty years ago, but my brothers resurrect the event whenever they think I need to be humiliated. A few years older than me, Gerald was the doted-on only child of Rachel, my mother's elder sister. Because the sisters had been rivals since childhood, my mother, when I was born, saw no reason why her sister should monopolise the name 'Gerald'. So began a lifetime's competition as each Gerald was continuously compared to the other. Not surprisingly we, the two main puppets in this play, early took on the colouration of our mothers. We competed with enthusiasm, failed to rejoice in the other's triumphs, and gloated at their disappointments. We followed different life-paths: he took to risky, quasi-respectable trading, and at one point I joined the Civil Service as a clerk.

As we grew older there was little contact between us. As a junior civil servant I was living a life of virtuous poverty. Auntie Rachel however, kept us very much up to date on Gerald's stratospheric progress: how he was increasingly well regarded in what we saw as the seedier side of Blackpool's more doubtful business activities. How he was now moving in the world of dud councillors and equally bent policemen, of whom there was no shortage in Blackpool at that time. He was progressing nicely in the Masons too.[1] We heard from her how he was increasingly involved in

---

1   There was a corrupt link at this time between Blackpool's Masons, the departments of The Town Clerk and Blackpool's Chief Constable, which lay behind the suicide of the one and the dismissal of the other. (See Ch 2. Footnote 6)

deals. And as he grew in wealth, so he grew in girth. He bought himself a nice new house in a good part of town and a smart car, and he married Millicent, a smart wife. We, on the other hand, were getting poorer – and more pious. Unsurprisingly, each of us despised the other.

Nonetheless, when Cousin Gerald, at forty-six, suddenly keeled over and died while driving his new car on the Promenade, I suggested 'the Brothers' meet up and attend the funeral. Now spread throughout the country, we four enjoyed being together and hadn't met for some time. We would have a good dinner before offering our respects to the newly-widowed Millicent.

We met, had a splendid time over an excellent meal, caught up with news of what we were each doing, and then, accepting what we were in Blackpool for, finally ceased our joviality and made our way to Millicent's.

It was a composed but clearly upset Millicent who, opening the door and surprised to see us, welcomed us in. There followed the usual and expected commiserations: we discussed her sad loss, exchanged pleasantries and gave reassurances. We had tea and biscuits, and finally at last came the time to depart. I clasped Millicent and gave her the expected peck. She saw us out and then in the doorway closed our visit by tearfully thanking us: 'It's so good of you boys to have come all this way.'

My brothers, as I saw it, looked to me, the eldest, to complete the occasion – and then stood appalled as a malicious poltergeist took over and uttered a dreaded, dreadful truth: 'That's all right, Millicent.' And he paused. 'It was a pleasure.'

# Auntie Daisy

I have always argued it was undue sensitivity on my part, rather than any inherent tactlessness, that caused the dreadful *faux pas* with Millicent. After that and a subsequent episode with Auntie Daisy, however, my brothers disagreed. A year separated the two, and their memories of the first were still raw. Again it was a scene involving all four of us – and a death.

Our dad had cancer. We had made numerous trips to see him, and then we received the final call. He was unlikely to recover. To see him before the end, we would need to move fast. We did: the four of us met at Blackpool's Victoria Hospital. We were too late. A brisk nurse told us that Dad had died a few hours before. The four of us mooched out, to face the vacuum that accompanies a death. What to do next? The obvious thing was a need to announce the sad news. 'Wait a minute,' I said. 'Auntie Daisy lives just round the corner. We had better tell her for a start.'

So we made our way to Auntie Daisy's. She was one of those utterly unselfish Christian ladies. Never married, thin and birdlike, without children of her own she had devoted her life to doing good, and over the years had been adopted as 'honorary aunt' to a host of families. She helped when people were sick; remembered everyone's children on their birthdays and at Christmas. She sent cards and presents well into their adulthoods. And when they in their turn had children, they too were similarly remembered. Yes – we must call on Auntie Daisy. We owed it to her. She would be the first. We would tell her in person.

We knocked on her door – but had not thought what to do next when Auntie Daisy opened it to find not one, but 'the four Mars boys' crowding her doorstep. Delighted, and selflessly overjoyed at seeing us, she cheerily ushered us into her front room and fussed about arranging chairs and cushions. 'I'll get some tea,' she trilled. 'There isn't much cake, but never mind, it's lovely to see you all.'

While Auntie Daisy – delighted in her 'giving mode' – came bustling back with tea and cakes and scones and jam, we sensed we were teetering on the edge of a social cliff. What had we to give her?

'Now, you boys, you must tell me all your news. First, how's your dad? He seemed so much better when I saw him on Thursday. And isn't he cheerful? And they're so good at the Victoria [Hospital] aren't they?' So she went, on and on, before she finally came crashing back full circle. 'So, how is your dad today?'

I was born to be the family's fall guy – as the eldest in a family like ours I felt I was expected to act. Auntie Daisy, her bright eyes fixed on me, cheerfully waited for the good news she so deserved. My brothers waited. I had no idea what to say or do next. How to let her down lightly? My poltergeist again took charge.

'Er... He's not so good.'

'Oh dear,' said Auntie Daisy.

'In fact, he's not at all good,' interjected the poltergeist, a little more firmly.

'Oh dear. And he seemed to be doing so well.'

'No. Not at all well,' asserted the poltergeist.

'Oh dear.'

'In fact,' insisted the poltergeist, 'he's dead.'

Why don't people in so-called 'simple' societies become enmeshed in the kind of embarrassments that arose with Auntie Daisy and Cousin Gerald?

Why do we face uncertainty and inadequacy in the face of death? Why do we lack adequate procedures for mourning and bereavement?

Part of the answer is due to the breakdown and physical spread of our extended and nuclear families and part to our widespread disillusion with traditional beliefs. In addition, care of the seriously sick and most dealings with death have largely been taken away from the family and out of the home: they are now professionalised and controlled by medical staffs in hospitals. Many of us have rarely seen a dead body. For these reasons then, we have become insulated from death. We have not just lost the rituals to do with death but the beliefs and the social support that buttress them.

So my defeatist advice, when dealing with death – for what it is worth – is that where no culturally defined course of action seems open – and if something needs to be done – you had best let someone else do it.

CHAPTER TWENTY

# HAMPSTEAD

## Rodents, Residents and Writers

'...rats are God's creatures. Just like you and me.'

Moving from one London district to another sometimes seems like emigrating – a cultural shift can be evident in less than half a mile. For six years we had lived by the traffic-blighted Archway Road. There were no other academics in the area, and before the university/poly expansion of the sixties, many working people had no experience of that occupation's erratic comings and goings. 'Why doesn't he go out to work?' was the unasked question, with, I suspect, a supposition that I must, at the very least, be living off illegal or possibly immoral earnings.

We hoped our move to Hampstead would prove stimulating. We have not been disappointed: for nearly forty years the borough's residents have intrigued us.

More eccentrics appear to live here than anywhere I have known – with the possible exception of Cambridge. And for similar reasons: individualism in both is untrammelled – is indeed encouraged. A high proportion of residents are self-employed or professionals following an individualised, competitive, time-constrained lifestyle – but without the controls and conformist constraints that most organisations impose.

In Hampstead there is much less of the intimacy and communality of The Avenues where everyone knew the personal details of everyone in the surrounding streets. There nobody put household waste on the street – it was seen as communal property and its residents felt responsible for what went on there. Yet it is not uncommon in bourgeois Hampstead to find a mattress dumped outside a house worth a couple of million pounds. And Hampstead people never put ornaments in their front windows facing out – as they did in The Avenues; their windows are more likely to have blinds that stop you looking in. Hampstead lives are largely privatised

In our second week, seeking a part-time secretary, I interviewed a tall, willowy, self-effacing, young woman. Her hobby she said was to go for long walks on the Heath. She explained shyly that it complemented her other hobby, she being a black-belt judoka. Baffled, I confessed to not seeing the connection. She murmured that most nights she went out about midnight. 'Oh yes, why was this?' She was hoping, she said, to be attacked – so she could test her self-defence skills. The stimulus of Hampstead's residents has never palled.

It is weak communality and lack of social controls then, that determines Hampstead behaviours.[1] Nobody much cares what others think – or blinks an eye at what elsewhere would send tongues into overdrive. And time is always at a premium. (In Cultural Theory terms, as outlined in Chapter 21, the former are strongly group-oriented; the latter, weak group.)

Our interest has been sustained by periodic waves of concern involving meetings, petitions and leaflets – though our lack of community means that few have led to sustained, organised long-term action. We are good and often very successful at running short, furious campaigns but find it difficult to sustain a vibrant ongoing and participative neighbourhood watch committee.[2] One neighbour, Diane, has long supported all the most progressive causes. She remains the country's foremost – probably only – Green Mother Christmas. She set up a stall one Christmas outside the local shops and, in a long, green, Mother Christmas robe (but without the beard), harangued passing shoppers as she handed out bundles of leaflets for the full range of Hampstead concerns – from sexism and feminism to 'Save the Environment and the whales to 'Free the Convicted Six' (or it may have been 'the Two').

Our most active inhabitants are nature lovers, especially defenders of animal rights – and of trees and theirs. Councillors are quick to respond. It is hardly possible to cut down a tree unless a diseased branch has actually fallen and killed someone – or at least injured or threatens to injure a dog or cat. Our tree-lined streets are festooned with notices – and photographs – plaintively offering rewards for missing pets. There might well be a profitable pet-napping fraternity at work, probably based in Camden Town. Trees are so full of notices they caused a split among the nature lovers. Friends of the Trees campaigned against damage from the drawing-pins used to secure animal-lovers' notices.

---

1   This again is to be understood as a comparison between Tönnies' *Gemeinschaft* and *Gesellschaft* categories as outlined in ch. 1, footnote 30.

2   One exception is the Heath and Hampstead Society which has a long history of good work but its membership is recruited from a very wide base, its consistency varies, and it fosters a multiplicity of social activities.

The local press closely fosters the views of its residents. A recent headline in the *Hampstead and Highgate Express* is typical: 'Outrage at yet another great tree massacre'. Another records a two-hundred-strong campaign group protesting at council plans to cut down an overgrown maple.[3]

It did not take us long to realise how unschooled in reformist causes we were. Soon after arrival, I was chatting to the man emptying our dustbins. As we both idly watched his mate lift a neighbour's bin, two rats jumped out – to scuttle away over the gardens.

'See those? Weren't they rats? Do you get many rats round here?'

'Oh no, Guv. Very rare round these parts. But nasty things, rats is. You'll want to get on to the council's pest control.'

But I soon found that rats are far from rare in Hampstead. Then I found out that teams of sweetly mad old ladies foster them. They service every piece of open ground in the borough to ensure that pigeons are nurtured, and in doing so they feed the rats. I once mildly remonstrated with one 'lavender and lace' old lady as I pointed to a rat among the pigeons – but had to retreat before a torrent of abuse that rivalled anything I had heard in the RAF.

We have a short circuit to the council – our own neighbourhood residents committee. Its shifting membership of mostly co-opted members seeks to defend us against the council's authority, neglect and oppression. And though it has done some good there is always difficulty in retaining volunteers. I went to see the secretary about our rat problem. An unsmiling old veteran from pre-CND days, she had supported campaigns from: 'No extra traffic lights in Hampstead' ('it will destroy our rural aspect') to 'Protect our Toads'.

I explained about the rats, elaborated on the likelihood of plague, the prevalence of Weil's disease and imminent attacks on babies. Here, I suggested, was a real campaign, the self-same problem that had rallied the burghers of Hamelin. She heard me out, smiled an arid smile and promised to put the problem to her committee. Perhaps I might, interestingly, be in at the start of a Hampstead Crusade? I was wrong of course. No response. I waited a week, a couple of weeks. She never came back. I called on her.

'Is anything happening on the rats front?'

'No, I'm afraid not.'

'What is the Council doing?'

'Nothing. But I did put it to the committee.'

'Yes? What happened?'

---

3    Hampstead and Highgate Express, 9 March 2009; 27 May 2010

'The committee decided not to proceed.'

'Why ever not?'

She paused, and grinned the mirthless grin she kept for nature-haters. 'The committee felt that rats are God's creatures. Just like you or I.'

I did not rate our shared affinity – but let it pass.

Not all Hampstead residents are as concerned about beauty and truth – as I discovered when my first book was published. When an author sees their book in print, especially a first book, it is known to affect their mental balance. Thus affected, I went to the main village bookshop to see if the owner might arrange a special display. Elderly, impatient, he had a reputation for being brusque, even abusive – this was apparently all part of his being 'a local character'. But I knew he had written several books himself. He just might be sympathetic to a beginner.

'I was thinking you might like to put this in a display?'

'What?'

'A window display. For a local author?' I showed him the book.

He stared in disbelief. 'A window display?'

'Yes, perhaps – in just a corner?'

'For a local fuckin' author?'

He started to swell – then he began to shout – in perfect rhythm. 'Look! [pause] Every single fucker [pause] that comes in this fuckin' shop [longer pause] – is a local fuckin' author…! Right?'

He had a point. Where else but in Hampstead would you find the local Oxfam charity shop with a shelf marked: AUTHORS' SIGNED COPIES?

I crept away, taking my miserable book with me. I wasn't sorry when, soon afterwards, Waterstones opened a massive bookshop opposite his.

But if hubris has the seeds of its own collapse, then authors' egos are resilient: they can be serially demolished – but they serially rise again. Dennis, our milkman, emerged as an effective demolition expert.

A streetwise everyman, Dennis is a hard-headed networker who has arranged all sorts of deals with his customers and knows the strengths and weaknesses of us all. Since my book was concerned with the fiddles and deviance of everyday work-life, including those of milkmen, I thought his comments might be useful – or at least interesting.

Dennis was quick to show he was aware of the book: 'I saw you on the box trying to push it.' No reverence here for TV appearances.

'Would you like a copy?' Well, yes he would.

I hurried to fetch a paperback and passed it over. Dennis glanced at it with disdain.

'John Le Carré always gives me hardbacks.'

# Hampstead's Hypochondria

As might be expected, 'People's attitudes to health and illness follow from their social situation.'[4] Since in Hampstead, competitive professionals and entrepreneurs predominate, illness can seriously limit their effectiveness. Accordingly they are open to the latest health fads and fashions, the most modern treatments, the most fashionable illnesses, and the newest diseases. And this concern is why the pavements sometime seem to be congested by joggers.

Hampstead medics, dentists, nurses and pharmacists are fully aware that many patients thoroughly research their symptoms. They scour the Internet and are quick to announce that they have close relatives who are eminent consultants or professors of medicine. They argue and readily seek second opinions. [5] GPs therefore, have to outwit and pre-empt them before they even begin to present symptoms. It is hardly surprising that in anticipating a patient's symptoms some Hampstead health professionals are as hypochondriacal as their patients. This is not a place for bland medical reassurance.

My last GP would invariably interrupt any presentation of symptoms with a distracted: 'Excuse me.' Then he would phone the local teaching hospital and arrange a priority specialist appointment. I cannot say what they thought of referrals for in-growing toenails ('but it could be gout: that's a kidney problem'); sprains and pains ('unlikely to be malignant – though best be sure'). I found such reassurance can be counter-productive – especially when hospital medics have a different agenda.

One Saturday afternoon I visited my dentist, Mr Rabinovitz, for a routine check. A hypochondriac himself, he has the finest Central European provenance: it seems the most intense hypochondriacs originate from there. Benign, even genial, he beckoned me to his chair as if about to offer a glass of sherry, and he smiled his dentist's crocodile smile:

'Open wide for me please.'

Bending from the waist, he looked in, poked about – then sprang upright – all geniality gone. 'You've lost your crown! What's happened to your crown? Didn't you notice? You *must* have noticed!'

But I had not noticed – though obviously I should have. I began to mutter an unhappy apology but he snapped that if I did not know where the crown was, then it was obvious: I must have swallowed it.

'Swallowed it? Is that serious?'

---

4    Helman (2007, p. 390)
5    Type 4 – Low group/Low grid'. The context is one of Individualism, as outlined in ch. 21.

'Serious? It's extremely serious. It can lodge in your appendix – that's how serious it is. You need an x-ray – and you need it now. I'll give you a note. He scribbled a note to Accident & Emergency at the Royal Free Hospital.

'Go. I'll telephone. They'll expect you'. He bundled me out.

'What a fragile envelope in which we dwell,' I mused. 'From a simple dental check-up to life-threatening crisis – all in a quarter of an hour.'

The A&E reception area was crammed with all ages, classes and ethnicities. That afternoon it seemed half North London needed emergency treatment. One lad of eight or nine being comforted by his mother had what appeared to be a broken arm. Several adults were bleeding from a variety of wounds. Others, pale and distraught, seemed unaware of anything except their own misery. And they all waited patiently as they suffered and bled. But none of them had a letter.

Waving mine I strode to the reception desk, explained to a nurse the urgency of my visit, and demanded an immediate x-ray. She responded with alacrity and hurried me to a doctor – the only one on duty.

She was a newly hatched child of a doctor, a pale, tired Glaswegian with mousey hair who looked as if she had been on night duty for a week. She looked me over without enthusiasm, then took the letter. Her lips pursed. She actually snorted. Tossing her head, she hissed: 'This is from a private practitioner?' It wasn't really a question, more an accusation, an assertion of class warfare. It sounded worse in Glaswegian. I confirmed it was indeed from a private practitioner. That was the wrong answer: I had stumbled into an ideological mantrap. Middle-aged, middle-class, probably a baby-eater, and a Hampstead resident at that. She glanced again at the letter then shoved it aside. 'I can't understand why he asks for an urgent x-ray.'

Wishing not to appear condescending – and aware that newly minted doctors can be sensitive, and tired ideological Glaswegian ones were likely to be even more so – I began to explain why my highly experienced dentist was so concerned.

'Well, you see, the crown, as she would appreciate, having been swallowed, could well have lodged in my appendix. In this case…'

A further snort. She changed tack. 'How old are you?'

I should have been prepared. 'Fifty five. Why?'

Another wrong answer. She seized her chance.

'Well – at your age…' She relished the phrase and repeated it. 'At your age, you've nothing to worry about. At your age it will have withered away!'

We understood each other perfectly. I thanked her and left. As I did so I caught the trace of a glacial smile. A clash of sub-cultures can be as potent as any.

# PART VIII:

# THEORY

## Introduction

'There is nothing more practical than a good theory'.
—Kurt Lewin

There is a lot written on the variety of theories that abound in the social sciences. For present purposes, and because this is not a textbook but primarily a memoir, then the reader's task (and mine) will be more manageable if I limit this next chapter to outlining one theory (called Cultural Theory, CT or Grid/Group) This is the principal theory I have used to guide in collecting, organizing and making sense of data in the different fields in which I have worked. Its effectiveness will I hope be evident by re-reading the accounts to determine where the theory is implicit.

The accounts hopefully demonstrate how anthropologists aim to see how a social system works – and how a particular feature which interests them relates to the system as a whole. This they do by carrying out fieldwork, by 'submerging' themselves in another culture.

In doing fieldwork, anthropologists note that it is the *situations* people are in that typically determines their behaviour, (and they note how extreme situations can lead to extreme behaviours).[1] In making their observations they compare situations within and between different cultures. Applying a comparative perspective can give new meanings to taken-for-granted aspects of a culture. And attempting to understand one's own culture can only benefit by being placed in a comparative perspective.

---

1   Extreme behaviour has been well noted in our own culture by social psychologists as being the product of extreme situations. See the classic study of a simulated prison by Zimbardo (1973) which had to be stopped because of the unacceptable, mounting viciousness of the 'guards', and Milgram (1963) who witnessed subjects prepared to give severe, even life-threatening, electric shocks because the authority structure in which they operated prevailed on them to do so.

CHAPTER TWENTY-ONE

# CULTURAL THEORY
# AND THE NEED TO CLASSIFY

As recounted earlier, the material on dockworkers' pilferage was rich and detailed. In possessing over thirty detailed accounts of pilferage and fiddling in other occupations I realised that if these could be extended to be comparable to the dockworker material, then here could be the basis of a very useful study.

Staff at the Cambridge Institute of Criminology were extremely hospitable. And so, with a Nuffield Fellowship I moved there and prepared to write 'The Great Work' on occupational crime. Oh hubris!

There was a massive problem: the data's variety. In some jobs fiddles depend on the collusion of management who accept it as a part of wages, as an incentive – albeit one sometimes paid by unaware customers; in other jobs fiddlers are not tolerated and are ruthlessly punished. Some fiddles are carried out by individuals in isolation; others require a group's co-operation, and some occur because of resentment... it is a way of hitting out at the boss, the company, the system, or the state. But how to accommodate all these variables? In particular, how to classify jobs and deviance, and how to compare them?

Without classification I had only a collection of disparate accounts. I was unable to compare, say, the group-based fiddles of collectively organised longshoremen with those of individually competitive journalists; the fiddles of waiters and autonomous entrepreneurs with those of accountants. Without classification (and its resultant comparisons and contrasts) there can be no science.

Attempts to classify occupations and their deviance by the usual occupational taxonomies – blue collar/white collar; lower/middle/upper class – all proved inadequate. None could be sustained because none met the two vital conditions for effective classification: that categories must be both exclusive and exhaustive. Otherwise someone can always say: 'Your categories and comparisons don't apply to the people I studied,' so that where they appeared to fit, 'They fitted like a poorly made frock fits – they fitted where they touched.'[1]

While involved with this problem I serendipitously came across the work of the anthropologist Mary Douglas. She was busy promulgating a system to classify all cultures[2] under one rubric. And just as I had a mass of data on occupational crime, she had a parallel mass of data on world cultures, and again, the same problem had faced her – how to classify them.

Douglas cracked her problem, and in so doing solved mine. Her approach, known as Cultural Theory (or CT or Grid/Group Theory) has the great benefit that it links people's values, attitudes and typical behaviours to the way their lives are organised.

Cultural Theory conceptualises four main ways by which[3] people's lives can be organised. These co-exist in different degrees of dominance in every society. They derive from two bases: how people relate to groups such as family, clan or neighbourhood, and the constraints and rules to which they are subject. These can each be rated on a scale from strong to weak and then be plotted on a graph with two axes to give a two by two matrix. The horizontal axis represents the strength of group norms; the vertical axis, the strength of grid constraints such as rules and rankings. A two by two matrix offers four categories.

We therefore have four 'ideal types'[4] of social organisation (often referred to as 'solidarities'. The place of a possible fifth solidarity is discussed below). Solidarities are not finite entities but represent 'fields'. And here the key contribution of Cultural Theory becomes apparent: each solidarity has a distinct bundle of identifiable values, attitudes and characteristic behaviours appropriate to it. These are thus products of the

---

1  Generally attributed to Christian Dior
2  Douglas (1982a)
3  Douglas (1982a); Perri 6 & Mars (2008, Introduction to Vol. I); Thompson *et al* (1990)
4  'Ideal types' are abstractions representing the totality of characteristics in a given category. In 'the real world' any specific example would possess some but not all of these defining characteristics – such that it would be recognizable as belonging to an overall 'ideal' category. The four quadrants in the grid/group diagram therefore represent 'fields' – they are not firm categories and they merge into each other.

four 'ideal type' ways that people are organised and do not derive from the psychological orientations of those involved.[5]

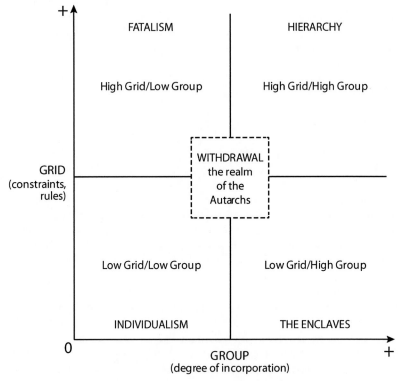

*Grid and Group, based on Douglas (1982b)*[6]

---

5    This is not to suggest that people do not have the independence to choose behaviours that suit them but rather that they will be oriented towards the appropriate solidarity in which they operate. If there is a mismatch between solidarity and personality they can move to another solidarity, change their personal orientation to better fit their existing solidarity, make attempts to alter the solidarity they are in, or they can crack. It should be apparent that Cultural Theory, dependent as it is on the *social* situation of actors, (on grid and group), is essentially a sociological theory. It does not aim to explain behaviour, values and attitudes by recourse to the psychological characteristics of individuals - a common cause of confusion in accounts of occupational and other kinds of criminality. Cultural Theory is most emphatically, not a psychological theory.

6    Douglas (1982b, p. 4)

The solidarities are each defined by their opposition to the others, and all exist in a state of mutual antagonism applicable to all societies at all times.[7] There is however, a need for alliances as part of the shifting processes of political adaptation. This need, provides the impetus for social change, whether in wider societies or at micro levels, in households and organisations.

The first solidarity, Hierarchy, is strong on both group and grid, and characterises hierarchical cultures as found in the caste systems of India, and in our own bureaucracies. They are noted for well-defined divisions of labour and have a marked sense of boundary that clearly distinguishes insiders from outsiders. They operate with long time spans and accordingly their policy-making seeks confirmation from the past and is based on strategies formulated by office holders at the peak of the hierarchy. These will be based on the validated advice of authorities – established experts.

It follows that Hierarchies value tradition, precedents and rules. Medieval cathedrals often took up to three hundred years to complete since perceptions of time didn't distinguish much between past, present and future. Modern Individualist-dominated construction is amortised over the prospective life of *individuals* - usually over a period of twenty five years.

In Hierarchies Space is used to buttress rank and is allocated to office while time is used as a social organiser and a source of control. Information is only validated from approved sources and tends to be restricted on a 'need to know' basis, as discussed in Chapter 8. Hierarchic strategies tend to be risk-averse unless risks are validated by experts or precedent. They do not readily adapt to change and are closely defensive of their members unless their behaviour is seen as a threat to the group – when punishments can appear relatively severe as demonstrated in Nigeria – Chapter 17.

The second, the Individualist solidarity, is weak on both group and grid. It characterises the innovative, entrepreneurial risk-taking and rule-breaking cultures that constantly seek change and do not regard rules or precedents as sacrosanct. Here competition and short time spans are marked, and networking is a perpetual activity. Conspicuous consumption, fad and fashion reign – as it does in the highlands of Papua New Guinea as well as, and increasingly, in the UK and the USA. There is a constant but unstable alliance between the Individualist and Hierarchic solidarities – since Hierarchy needs the innovative but risk-prone drive of the

---

7   Douglas (1996, pp. 41-49)

Individualists, and Individualism needs the institutionalised security of the ruling structures and legal processes provided by Hierarchy. Both are opposed to but both need society's 'conscience bearers' the third solidarity, the Enclavists, who act as 'watchdogs' of what they consider are the excesses of both Hierarchy and Individualism.

The Enclaves are noted for strong group involvements and weak constraints. In their firmer forms they are located within communes, sects, environmental and libertarian movements. They tend to have distaste, sometimes even fear, of what they see as 'the controlling 'outside' – (sourced from Individualism and Hierarchy) - which they see as the source of risk and danger They eschew internal controls, embrace egalitarian values and are reluctant to recognise authority. They have difficulties, for example, in validating arbitrators and are therefore commonly subject to schism (Flanagan & Rayner, 1988). At their most extreme, Enclaves are represented by the more intense animal liberationists and the active units of terrorist organisations. At more common less extreme levels we find vegetarians and organisations such as Greenpeace. Overt competition is eschewed but enclaves often demonstrate competitive piety.

The fourth solidarity, Fatalism, is marked by weak group involvement but strong constraints such as derive from poverty. This is the home of 'isolates' – such as asylum seekers and the chronically unemployed who, lacking the security of group membership, are subject to the constraints and controls their situation provides. Fatalists see the world passively, and events as being beyond their control, as capricious, with causality due to fate or luck. They may however, revolt and commit sabotage if pressed too far and their constraints too oppressive. There is the tendency for an unstable alliance to exist between members of Enclaves who see themselves as representing society's conscience and Fatalists on whose behalf they seek to act.

Many Cultural Theorists are now coming to accept a fifth solidarity. Set at the centre of the Grid/Group chart it expresses the world view of those who consciously withdraw from the constraints arising from each of the other four solidarities. These are the Autarchs.[8] Their position is discussed in Chapter 18.

Applying this model to the world of work means focusing on how jobs are structured – on the two dimensions of social organisation – Grid and Group – as these apply to the workplace. In doing so it reveals, as we would expect, four characteristic and distinct kinds of deviance, and the

---

8   Michael Thompson postulated this fifth solidarity which he calls 'Hermits' (Thompson, 1996, pp. 75-92).

values, attitudes and behaviours appropriate to each: Hierarchy is the category that strongly fits the group-based longshore dockworkers discussed in Chapters 10 and 11; Individualism is represented by those entrepreneurial risk-taking bankers who led us to the financial crisis of 2007-8 and whose ideology was well represented in Blackpool (Chapters 2-4). The Enclave is the home of driver/deliverers and waiters doing similar jobs who are brought together by subordination to a common boss but otherwise compete for benefits (Chapter 5). Fatalists (sometimes called Isolates) are epitomised by isolated dial-watchers, conveyor belt and call-centre workers whose jobs largely preclude interaction and whose deviance involves aiming to wrest a degree of control over jobs that exert controls over them. It is usually manifest as sabotage – 'throwing a spanner in the works'.

Cultural Theory – later termed 'Grid/Group Theory or CT – not only fitted my material when I was seeking a system to classify work and its correlated deviance but has fruitfully and repetitively suggested new areas of enquiry ever since. It has been a constant source of inspiration and applicability as evidenced by the accounts of different cultures that appear throughout this book. The four (or five) grid/group solidarities with their correlating clusters of values, attitudes and preferred behaviours are implicit and manifest in the accounts

For the fieldworker, the correlation of values, attitudes and appropriate behaviours that derive from a solidarity's grid/group position can provide a ready checklist against which variations may suggest fruitful lines of enquiry. If, for instance, Individualist actors display unexpected risk-aversion, or Hierarchs manifest reckless risk-taking, then we can be alerted to the likelihood of a shift in their organisation. We can also look with clearer understanding at the competitive interplay of different solidarities within the same context – in a household or workplace for example – to better understand the bases of conflicts, alliances and reconciliations within them and to have clearer understanding of the processes of social and organisational change.

# PART IX:

# CONCLUSIONS

CHAPTER TWENTY-TWO

CONCLUSION:
BECOMING AN ANTHROPOLOGIST

Having lived in a variety of different cultures before undergoing professional training, I already possessed some experience of what can be called 'naïve fieldwork.' This gave me the early bonus of a relatively broad base from which to draw comparisons between cultures, some appreciation of what participant observation entailed and a minimum awareness of the 'sin' of ethnocentricity. To this background Cambridge then added awareness of theory, an appreciation of the connectedness of a society's different institutions, some understanding of research methods and an academic knowledge of other cultures.

After Cambridge, armed with a greater degree of academic understanding, it was time, to reconsider and refine the methods and concepts I had previously used in attempting to explain the cultures I had already experienced. I then had, in effect, a store of personally experienced, comparative and concrete material to draw on – useful not only in analysing the past but that would be applicable to future assignments. Most anthropologists agree that their first full scale study is the most formative in becoming an anthropologist.

The first thing Newfoundland demonstrated was the mundane reality of early being overwhelmed by a mass of data that seemed to make little sense. It needs patience and a degree of faith to daily record such details in a diary so as later to see the connections between apparently disconnected events. These, when considered together, later revealed aspects of a wider social system. This was demonstrated, for instance, when identifying and contextualising the trouble case discussed on page 137.

It was only towards the end of fieldwork in Newfoundland that a wider system began to emerge and the interactions of its parts became evident. Then the value of detailed and recorded daily observations became apparent. Sometimes this doesn't happen until after one has left the field and enters the 'analysis and writing up' phase. Then one can bring further data to bear through wider reading and discussion with co-academics This

I was able to achieve at the London School of Economics with the support of a talented body of 'same stage' academics and the benefit of an insightful and facilitative supervisor. I found it particularly useful to then schedule a short return visit to the field to fill in gaps and explore further questions that had arisen. Unfortunately this is not often possible for most researchers.

Newfoundland brought to the fore and refined three important academic concepts that I had previously only half glimpsed: comparison, participant observation and ethnocentrism that are central to social anthropology.

## Comparison (and its Twin, Contrast)

To understand a people's thinking and behaviour means relating their concepts, symbols, justifications and values to the structure of their society. It does this by comparing similarities and differences. The manipulation of debt relationships in Manchester, for instance, (p. 15, footnote 15) alerted me to their role in mitigating the effects of poverty among striking longshoremen in Newfoundland (p. 140).

This is why I was so fortunate to find myself, a Jew, growing up on a largely non-Jewish working-class estate whose values, attitudes and behaviours were often startlingly different from those of my own culture. Living with these differences forced me to make comparisons. A comparison of working-class and Jewish attitudes to education for instance (page 8) and the different ways that Jews and Catholics showed respect to their clergy (page 11) revealed markedly diverse cosmologies – with all the implications these raised for family organisation and social controls.

Moving from Manchester's integrated, cooperative and personalised culture to the individualist, competitive, impersonal culture of Blackpool, again threw up stark comparisons.[1] These were evident in their different schooling styles (pp. 29-30) and the different acceptance of class roles. In Manchester, life's progression was seen as largely fixed – in contrast to the prevailing view in Blackpool. There, individualist, achievement-oriented rule-breaking entrepreneurs held that position in life was largely self-determined. Comparison of their differences sharpened perceptions of both.

And then came the RAF, manifesting two markedly contrasting sets of values: hierarchy, with coercion from the top, matched by covert

---

1   The *Gemeinschaft/Gesellschaft* dichotomy as defined by Tönnies (1887) is evident here. See p. 24, footnote 30.

opposition from below: the one attempting to subjugate individuality, the other to sustain it. Observing, comparing and contrasting such 'undercover' or 'informal' behaviour and values has been a dominant interest ever since. Much of the teaching about organisations (taught as 'organisation theory' in business schools) cannot be understood without awareness of it – though it is often attempted.

Comparison involves contrasts – searching for similarities *and* differences – looking at what one expects to find – and noting its absence. This recalls the famed example of Sherlock Holmes about the dog that did *not* bark in the night. The significance here is the comparison with contexts where a dog *would* be expected to bark – and its absence – when it did not (Conan Doyle, 1892). A similar comparison of absence was offered by the case of the two Newfoundland longshoremen sacked for being drunk (p. 137). I puzzled over this because drunken longshoremen were normally protected by fellow gang members who covered them under tarpaulins and did their work for them. In this case protection was absent. Sussing out why this had not been so on this occasion altered my understanding of gang relationships and the links between foremen and their gangs. In its turn these gave insights into management's (doomed) attempts at control, to fruitful enquiries about the operation of kinship obligations and to the gangs ability to obtain and allocate pilfered cargo.

## Participant Observation

Before starting formal training, I had the benefit of having gained at least a partial appreciation of anthropology's principal fieldwork method: participant observation.[2] A second big advantage – the essence of participant observation – was the much-emphasised value of noting what is seen and - importantly – listening to what is heard (by keeping your eyes and ears open as it was hammered home to me). These tools were well demonstrated when I was selected as a scapegoat by the NCOs responsible for basic training in the RAF (Chapter 7). This (albeit reluctant!) participant observation led to understanding the collectivism their training regimen was designed to achieve; how its practice was intended to be supplemented within the barrack hut, and how it served to deflect antagonism from its formal controllers – the drill corporals – onto the scapegoat, who happened to be me. In a real sense I enjoyed a privileged role.

---

2   For a clear, succinct and fuller discussion of participant observation see Frankenberg, (*op cit*), pp. 190-199.

Intensive participant observation is undoubtedly the most fruitful research method available to social scientists. But it is expensive in time, training and the intensity it demands.[3] Yet no other means of collecting data on occupational crime, for example, as in Blackpool and Newfoundland, could have uncovered such rich data. With participant observation it proved possible to explore well beyond noting the pilferage techniques involved; it required the researcher to 'go to wherever the material leads'.[4] It led me to appreciate the nature of illicit training, showed how pilferage influenced industrial relations, revealed how it determined high or low prestige, and demonstrated its effects on marital and community relations. Such insights proved invaluable in other contexts and when working as a consultant. They were most unlikely to emerge from straight interviewing, and even less by issuing questionnaires since their avenues of enquiry are largely pre-determined. I continue to use and advocate participant observation as a prime research tool.

## Ethnocentricity

It has been asserted that the arch anthropological sin is to be ethnocentric – attempting to understand and explain behaviour in another culture by reference to one's own assumptions and values. And not least, to be aware of what these are. This was well demonstrated in discussing consultancy work in Nigeria (Chapter 17).

Yet ethnocentricity is not just widespread – it is universal. Every culture, subjects each new generation to a process of cultural conditioning that results in the issue of 'cultural blinkers'. These cause people to see their way of doing things as not only 'natural' – but best. The problems that result from mutual misunderstandings have resulted in development projects being unsuccessful (p.181) and diplomatic discourses being disastrous. An alertness to one's own ethnocentricity and awareness of the ethnocentricity of others is a characteristic that influences an anthropologist's day to day interactions.

---

3   It is acknowledged that 'submergence' in a culture makes heavy demands on a researcher. Accordingly I have devised a 'quick and dirty' method of attenuated fieldwork that was originally designed for use in organisations. Though far from ideal, it will nonetheless prove useful in circumstances where time is short. This is described in the Appendix to Mars (2013) 'A Practical Guide to Doing Organisational Ethnography: LISTOR/SPARCK', (an anagram). It can be used in contexts other than organisations.

4   As emphasised by Max Gluckman in his postgraduate teachings on research methods.

Comparison, participant observation and awareness of ethnocentricity often interact in the same context. But awareness of the three, though valuable and useful in travel writing, is not enough: anthropology requires that the collection of data and its analysis be shaped and moulded by theory – as the previous chapter has hopefully demonstrated. And as Kurt Lewin has it: 'There is nothing more practical than a good theory.'

Working as others work, thinking as they think, learning about the lives of factory-hands, watching a shaman cast out devils, 'spieling' on a fairground, learning about 'the weed' or patronising a witch and working out how she foretells the future – these have proved fascinating. Being an anthropologist, as well as offering insights into the lives of others also offers insights into one's own. And seeing how a theory works in practice and being able to add to – and if necessary amend it – is extremely satisfying. But beware – as I have found – anthropology can become an obsession: becoming an anthropologist involves being always 'in play'.

# BIBLIOGRAPHY

Adams, J. (2000) The Hypermobility of Western Society, *Prospect Magazine*, 20 March 2000.

Allen, B. (1994) Perceptions of Time, in Tim Ingold (Ed.) *The Companion Encyclopaedia of Anthropology*, Routledge.

Bordieu. P. (1984) *Distinction: A Social Critique of the Judgement of Taste*, trans. R. Nice, Harvard University Press.

Brandon, H. (1839) Poverty, Mendacity and Crime.

Encyclopaedia Britannica (2006) Britannica Concise Encylopedia 2006: Revised and Expanded Edition, Encyclopaedia Britannica Ltd.

Campbell, J.K. (1964) Honour, Family and Patronage: a study of institutions and moral values in a Greek mountain community, Oxford: Clarendon Press.

*Cassell's Dictionary of Slang*, (Ed. J. Green) (2000) Cassell and Co.

Channel 5 TV (2005) *Bad Boys of the Blitz*, UK broadcast 13 Dec. 2005.

Clark, C. & Pinch, T. (1992) The Anatomy of a Deception: Fraud and Finesse in the Mock Auction Sales Con, *Qualitative Sociology*, Vol. 15, No. 2, pp. 151-175.

Conan Doyle, A. (1892) Silver Blaze, in *The Memoirs of Sherlock Holmes*, George Newnes.

Dake K. & Thompson, M. (1999) Making ends meet, in the household and on the planet, *Geojournal*, 47, pp. 417-424.

Dennis, N., Henriques, F. & Slaughter, C. (1956) *Coal is Our Life: an Analysis of a Yorkshire Mining Community*, Eyre and Spottiswood. Reprinted 1969, London: Tavistock.

*Dictionary of the Underworld* (1950, 1989) (Ed. E.Partridge), Wordsworth Collection.

Douglas, M. (1982a) Cultural Bias, in *In the Active Voice*, Routledge & Kegan Paul.

— (1982b) *Essays in the Sociology of Perception*, London: Routledge & Kegan Paul.

— (1988) Constructive Drinking: Perspectives from Anthropology, Cambridge University Press.

— (1992) Risk and Blame: Essays in Cultural Theory, Routledge.

— (1996) *Thought Styles*, Sage Publishers.

Etzioni, A. (1961) *A Comparative Analysis of Complex Organizations*, The Free Press.

Evans-Pritchard, E.E. (1940) *The Nuer: The Modes of Livelihood and Political Institutions of a Nilotic People*, Oxford: The Clarendon Press.

Flanagan, J.G. & Rayner, S. (Eds) (1988) *Rules, Decisions and Inequality in Egalitarian Society*, Avebury Publications.

Fortes, M. (1974) The First Born, *Journal of Child Psychology and Psychiatry*, pp. 81-104.

Freedman, J. (1977) Joking, Affinity and the Exchange of Ritual Services Among the Kiga of Northern Rwanda: An Essay on Joking Relationship Theory, *Man*, New Series, Vol. 12, No. 1, pp. 154-165. Published by: Royal Anthropological Institute of Great Britain and Ireland.

Frankenberg, R. (1990) *Village on the Border*, Illinois: Waveland Press Inc.

Gardner, H. (1999) *Intelligence Reframed: Multiple Intelligences for the 21st Century*, Basic Books.

Gluckman, M. (1955) *Custom and Conflict in Africa*, Basil Blackwell.

— (Ed) (1962) Essays in *The Ritual of Social Relations*, Manchester University Press, ch. 1.

— (1963) Papers in Honor of Melville J. Herskovits: Gossip and Scandal, *Current Anthropology*, Vol. 4, No. 3, pp. 307-316.

— (1967) *The Judicial Process Among the Barotse*, Manchester University Press.

Goffman, E. (1961) *Asylums*, Penguin.

Goodall, A.H. (2009) *Socrates in the Boardroom; Why Research Universities should be Led by Top Scholars*, Princeton University Press.

Haas, J. (Ed.) (1990) *The Anthropology of War*, Cambridge University Press.

Haviland, J. (1977) 'Gossip, Reputation and Knowledge' in *Zinac*, Chicago Univ. Press.

Heilman, S. (1978) *Synagogue Life Chicago*, Chicago Univ. Press.

Helman, C.G. (2007) *Culture, Health and Illness*, 5th ed., Hodder Arnold Publication.

Hoggart, R (1957) *The Uses of Literacy: Aspects of Working-Class Life*, London: Chatto & Windus.

Hotten, J.C. (1887) *Slang Dictionary*, London: Chatto & Windus.

Jensen, A.R. & Eysenck, H.J. (Eds) (1982), *A Model for Intelligence,* Springer-Verlag.

Janis, I.L.L. (1972) *Victims of Group Think: a Psychological Study of Foreign Policy Decisions and Fiascos*, Boston: Houghton Mifflin.

Kipling, R. (1902) *Just So Stories*, Macmillan.

Kuper, A. (1973) *Anthropologists and Anthropology*, Penguin Books.

Larrowe, C.P. (1956) *Shape-Up and Hiring Halls*, California University Press.

Lawrence, T.E. (1955) *The Mint*, Jonathan Cape.

Lewin, K. (1952) Field Theory in Social Science: Selected Theoretical Papers, London: Tavistock.

Mair, L. (1972-92) *An Introduction to Social Anthropology*, 2nd ed., Oxford: Clarendon Press.

Malinowski, B. (1954) *Magic Science and Religion and Other Essays*, New York: Doubleday Anchor Books.

Mars, G. (1974) Dock Pilferage: A Case Study in Occupational Theft, in P. Rock & M. McIntosh, (Eds) *Deviance and Social Control*, London: Tavistock, pp. 209-228.

— (1979) The Stigma Cycle: values and politics in a dockland union, in S. Wallman (Ed.) *Social Anthropology of Work*, ASA Monographs, Academic Press.

— (1982) *Cheats at Work: An Anthropology of Workplace Crime*. London: Allen & Unwin. Reprinted 1994, Aldershot: Dartmouth. New ed. *Cheats at Work Revisited*, Cambridge Scholars Publishing, 2015.

— (1988) Drinking among Dockworkers and the Politics of Union Turbulence in M. Douglas M. (Ed.) *Constructive Drinking: Perspectives from Anthropology*, Cambridge University Press.

— (Ed.) (2001) *Workplace Sabotage*, Ashgate/Dartmouth.

— (2003) Advice to a Potential Academic Politician, *Times Higher Education Supplement*, March 2003.

— (2008) From the Enclave to Hierarchy and on to Tyranny: the micro politics of a consultancy group, *Organization and Culture*, Vol. 14, No. 4, Dec. 2008.

— (2013) *Locating Deviance: Crime, Change and Organizations*, Ashgate Publishers.

Mars, G. & Altman, Y. (1983) The Cultural Bases of Soviet Georgia's Second Economy, *Soviet Studies*, 35/4. Reprinted (1985) in Dutch in *Russland Bulletin*, Vol. 9 (3).

— (1988a) The Role of the Factory in Illicit Production in the Second Economy of Soviet Georgia, in B. Dallago & A. Alessandrini (Eds.) *The Unofficial Economy: Consequences and Perspectives in Different Economic Systems*, Gower Press.

— (1988b) The Role of the Store in Illicit Distribution within the Second Economy of Soviet Georgia, in B. Dallago & A Alessandrini (Eds.) *The Unofficial Economy: Consequences and Perspectives in Different Economic Systems*, Gower Press.

— (2008) Managing in Soviet Georgia: an extreme example in comparative management, *European Journal of International Management*. Vol. 2, No. 1.

Mars, G. & Nicod, M. (1984) *The World of Waiters*, Allen and Unwin.

Mars, G. & Weir, D. (Eds) (2000) *Risk Management* (two volumes), The International Library of Management, Aldershot: Dartmouth Publishing/Ashgate.

Mauss, M. (1954) *The Gift,* (English translation), London: Cohen and West.

Melville, K. (1973). Rites of Reversal, *The Sciences*, 13(1), pp. 19-21.

Merry, S.E. (1984) Rethinking Gossip and Scandal, in D.J. Black (Ed.) *Towards a General Theory of Social Control*, Academic Press.

Milgram, S. (1963) A Behavioral Study of Obedience, *Journal of Abnormal and Social Psychology*, 67 (4), pp. 371-378.

Myers-Briggs, I. with Myers, P.B. (1980) *Gifts Differing*, Consulting Psychologists Press, pp. 83-116.

Newman, O. (1972) *Defensible Space: Crime Prevention Through Urban Design*, NY: Macmillan.

*Oxford Dictionary of Modern Slang* (2008), Oxford University Press.

Paine, R. (1967) What Is Gossip About? – an alternative hypothesis, *Man*, New Series, Vol. 2, No. 2.

Peet, T.E. (1924) A Historical Document of Ramesside Age, *Journal of Egyptian Archaeology*, Vol. 10, pp. 116-126.

Perri 6 & Mars, G. (Eds) (2008) *The Institutional Dynamics of Culture*, (two volumes), International Library of Anthropology, Farnham: Ashgate Publishing.

Radcliffe-Brown, A.R. (1940) On Joking Relationships, *Journal of the International African Institute*, 13 (3) pp. 195-210.

Shindler, C. (2012) *National Service: from Aldershot to Aden, Tales from the Conscripts*, Sphere Books.

Sharpe, Tom (1974). *Porterhouse Blue*. Martin Secker & Warberg.

Simey, T.S. (1956) *The Dock Worker*, Liverpool University Press.

Smith, H.L. (1996) *Britain in the Second World War: A Social History*, Manchester University Press.

Strinberg, A. (1900) *The Dance of Death*.

Taylor, L. & Walton, P. (1971) Industrial Sabotage: Motives and Meanings, in S. Cohen (Ed.) *Images of Deviance*, Pelican.

Thiong'O, N. (2011) *Dreams in a Time of War*, Vintage Books.

Thompson, M. (1996) Cultural Theory Without Grid and Group, in M. Thompson (Ed.) *Inherent Relationality: an anti dualist approach to institutions*. Report 9608, Bergen: LOS Centre.

Thompson, M., Ellis, R. & Wildavsky, A. (1990) *Cultural Theory*, Westview Press.

Tönnies, F. (1887) *Gemeinschaft und Gesellschaft*, Leipzig: Fues's Verlag. (Trans. 1957 by C. P. Loomis as *Community and Society*, East Lansing: Michigan State University Press.)

Turner, V. (1967) Ceremonial Ritual and Play in Rio de Janeiro, in A. Falassi (Ed.) *Time out of Time: Essays on the Festival*, University of New Mexico Press, pp. 74-92

— (1987) Betwixt and Between: Patterns of Masculine and Feminine Initiation, in Mahdi LC, Foster, S and Little M. *Betwixt and Between: The Liminal Period in Rites of Passage*, Part 1, pp. 3-23, Open Court Publishing Co.

Vaux, J.H. (1819) *Memoirs*, London: Clowes Publishers, Glossary.

Walton, J.K. (1978) *The Blackpool Landlady*, Manchester University Press.

Whyte, W.F. (1955) *Street Corner Society*, University of Chicago Press.

Whyte, W.F. & Gardner, B.B. (1945) The Man in the Middle: facing the foreman's problems, *Applied Anthropology*, Spring 1945, pp. 1-28.

Young, M. & Wilmott, P. (2007) *Family and Kinship in East London*, Penguin Modern Classics.

Zartman, I.W. (Ed.) (2000) *Traditional Cures for Modern Conflicts: African Conflict Medicine*, Lynne Rienner Publishers, Inc.

Zimbardo, P. (1973) A Study of Prisoners and Guards in a Simulated Prison, *Naval Research Reviews*, 9, Washington DC, pp. 1-17.

Zweig, F. (1953) *The British Worker*, London: Pelican Books.

# INDEX